Richard Obenshain

A Spirit of Fire

Joel L. Hensley

ISBN: 9781073364664

DEDICATION

Dedicated to all of my family and friends who supported me and were patient with me while working on this project. This is also dedicated to all grassroots activists in Virginia seeking to make a difference in the Commonwealth, your efforts do not go unnoticed and are not forgotten.

Preface

My purpose is to highlight the life of Richard D. (Dick) Obenshain and his role in the political realignment that took place in the South at the turn of the 20th Century, and to add a human touch to his story. This important period paved the way for the Reagan Revolution. Over the course of two decades in politics, Obenshain influenced the lives of many and inspired an entire generation of young conservatives, including many significant names in recent history such as George Allen, Jim Gilmore, and Karl Rove.

It is astonishing to both myself and many others that there has yet to be a biography dedicated solely to Dick Obenshain. While this is his biography, I also included biographical chapters on his three Republican opponents in order for readers to fully grasp the challenge he faced and the enormity of the 1978 primary, the climatic event in Obenshain's political life. This is his first biography to be published but I hope it is not the last. At the very least I hope that it serves as a foundation for future writers to write about the influence that Richard Obenshain had on Virginia and national politics. I do not feel that it is an overstatement to say that he was the Ronald Reagan of Virginia.

It is important to note that the issues which defined the political terms; conservative, liberal, and progressive, are somewhat different today than they were fifty years ago. You will see these descriptions used frequently throughout the book but remember the context of the times. No matter what side of the political aisle you are on, I hope that you can find inspiration in his story. I meant for his to be as personal of a story as possible: a story about a human being with a dream and the obstacles he faced to achieve that dream. Whatever your dream is, I hope this book helps you find that spirit of fire to pursue it.

I am thankful to the Obenshain family and the many people who were generous with their time on this project, and to scholars such as Frank B. Atkinson and John Stanley Virkler, who provided the framework for understanding the importance of this historic figure. Some of the political intrigue and analysis has been trimmed as these stories have already been written by the authors mentioned above. This allowed the space for more personal tales. Some of these stories are intended to provide insight as to the kind of man Dick Obenshain was, to inspire, and in some cases, to make you laugh.

I am grateful to the Honorable A.R. "Pete" Giesen, Jr. who encouraged me to pursue this project and to my friends over at The Printing Express who created the cover for this book. I am also thankful to the staff at the Library of Virginia, the Republican Party of Virginia, the Richmond Times Dispatch and countless others for allowing me access to their archives and scrap books. I would like to thank my family and friends for their support over the years that I have been working on this project. I certainly did not intend for the project to take this long, but the book relies heavily on interviews from first-hand accounts. Some of the interviews took months and even years to arrange. Unfortunately, many of the folks who knew Dick best have long since passed. Those who have not, found it difficult to remember many of the smaller, yet important details which required much cross-referencing to verify. It has now been forty-one years at the time of this writing since that tragic day, August 2nd, 1978.

-Joel L. Hensley

June 1st, 2019

Chapter 1:

A Convention Defeat

"Electrifying" is a term frequently used to describe the atmosphere of a state political convention in Virginia. Those who have had the privilege of attending such an event, on either side of the political aisle, fondly remember the feelings of enormity as nothing short of epic.

The first political convention occurred in Hartford, Connecticut in 1766, before the nation's birth and long before the advent of organized American political parties. This convention was organized in response to the implementation of the Stamp Act. As is often true in politics today, the primary issue of debate had been taxes. The incumbent, Governor Thomas Fitch, had been ousted by the Sons of Liberty in favor of William Pitkin, who opposed the Stamp Act. Early in the 19th Century, voting citizens wanted more control over their party's nominating processes, and conventions became a favorable alternative to secret caucuses, which could easily be manipulated and corrupted. Primaries eventually became another way for parties to nominate their candidates and allow more inclusiveness to the process.

For Republicans in Virginia, as at the national level, a state convention delegate is someone selected by the local political party, typically organized by city and county, to nominate a candidate to run for an elected office under the party label. There are almost no limitations as to who may attend, but the more delegates voting, the less their individual vote is worth. Voting points per locality are based on the party's previous election year strength within that locality. To attend is to witness history in the making, and to lay claim to an active role in the making of that history. It is participatory democracy at its liveliest. At the state level, friends, family, and others with personal connections to a candidate make up a significant portion of the convention delegates, which only intensifies the emotions that stir during these political boxing matches. Those involved in a candidate's campaign invest their time, money, and energy supporting and promoting their candidate. If the person seeking the party's nomination is defeated, it can be personally, professionally, or politically devastating for the candidate as well as those involved on the losing end of the race. Ideological differences, personal rivalries, and other fiery-spirited elements come to the forefront at these political events as the nominees are chosen and the direction of the party is decided.

Conventions are largely fickle and unpredictable. The momentum of a winning candidate can shift suddenly because another popular candidate endorsed his opponent; the slightest smear or rumor, an incorrect vote tally, and even the time of day can decide who wins and who loses. If it's a hotly contested race, no outcome is certain and anything can happen. Undecided delegates are more common in these settings because a candidate has the opportunity to make his case before a large audience immediately before voting. If a race is close, it may go to multiple ballots until a winner is declared. This allows the unpledged delegate to switch sides multiple times. Without pledging, a delegate is free to switch from one candidate to another. Appearances are everything during these crucial hours, and if a candidate shows signs of losing or has lost some momentum, it can have a snowball effect and make vote switching a convenient option. If it is late and a delegate is simply ready to go home and has no particular allegiance to that candidate, votes can be lost. Nobody knows for sure why some delegates switch their votes, but the mystery of the convention is enough to keep the candidates on their toes throughout the day and cause plenty of anxiety for the candidate's staff.

The details describing what happens at most of these conventions—the campaigns, the speeches, the candidates, and their faces—are scarcely remembered. However, there is one that is still talked about today by those who were there, as if they were veterans of a great battle deciding the fate of all mankind. The stories are told and retold, and the effects of this event are apparent even decades later. It has become interwoven into the history and culture of the Commonwealth of Virginia. This particular convention represented something more than an annual rallying cry for party members; it reflected a deep-rooted political clash at the heart of the American political fabric and the conservative movement. Virginians refer to it as "the Great Indoor Primary," which took place in 1978.

A year prior to that, the 1977 Republican Convention at the Roanoke Civic Center had nominated John Dalton as its gubernatorial candidate, Joe Canada for Lt. Governor, and Marshall Coleman as the candidate for Attorney General. It was no different than any other convention in regard to its electrifying atmosphere, but it was also something the Republican Party of Virginia had not been very accustomed to until recently. It was not long ago that a republican candidate would have to be persuaded to run for statewide office. The 20th Century proved to be a tumultuous period for Virginia Republicans as they grew from being a meek, ideologically confused party in the western mountain regions to a dominant majority covering the Commonwealth from all corners. Their conventions became the frontline catalysts for their movement. The Democratic Party had dominated Virginia politics for a century, mostly by a political organization informally known as the Byrd Organization, or the Byrd Machine. An outdated brand of alleged conservatism defined by archaic pay-as-you budgeting philosophy, racism, and an authoritarian political style. It tried to hold on to its conservative base while increasingly becoming more ideologically ambiguous at the state level and disenchanted by its more liberal counterparts at the national level.

"I have just seen my political life pass before my eyes," Dick said to his friend and political ally, John Alderson, as they exited the Roanoke Civic Center on June 4th, 1977.[1] This electrifying, unpredictable, hotly contested Republican convention left him in despair after two of the candidates he openly endorsed were defeated.

Richard (Dick) Dudley Obenshain dedicated most of his life to rebuilding the Republican Party in the Commonwealth of Virginia in the midst of a floundering Byrd Machine and through the Watergate scandal that devastated Republicans nationwide. He led a conservative coalition that had

---

[1] Atkinson, Frank B. *The Dynamic Dominion: Realignment and the Rise of Two-party Competition in Virginia, 1945-1980*. Lanham, MD: Rowman & Littlefield Publishers, 2006. p. 366

held together since 1972, which had now splintered in 1977 for the first time, a year prior to finally pursuing his lifelong dream.

Every few years it seemed as though that dream had been thwarted, either by a choice of his own or by circumstances out of his control. In the fall of 1977, he had planned on announcing his intent to run for the U.S. Senate. His dream had always been to become a United States Senator as a Republican while remaining principled to his distinct brand of conservative values throughout his pursuit. More importantly was the goal behind that dream, which was to have a role in expanding individual liberty in the United States. The Richmond Times summarized his career precisely by saying, "For here was a man whose every considerable achievement was the result of fierce adherence to principle. As early as 1960 he foresaw that the Virginia Republican Party—and Republican Parties throughout the South—would have to become vehicles of responsible conservatism for voters tired of being taken for granted by Washington".[2]

Frustrated and discouraged, he later vented to his mentor, Dr. Lewis Williams, "This convention has made the decision for me. There isn't any way I am going to run for the Senate".[3]

After defeat, many politicians become obsolete as quickly as they had risen to the top. Dick Obenshain had lost before—many times, in fact—yet managed to re-emerge more popular each time. His advisor, Kenny Klinge, chuckled, "Dick thought his political career was over almost every year".[4] The 1977 Republican convention would be the first time, however, that Dick suffered a loss so great within his own party. His previous losses were victories in disguise, as they showed that Dick was very capable as a candidate, an organizer, and a leader. This time he found little to be optimistic about as he and the 3,000 in attendance left that day. But the ideological leader known to many as the architect of the modern Virginia Republican Party would return to fight again.

---

[2]"Richard Dudley Obenshain." Richmond Times Dispatch, August 4, 1978.
[3] Atkinson, p. 366
[4] Kenny Klinge interview, February 10, 2010.

Chapter 2:

Spirits of Fire

This tale begins, like many, centered around money and political corruption. During the antebellum period, Virginia was prosperous, modestly progressive, and stable. Railroads were the largest new industry in the country during the Industrial Revolution. Due to seemingly endless years of prosperity, making payments on long-term debts for infrastructure projects was mostly a non-issue. As a result of her wealth, the Commonwealth confidently accrued $34 million in debt to finance new capital projects such as turnpikes, bridges, canals, and railroads that were guided under the auspices of the Virginia Board of Public Works. The agency skillfully found clever ways of financing and overseeing the direction of these endeavors. While Virginia had the 3rd largest debt of any other state, the long term goal was to make Virginia the primary connecting seaboard state between nations across the Atlantic Ocean and the booming Ohio Valley.[1] In short, Virginia was fast becoming the forward-thinking standard for the South and the nation.

Virginia also held a rich political history. The Commonwealth led the colonies in the American War for Independence and was called home by famous patriots such as Patrick Henry, Meriwether Lewis, George Mason, Sam Houston, Nathaniel Bacon, and Stephen Austin. Along the way, the Commonwealth acquired the nickname "Mother of Presidents." Home to eight presidents to be exact, seven of whom were president before the Civil War. This included Presidents George Washington, Thomas Jefferson, James Madison, James Monroe, William Henry Harrison, John Tyler, Zachary Taylor, and later, Woodrow Wilson. All of these men had a fire in the belly, defining themselves by an intense will to survive and an unbreakable determination to push boundaries and succeed in their endeavors.

Patrick Henry was the first of many in this ancestral line of kindred spirits. Self-learned, he made a name for himself after advocating for colonial rights during the "Parson's Cause" dispute. During this case, he gained a reputation as an exemplary and enthusiastic orator. He became a leading figure for American independence and was elected as Virginia's first post-colonial governor in 1776.

In the halls of St. John's Episcopal Church in Richmond, on March 23rd, 1775, Henry attended as one of 120 delegates to the second Virginia Convention. The convention was dominated by moderates and many who hoped that peace with Great Britain remained a viable option. Patrick Henry sat patiently, listening to prolonged speeches. When it was finally his turn, a Baptist minister in the room noted that he "had an unearthly fire burning in his eye," a look shared by those equally passionate for liberty. Yet he began his speech softly. The veins in his neck popped and his voice rose louder to the point that it nearly shook the walls. While his exact words remain unclear, there can be no doubt regarding the enormous effect his speech, popularly known for its famous line, "Give me liberty or give me death," had on the delegates that day, the children of that era, and the generations to come. It was his speech

---

[1] Morton, Richard L. "The Virginia State Debt and Internal Improvements 1820-1838." *Journal of Political Economy* 25, no. 4 (April 1917): 339-73.

that motivated the delegates to adopt an amendment allowing for the armament of militias for the coming war.[2] A few weeks later, the American War for Independence began after fighting broke out in the towns of Lexington and Concord, Massachusetts.

Less than a century later, after the attack on Fort Sumter, Virginia became the eighth state to secede from the Union, leading to the Civil War. Again, Virginia became the leader of yet another war for political independence, which ended in defeat for the southern states at Appomattox, Virginia in 1865. The results cast a dark shadow on Virginia's future that would last for a century. What was once a flourishing economic, cultural, and intellectual epicenter in the United States became burdened by despotism, debt, usury and ignorance. Opportunists emerged to take advantage of the chaos that afflicted all of the now impoverished southern states.

Most of the infrastructure built prior to the war, still unpaid for, had been completely destroyed. Virginia still owed much of this pre-war debt to northern interests. The years following were a politically vibrant, turbulent, chaotic scene which centered around how to pay back these loans. The conservative Democrats at the time believed in paying the debt at full interest, lest the state risk bankruptcy. The Readjuster Party emerged as a popular alternative to the Democratic stance and believed in "readjusting" the state's debts to accommodate a lower interest rate. It was a coalition party that consisted of Republicans and some conservative Democrats and won the support of both white and black men. Their stated goal was to break the power of wealth and established privilege. A similar statement would be echoed by the progressive movement several decades later.

Virginia had been split into two states—Virginia and West Virginia—and there was controversy over how much West Virginians owed as their share of the debt. The Panic of 1873 created an even deeper economic crisis. Finally, the racially charged Danville Riot of 1883 led to the dissolution of the Readjusters and marked the end of coalition building. This was followed by the election of John S. Bourbor Jr. to the U.S. Senate. Bourbor Jr. immediately

[2] Kukla, Jon. Patrick Henry: Champion of Liberty. New York: Simon and Schuster Paperbacks, 2018.

organized the top-down dominant political structure that led to the Byrd Machine.

On a national scale, political machines exploded in nearly every major city in the latter half of the 19th century. These machines were dominated by one individual, known as a "boss," who would become the center of power within the machine, conventionally motivated by his own self-interest. Machine politics often led to corruption in many forms, including graft, kick-backs, patronage, and voter fraud. This system could be seen across the nation's cities: Mayor Richard Daley in Chicago, James Pendergast in Kansas City, and Edward Crump in Memphis. But the most notable and heavy-handed was the New York City political machine known as Tammany Hall, dominated by William "Boss" Tweed. The Byrd Machine was one of the last state-wide machines left standing.

The machines had little to do with any sort of philosophy but were more about power for the sake of power. They were fundamentally at odds with the founding principles of liberty and radical individualism. While machine power grew, the United States was experiencing vast urban expansion and population growth, and with it, philosophical changes. The previously unchallenged power of the machines reached a boiling point that resulted in the progressive era, which began close to 1890. It lasted until around 1920, after the 19th Amendment passed, granting women the right to vote. This was not necessarily a monolithic movement, nor was it easily definable, but one thing progressives did do was directly target the existing political bosses and their machines. The primary goals of this era were to end political corruption, regulate monopolies, and reform the way government operated. The progressives were modestly successful in this pursuit.

In the early 20th century, before the Democrat and Republican parties defined themselves along the lines of polarized terms such as conservative and liberal, their opposition to each other was seemingly superficial. Diverse ideas existed within both party structures. Even members in the conservative coalition that emerged in the 1930s fundamentally disagreed on certain matters of economics and foreign policy. There were, however, and still are to this day, elitists and populists on both sides. The elitists were not necessarily what one would call "moderates," but they were essentially without principle and committed only to maintaining power. Professor Carroll Quigley, a mentor to President Bill Clinton, summarized the elitist position by saying, "The argument that the two parties should represent opposed ideals and policies, one, perhaps, of the Right and the other of the Left, is a foolish idea acceptable only to doctrinaire and academic thinkers. Instead, the two parties should be almost identical, so that the American people can 'throw the rascals out' at any election without leading to any profound or extensive shifts in policy."[3] Opposite of this, Obenshain staffer Bill Hurd said it best, that, "A party without principle is a conspiracy to take power."[4] It would take spirits of fire on both sides of the aisle to burn down this type of political control.

It is important to note that what defined conservatism to the Byrd Machine is not what defined conservatism on a national scale. Also, what defines conservatism today is not what defined it in the 1960s and 1970s. Environmental, religious, and social issues were not prevalent political issues at the time.

For the first half of the 20th century, conservatism found it difficult to define itself. Prior to World War Two, there was no self-described movement or even the title "conservative." However, there were those who referred to themselves as southern agrarians, individualists, isolationists, and nationalists who found themselves under the new label in the 1940s. With the political ascension of Franklin Roosevelt and the passage of the New Deal, like-minded people began to fear the perceived increase in power by the state, growing labor movements, and the communist threat. Still, it was rather unorganized.

Most would find the roots of conservatism in what was called classical liberalism. Classical liberalism, in essence, is defined by an adherence to the rule of law, the representative democratic process, civil liberties, natural rights, private property, and economic liberalism (capitalism).

Historian George H. Nash wrote a comprehensive summary in his work *Conservative Intellectual Movement in America Since 1945*. In it, he identified three strands of thought which had previously been considered independent of

---

[3] Quigley, Carroll. *Tragedy And Hope: A History Of The World In Our Time*. Macmillan, 1974. p. 1247.

[4] Gary Byler interview, December 26, 2009.

one another: libertarianism, traditionalism, and anti-communism.[5] The movement was able to find footing and harness its ideals around Senator Robert Taft in 1948.

In 1890, with the emergence of a strict political machine in Virginia, the vibrant dialogue and struggle that had been Virginia's heritage—highlighted especially in the past two decades—finally came to a screeching halt. Virginia was unique in that it became a state-level machine whose power was derived not so much in the municipalities, but in the rural counties dominated by the circuit courts. Harvard political scholar, V.O Key noted in his work *Southern Politics in State and Nation* that, "Of all the American states, Virginia can lay claim to the most thorough control by an oligarchy. Political power has been closely held by a small group of leaders who, themselves and their predecessors, have subverted democratic institutions and deprived most Virginians of a voice in their government...It is a political museum piece."[6]

---

[5] Nash, George H. *The Conservative Intellectual Movement in America since 1945*. Wilmington, DE: ISI Books, 2008. p. 5.

[6] Key, V. O. *Southern Politics in State and Nation*: (2. Print.). New York: Alfred A. Knopff, 1950. p. 19.

Chapter 3:

Boss Byrd

The heavy debt certainly made things worse for Virginia's already impoverished economy. Many children growing up in the rural parts of Virginia were very poor. Their lifestyles certainly influenced their later disdain for debt of any kind. Despite relative affluence, disdain for debt also influenced the thinking of a young future leader named Harry F. Byrd, who also had a "phobia of deficits".[1]

The Byrds are considered to be one of the First Families of Virginia; they first came to the colonies by way of William Byrd I in 1669. The family helped to establish the City of Richmond while growing their fortune as fur traders, slave dealers and landowners. They eventually amassed 180,000 acres around Charles City County, Virginia. Byrd Park was named after William Byrd II, a man known for his cruelty and womanizing ways. His son, William Byrd III, committed suicide in 1777 after alienating most of his relationships for

[1] Heinemann, Ronald L. *Harry Byrd of Virginia.* Charlottesville, VA: University Press of Virginia, 1996. p. 122.

supporting Great Britain during the Revolutionary War, and squandering most of his family's wealth through gambling. Although the Byrds of Virginia lost some of their status, they still maintained deep political and social connections throughout the 19th century.[2] William Byrd III's son, Thomas Byrd, fought for the crown and moved the family to Frederick County in 1786. Thomas's son Richard Evelyn Byrd was elected to the General Assembly in 1839. Two generations later, another Richard Byrd (and friend of Woodrow Wilson) would be elected to the House of Delegates. In 1886 "Dick" Byrd married Eleanor Bolling Flood, who also had a strong political heritage.[3] Her grandfather had been an ambassador to France, and her younger brother Hal would be elected to both chambers in the Virginia General Assembly and to the U.S. House of Representatives.

After the Civil War and the period of Reconstruction, a wealthy railroad lawyer by the name of Thomas Staples Martin emerged as the leader of Virginia's political future. Martin grew his financial standing by representing the Chesapeake and Ohio Railroad (also known as C&O) as their counsel.[4] The C&O was developed by one of the most hated and corrupt railway men of the time, Collis Potter Huntington, a member of "The Big Four," a group of influential businessmen who built the Central Pacific Railroad. The Big Four had developed a political machine of their own in which Huntington played a huge role: lobbying and bribing politicians. It was openly rumored that Martin had utilized these funds to bribe members of his caucus against Fitzhugh Lee for his United States Senate seat.[5] Lee assisted southerners in reconciling after the war as the Governor of Virginia, and was also the popular nephew of General Robert E. Lee.

A powerful figure in Martin's inner circle who helped his rise to power was none other than Hal Flood, the uncle of Harry F. Byrd. Flood was a member of the Virginia state Senate and helped Martin build a political organization which relied on railroad money and the New York banks which financed them. The Martin Organization, as it was called after John S. Barbour's

---

[2] Heinemann, p. 1.
[3] Heinemann, p. 3.
[4] Heinemann, p. 11.
[5] Ibid.

departure, experienced many wins but also a few losses after Virginia elected a progressive governor by the name of Andrew Jackson Montague in 1901. The progressive democrats argued for a new constitutional convention in Virginia in 1902, which ironically increased the power of the Martin Organization. The result of this convention was the creation of a $1.50 poll tax and a literacy test requirement in order to vote, which alienated most blacks and half of white voters in poor, mostly Republican areas in the Valley and Southwestern regions of the State.[6] Decreasing the size of the electorate made it easier for the organization to control the state at all levels through money and patronage. The new constitution created the circuit court system in Virginia, and all judges were to be appointed by the General Assembly. Judges could then appoint people to the county electoral board. The foundation for the circle of power was at the local level, primarily with the courthouses. Elected positions such as Commonwealth's Attorney, Clerk of Court, Commissioner of Revenue, Sheriff, and Treasurer were all responsible for getting out the vote and dispersing the patronage. There was no transparency. "In those days everything was done in secret; I was once sent to the library to dig for records about what supervisors were paid as a salary, that was also a secret," said republican political activist Barbara Hildebrand.[7] All elected officials became interlocked, dependent on each other for their own job security. This allowed the machine to run on its own, without a boss having to micromanage.

Martin and Flood publicly disagreed on having a convention, with Flood in favor while Martin was strongly against. However, considering the results, which strengthened the organization, it remains suspect whether this disagreement was a ruse from the beginning. Hal Flood was elected to Congress in 1901, where he stayed until his death in 1921. His brother-in-law, Dick Byrd, was elected to the House of Delegates in 1908, and was elected as Speaker of the House that same year. A suspiciously rare position of authority for a newly elected legislator. Dick Byrd was later appointed to United States District Attorney in 1914 by his friend, then President Woodrow Wilson. While the

---

[6] Heinemann, p. 12

[7] Barbara Hildebrand interview, March 3, 2010.

machine had contentious bouts with its members, it was able to survive and grow by putting pragmatism over principle.

Other notable colleagues of the organization included Representative Carter Glass, Senator Robert Owen, and Senator Claude Swanson. Glass was extremely influential during the Virginia Constitutional Convention of 1902, advocating for many progressive policies and for the creation of the State Corporation Commission, which replaced the old Virginia Board of Public Works. He also owned the Lynchburg Newspaper.[8] He is most remembered for his central role in helping President Wilson pass the Federal Reserve Act of 1913. After a brief stint as U.S. Secretary of the Treasury, in 1920 he was elected to the U.S. Senate, where he remained until his death twenty-six years later.

While not necessarily a direct member of the Martin Machine, Senator Robert Owen, like Congressman Carter Glass, was also originally from Lynchburg. However, he was elected to the United States Senate in the state of Oklahoma. He was born into a wealthy home, but his family lost their fortune during the Panic of 1873. He helped co-sponsor the Federal Reserve Act with his friend Carter Glass. Lastly, Senator Claude Swanson also identified himself as a progressive "Wilson" democrat. He was elected Governor of Virginia in 1905, shortly after the constitutional convention, and governed in a progressive way. He was appointed to the U.S. Senate in 1910 after the death of Senator John Daniel. Years later he was appointed by President Franklin Roosevelt to Secretary of the Navy in 1932, where he remained until his death. His successor to the U.S. Senate was none other than Harry F. Byrd. All three of these senators supported interventional foreign policy as well.

Perhaps the most powerful political figure in Virginia history, Harry Flood Byrd, was actually born in Martinsburg, West Virginia in 1887. He dropped out of school at a young age to run his father's newspaper, the Winchester Evening Star, which he purchased from him in 1902, then the Southern Bell Telephone Company. Finally, in 1906 he grew his fortunes and began leasing apple orchards near Winchester. This became his wealth-producing vocation and led to his title as "The Apple King" of America.[9] In

---

[8] Heinemann, p. 47.
[9] Heinemann, p. 125.

1915 young Harry Byrd ran for state Senate and won. Ten years later he ran a successful campaign for governor. His earnings increased substantially after running for public office.

He had grown up close to power, not only within his family, but also in his friendships. As a boy he became friends with Lewis Strauss, who he would eventually defend during Strauss's contentious nomination to become Secretary of Commerce.[10] Strauss was accused of withholding important information from Congress during the hearing, and Byrd used the power of his media outlets back home to try and write up supportive articles about Strauss. Strauss was born in West Virginia but grew up in Richmond. He had a decorated career as chairman of the Atomic Energy Commission and became wealthy after joining as a partner at Kuhn & Loeb bank as his friend Harry was finishing his last term as Governor of Virginia. His bid for Secretary of Commerce was ultimately unsuccessful.

Byrd maintained ironic friendships with people in high positions of power. One of which was Bernard Baruch.[11] Baruch served as a liaison and adviser under many presidents and was a very wealthy financier known as the "Czar of the War Industries Board" during World War I. Harry Byrd also adamantly defended accused communist Alger Hiss, something that at that time should have been politically risky for him to do.

Despite being perceived as an ultra-conservative, Byrd implemented progressive policies. When he was elected governor, his administration became one of the busiest in the nation. He turned a deficit into a surplus, implemented tax reforms, promoted electrification and conservation efforts in rural areas.[12] Under the guise of efficiency, he reformed (consolidated) Virginia's government by simplifying and merging hundreds of agencies, boards, and departments.

---

[10] Heinemann, p. 376

[11] Heinemann, p. 218

[12] Wilkinson, J. Harvie. *Harry Byrd and the Changing Face of Virginia Politics: 1945-1966.* Charlottesville: University Press of Virginia, 1984. p. 6.

As a U.S. Senator he supported and assisted with the election of Franklin D. Roosevelt, but later resented the man. Byrd himself voted with Republicans almost half of the time, while the rest of the conservative Democrats voted against the Republicans 70% of the time. He was certainly one of the least conservative of the southern democrats by comparison. The conservative coalition of the 1930s to 1960s, as well as Byrd's role in it (despite having much seniority in later years), is slightly exaggerated, according to V.O. Key.[13] He only voted against New Deal programs which would have paid workers a higher wage than what he was paying his own.

During the implementation of the New Deal, Byrd was initially supportive of the measures, which had a profound positive effect in temporarily relieving the burden that many Virginians faced. However, the Byrd organization failed to meet federal matching requirements, which prevented them from receiving continued assistance. Byrd and his machine were committed to governing 20th century Virginia in a 19th century manner. The fear was that the influx of money into the commonwealth, and the reforms that would come with those monies, would lead to Byrd losing his political control over the state.

Yet it was not the New Deal that brought down the Byrd Machine. What weakened and eventually destroyed the machine altogether was a growing population of Washington, D.C. transplants in northern Virginia. A growing suburbia brought with it a modern conservative base whose ideas clashed with the Byrd Machine's adherence to; segregation, the embarrassing failure of Massive Resistance (which the conservative Richmond business community also rejected), and pay-as-you-go financial methods which could no longer meet the emerging needs of the Commonwealth. Failure to respond to societal change is what ultimately killed the outdated Byrd Organization.

The Byrd Machine looked to rule indefinitely by the time Harry Byrd became a U.S. Senator. At the height of his power, he had obtained control over most of the newspapers in Virginia, restricted the electorate, and consolidated power within the Governor's office, which held the patronage for all of the county courthouses. This was the cornerstone of his power. Byrd also

---

[13] Wilkinson, p. 63.

had a consensus group, one in which his vote was the only one that mattered. "As long as he controlled things at the local level, it was 'pass the word' along. The henchmen would pass the word to their constituency and there were all of these little rewards. When time came to distribute license plates, you would be the one hired to distribute the license plates, so to speak", said republican activist Kenny Klinge.[14] While Byrd retained dominance in most of the Commonwealth, his power was weaker in the western and southwestern mountain regions of Virginia.

According to Judge J. Harvey Wilkinson in his book *Harry Byrd and the Changing Face of Virginia Politics 1945-1966*, "The Republican Party has often been called the 'liberal party in Virginia. Prominent Republican leaders objected to this definition, however. They preferred to characterize their party as more 'progressive' or less 'segregationist-minded' than the Virginia Democrats."[15] Byrd had occupied extreme conservative space with pay-as-you-go policies at the state level. Therefore, as an opposition party, Republicans had nowhere else to go but to the left of Byrd, however slightly it may have been.

Much of the regional divide was due to remnants of the Civil War: there was strong Unionist support in Southwest Virginia. It was also a classic "West versus East" cultural divide. The Democrats that dominated the central and eastern parts of Virginia considered themselves more sophisticated, while Republicans to the west were less affluent and were seen as being somewhat backwards. Those in the western part of the state were far removed from Richmond, with poorly maintained roads and insufficient aid for schools and internal improvements. For these reasons, while the Republican Party still wasn't a statewide threat to Byrd, they were able to maintain pockets of support in some parts of the western region during this era.

---

[14] Kenny Klinge interview, March 3, 2010.
[15] Wilkinson, p. 209.

Chapter 4:

A Philosopher's Walk

The Byrd Organization had solidified its stranglehold over Virginia after the election of Harry F. Byrd to the U.S. Senate in 1933. The Virginia Constitution had been rewritten in 1929 to further benefit Byrd, enhancing his ability to control the purse strings from afar through his handpicked governors. This would be the new normal in Virginia for nearly forty years. Byrd's attempts at political consolidation and domination were made easy by the distractions caused by the Great Depression and the second World War which loomed on the horizon. It was in the midst of this dark political era, on Halloween night of 1935, that Richard (Dick) Dudley Obenshain was born.

Up to this point the Obenshain family's political and social heritage had differed greatly from that of the Byrd lineage. While Harry Byrd's ancestors William Byrd III and Thomas Taylor Byrd were both well-known British loyalists, the first generation of American Obenshains fought for independence. The Obenshains had come to the colonies as poor farmers from Germany, while the Byrds had come from a family of wealthy goldsmiths from England. The Byrds were staunch Democrats; the Obenshains, staunch Republicans.

The Abendschoen family, as was their Germanic surname, resided in and around the country town of Schwaigern in the southwestern region of Germany between the cities of Heidelberg and Stuttgart. There is some debate over the meaning of the family name, but it is popularly accepted to mean "beautiful evening." The nearby City of Heidelberg is known for its ancient architecture and the famous "Philosopher's Walk," an old pathway used by local philosophers, professors, and priests. The intellectuals of the city and surrounding area would commonly walk, think, pontificate, and converse among the scenic views and the old buildings and churches.[1]

By the mid-18th century, the area had already experienced decades of conflict between Catholics and Protestants after Charles III Philip, Elector Palatine, gave the ancient Church of the Holy Spirit exclusively to the Catholic Church in 1720. It had previously been shared by both groups. Just three years before, Count Wilhelm Reinhard von Neipperg, who ruled the town of Schwaigern, reversed two hundred years of Protestant tradition within his family by converting to Catholicism. While it is unclear why the Abendschoen family left the prolific Protestant town of Schwaigern, it is possible that these conflicts contributed to their decision to leave.

Regardless of their reasoning, Samuel Heinrich Abendschoen and his family of nine others boarded a ship called "Fane" and left Germany for Pennsylvania, arriving in Philadelphia on October 17th, 1749. They settled in the northern part of Lancaster County, which broke off and became Berks County a few years later. At that time, Pennsylvania was governed by proprietors, but it was known as a beacon of religious freedom with a growing economy.

At some point the Abendschoens changed their name to the more English-sounding "Obenshain." The sons of Samuel Heinrich fought in the American War of Independence. One of these sons, Christian, had a son named Daniel, who continued to farm and later moved his family to Botetourt County in the southwestern part of Virginia between Roanoke and Lexington. Daniel also had a son named Samuel, who was known in the community as "Hotel"

---

[1] Heidelberg Castle. Accessed April 02, 2019. https://www.heidelberg-marketing.de/en/experience/sights/heidelberg-castle.html.

Sam—by this time, there were so many Obenshains in Botetourt County that many of them took up nicknames to distinguish themselves. There was "Paper Mill" Bill, "Wagon Maker" Bill, "Potter Maker" Pete, and of course "Hotel" Sam, who owned a local inn and was a stagecoach driver, and like many Obenshains before him, worked his own land. In fact, he was killed while doing so: one day while out plowing his field, his plow horse suddenly sprinted, dragging the 78-year-old "Hotel" Samuel Obenshain to his death in 1890. [2]

"Hotel" Sam had fourteen children from two marriages. Many of these Obenshains fought for the South and joined the Blue Ridge Rifle Regiment, which organized at Blue Ridge Hall, owned by "Hotel" Sam.[3] The smaller regiment served in the 28th Virginia Volunteer Infantry Regiment, which raised volunteers from Botetourt, Craig, Bedford, Campbell, and Roanoke counties. The infantry unit served throughout the war under famous generals such as James Longstreet and George Pickett, fought in 18 battles and campaigns, and participated in Pickett's Charge at the Battle of Gettysburg. Most of the Obenshains were captured at Gettysburg and remained as prisoners until the end of the war.

Of the fourteen children by "Hotel" Sam, Boyce Putney Obenshain was one of the youngest, born after the war. Boyce was the first known politician in the family. At some point in his life he befriended Congressman C. Bascom Slemp. Slemp was the sole Republican congressman from Virginia, succeeding the position from his father, Campbell Slemp, after he passed away in October of 1907. Bascom Slemp served until his appointment as Secretary to President Calvin Coolidge in 1923, where he served for two years. It was Congressman Slemp who encouraged his friend, Boyce Obenshain, to run for Sheriff of Botetourt County in 1919. Their relationship was allegedly so close that Boyce could walk into Washington, D.C. and go right into the Secretary to the President's office in the Capitol without an appointment.[4]

The Republican Boyce Obenshain likely shared the traditionalist, non-interventionalist mindset. There was a wave of resentment and backlash

---

[2] Joseph (Joe) Obenshain interview, September 1, 2017.
[3] Mark Obenshain interview, March 23, 2018.
[4] Joe interview, September 1, 2017.

towards Woodrow Wilson after getting the United States involved in World War I. After winning, Sheriff Obenshain would serve in his post for several years and would be the first Obenshain to confront the Democratic operation that Byrd took over in 1925.

Boyce made a successful living not only as a farmer but as a businessman, and was well-respected within a community dominated by Democrats. Yet it was a small county, and people knew him personally. Evidence suggests that Boyce was the first Republican to ever be elected to any local public office in Botetourt County. Boyce was not a professional law enforcement officer; in those days the position was mostly political. Most of the duties involved directing traffic at funerals and keeping order at the county Board of Supervisor meetings. However, after 1920, when Prohibition went into effect nationally, the job did entail raiding bootleggers. According to his grandchildren, one of Boyce's deputies got into some trouble during his term, and another turned out to be a crook. The incidents were so disheartening to Boyce that he decided not to run again in 1923. However, another Republican followed and was elected as Sheriff.[5]

Boyce had one son and six daughters. He would pass on the Republican tradition to them. Samuel Shockley Obenshain, his only son, was a very bright and talented individual who became a Professor of Agronomy at Virginia Polytechnic Institute (Virginia Tech), as well as an internationally renowned soil specialist. Dr. Obenshain never wavered in his beliefs as a Republican, but it did prevent him from ever becoming the chair of his department, despite having many accolades. While teaching at VPI, some of his friends and colleagues voiced their concern over his outspoken politics. Faculty colleagues told him numerous times that he was crazy for admitting to people that he was a Republican, warning him that he could lose his job. His daughter, Beth Obenshain, recalled him coming home one day distraught because his department chair was angry with him and had said, "Nobody in our department is going to get a raise this year, because we have a known Republican in our department!" Whether or not that was true, the constant badgering had to have been a point of frustration for the elder Obenshain. The department he worked

---

[5] Joseph (Joe) Obenshain interview, July 20, 2011.

for was headed by a prominent Democratic family from the eastern shore of Virginia. Dr. Obenshain was never afraid of a good argument. His family took note of his convictions as well, especially his oldest son, Richard Dudley Obenshain, whom they called "Dick." [6]

Dr. Obenshain married Josephine Dudley (Jo), who he had met while he was a student at Iowa State getting his Ph.D. Josephine was a librarian at the college. She was born in Augusta County but grew up in New York, where she was valedictorian at her school. She was very bright and edited many of Dr. Obenshain's papers, helping him get through his doctorate program. Once married, the two moved back to Virginia. Life in the country was initially difficult for Josephine, who was raised as a city girl and had to adjust to being a full-time homemaker.[7] Once settled, she became an active participant in her new community. She joined various community groups and clubs in Botetourt County such as the Association of American Women and the Faculty Wives Club. Josephine also taught Sunday school at the Blacksburg Baptist Church, which they attended. She was an avid reader and helped establish a local library and a book-mobile. Her active involvement in the community had an enormous influence on her children.[8]

Dr. Obenshain was a bit louder and more of an outspoken individual, while Josephine was the quieter and more introverted spouse, but "she was the sun that they all revolved around".[9] Despite their different personalities, together they made a wonderful pair. If there was any disagreement between them, the children were not aware of it. It was a very loving, affectionate, devoted relationship that created a stable environment for their children to flourish in. "Our parents gave us a model as to what a marriage should be," said Beth. As parents, they were very stern yet gentle with their children. Dr. Obenshain was particularly strict with the boys. The family tried to instill a love of farming while also placing great emphasis on the importance of an education. While they were not wealthy, they never went without their basic needs; they

---

[6] Beth (Betty) Obenshain interview, July 20, 2011.
[7] Scott Obenshain interview, September 18, 2017.
[8] Beth (Betty) Obenshain, September 13, 2017.
[9] Ibid.

were what some would call "land rich." Samuel and Josephine had three sons and one daughter: Richard (Dick), Scott, Joseph (Joe) and Beth (Betty).[10]

Dick Obenshain was born in Abingdon shortly after the couple had moved back to Virginia. The Obenshains moved near Blacksburg when Dick was one year old and rented a farmhouse. The home was small and only had four rooms, with no indoor plumbing. Meanwhile, Dr. Obenshain was working on building their future home on a 140 acre farm property that he had purchased two miles outside of Blacksburg. He wanted a place to call his own where he could continue the family tradition of farming. Perhaps the farm provided necessary security in case he ever lost his job over politics. Luckily, Dr. Obenshain was a good judge of property and happily offered 25 dollars more than what the neighbor was willing to sell it for. He completed construction on the house in 1942.[11]

Dick and Scott were only three years apart. The two were typical brothers who had different interests yet shared a lot in common, including a bedroom, October birthdays, and hot tempers. While they generally got along, it wasn't unusual for the two of them to fight, often times in the barn. "Dick had a good sense of humor. He also had a temper. He'd get upset and that's when we would fight. We both had tempers. It was easy to push," said Scott. This mostly stopped when Scott was big enough to hold his own.

Both had much responsibility on the farm. Their father travelled often, which made Dick the man of the house. It was a difficult farm operation: they would wake up at 6 a.m. and do everything from milking the cows, making hay, hoeing corn, driving horses, making silage, feeding the hogs, and whatever else needed to be done.

Scott recalled, "When each of us would turn six years old, my dad would buy us our own purebred jersey calf." It was a wonderful part of their childhood, but life on the farm was somewhere in between constant adventure and drudgery. None of the children could understand why they had to use outdated techniques, tools, and methods that made the work twice as hard.

---

[10] Ibid.

[11] Scott Interview.

"Growing up on the farm was frustrating," Scott continued. "Here our father was a professor in ag, and we were still doing things the ancient way by chocking it up and dragging it up on a haystack with a horse and long stick that we just tied the shock on and pulled it in. We thought we should be doing things like everybody else."[12]

He wasn't alone in his sentiment. While Dick was naturally a hard worker and did well on the farm, he did not develop the same love for agriculture that his father had. He despised getting up early every morning. The farm life was not something he could ever imagine himself pursuing as an adult.

Despite all of his responsibilities at home, Dick did well in school and participated in a lot of activities at Blacksburg Elementary School. In fourth grade, he played the trumpet in the school band, and later tried to help get Scott into the school band as well by mentoring him on the drums. Scott, admittedly, wasn't very good. "I remember them sitting on the front porch practicing," said Betty, which made the farm dogs howl. Dick was also a proficient reader, and later became a skilled writer. He tried a little bit of everything. It was in fourth grade that he met his lifelong best friend, Rodman Layman. Rodman and Dick were "joined at the hip" from that point on.

Mother Josephine was always involved with trying to improve the public schools. Funding for schools was always an issue, especially since the western region of the state was far removed from the state capitol. Beth recalled finding old letters that Josephine had written to the local school board asking for certain fees to be waived for lower income families who lived in the area. To help remedy the situation in her own household, she read often to her children, including each night before bed.

The importance of family was emphasized in the Obenshain household as well. All of Dr. Obenshain's six sisters lived close enough to meet for every holiday. This made for massive get-togethers. Dick's Aunt Lucy's was the place to be every year, and numerous cousins swelled her home. Dick's Aunt Elizabeth wrote a Halloween story about him when he was a little boy. She was actively writing children's stories at the time and decided to write one in which

---

12 Ibid.

a boy named "Dickie" was the hero of the story. Since Dick's birthday was on Halloween, the character who shared his name would go off on Halloween adventures every year with an elf, a witch, or a ghost, and his little brother Scott had to stay home, since his birthday was not on Halloween. The countless family get-togethers allowed the Obenshain children to have a much closer relationship with their extended family members.

Dick's maternal grandfather, Joseph Dudley, moved in with the family for ten years after his wife passed away. At one time he had been a director at the YMCA in New York, and he was a card-carrying Democrat. Grandfather Dudley knew Boyce Obenshain long before they became interwoven through their children's marriage, and they were on opposite sides of nearly every political issue in Botetourt County during that ten year period. Eventually there had to be an agreement between Sheriff Obenshain and Grandfather Dudley that there would be no discussion of politics between the two of them. Joseph Dudley was always reading, and was an intensely religious man whose daily proximity likely helped launch Dick's interest in spiritual matters.[13]

The church was also an important part of the family's social life in Blacksburg. The family attended Blacksburg Baptist Church, but also had a hand in helping nearby Mill Creek Baptist church when in 1910 Boyce P. Obenshain donated land space for a new building.[14] Dr. Obenshain became a deacon at the Blacksburg Baptist Church, but it was Josephine who seemed more interested in contemplating the great theological issues. From an early age, religion was important to Dick. His religious upbringing deeply guided him and his decision making, beyond even what most had known. His brother Joseph put it best when he said, "Religion was important to Dick, but he didn't wear it on his sleeve. He believed in freedom of religion more than just a secular position. Religion provided a base for his actions."[15]

Upon entering Blacksburg High School (at an earlier age than most), Dick continued to stay busy and aimed for high achievement. His grades were good, and he made time for extracurriculars. The Obenshains were not natural

---

[13] Ibid.
[14] Joe Interview, September 1, 2017.
[15] Joe interview, July 20, 2011.

athletes, but they were tough. Dick ran cross-country track, and in his senior year he joined the football team, something his siblings noted he was most proud of. He was scrawny at 5'11, but he was quick, which made him an acceptable enough player to earn a spot as a second stringer. But that became a staple of Dick's personality. He wasn't afraid to try new things, and he thrived off of being the underdog in any situation. Academic activities were more his pace; he joined the school's debate team and was Speaker of the House for the YMCA's model General Assembly during his senior year. It was 1952, the same year as the famous Democratic senatorial primary between Harry F. Byrd and challenger Francis Pickens Miller. During the deliberations at the model General Assembly, someone introduced a resolution to support Miller in the primary against Byrd; almost everyone except for Dick opposed the mock resolution.[16]

Dick was interested in a little bit of everything. In particular, his most loved subjects were history, economics, philosophy, theology, and government. Teachers and colleagues jokingly recalled him walking around the high school with a copy of the Constitution in his pocket. His senior year, he edited the sports section of the school newspaper and ran for mayor of the school's town government. One of the perks of being school mayor would be to hold mayor's court in the actual office of the town mayor. Scott Obenshain recalled continuing to rib his older brother by campaigning against him for the other candidate, Tommy Clemens, who ended up winning. All in all, there were four total candidates, and Dick's first attempt at running for office was unsuccessful. Tommy, however, was a friend of Dick's, although they weren't nearly as close as he, Rod and the most recent addition to the inner fold, Jay Price. Jay entered this close circle in high school. Together, the three of them were likened to the Three Musketeers. Tommy remembered them as being "nice guys; they all thought they were the best (academically), but they weren't arrogant." There were a little over one hundred students in their graduating class, and five were chosen as speakers for graduation. Dick was one of those speakers, as he was

---

[16] Ibid.

one of the top leaders in the class. Dick, Jay, Rod and Tommy, were all ambitious students.[17]

Dick was considered by all accounts to be a good child. He was obedient to his parents, he worked hard around the family home, and studied hard at school. He looked out for his siblings and took his faith seriously, even at a young age. Aside from the occasional mischievous behavior that all children get into, he was never in serious trouble in school or at home.

It wasn't until around the age of nine that Dick really began to take a more serious interest in politics. He felt that he came from a political heritage and reveled in the fact that being a Republican meant being an automatic underdog. Dr. Obenshain made an effort to bring his children along to county political meetings as part of their education. "We learned that it was just a part of good citizenship, that you participated in the political system, you voted, but you were also active in the local party," Betty reflected on her earliest political memories. "Going to committee meetings was just like going to church, it was a part of being a citizen." Dr. Obenshain never forced his children to go, but to them it was another social event. Their friends at school were mostly Democrats, so they had to learn to defend themselves early on. Even their mom would participate and was counted on for organizing things for the local party. But Dick was the one who truly "caught the bug."[18]

To the Obenshain family, which had traditionally been Republican and stood opposed to the Byrd Machine, it always seemed natural and inevitable that conservatives should rally to the Republican Party. The family believed that if a state did not have at least a two-party system, it would fall victim to cronyism, with nobody to investigate or hold people accountable for their actions. Republicans in Virginia were not necessarily liberal, but they sought to be a modern conservative party: a modern solution to outdated problems. Dick, of course, adopted these views at an early age. In 1944, at the age of nine, Dick campaigned for Thomas Dewey against Franklin Roosevelt. Dewey ran on the idea of compassionate capitalism and was considered a moderate. However, it

---

[17] G.O. (Tommy) Clemens interview, October 18, 2017.

[18] Betty interview, September 13, 2017.

was Dewey's running mate, John W. Bricker, backed by Senator Robert Taft, who reflected Dick's emerging political philosophy.

Dick graduated early from Blacksburg High School in 1952 at the age of sixteen. He and his best friend, Rod Layman, were chosen as pages to the Republican National Convention and Dick was allowed to go as a graduation present. The event was held at the International Amphitheater in Chicago. Their family friend and state senator Ted Dalton accompanied them to the event and even managed to get them onto the floor at the convention. Dalton was gearing up to mount a campaign for governor against a Byrd man by the name of Thomas Stanley. "Mr. Republican" Ted Dalton must have also inspired Dick's early political dreams. He was the first Republican who came close to successfully challenging the Byrd Machine.

This convention witnessed Dwight D. Eisenhower, the eastern establishment's man, versus Robert A. Taft, son of former President and Chief Justice William Howard Taft. For years Taft was the main opponent of Roosevelt in the Senate. He became the Senate Majority leader and fought the inflating power of labor unions by passing the Taft-Hartley Act of 1947. He was also coincidentally nicknamed "Mr. Republican" as a national leader of the conservative wing of the Republican Party. Taft had previously made two unsuccessful attempts at the Republican nomination for president, once in 1940 and again in 1948. He continued to make a strong showing, and with Thomas Dewey no longer a candidate he was considered to be the frontrunner heading into the 1952 Republican convention. Taft's non-interventionalist foreign policy ideals were now becoming less attractive as the fear of communism grew. The Eastern Establishment of internationalists, moderates, and liberals capitalized on these fears by talking NATO Commander General Dwight D. Eisenhower into running for president. Eisenhower was also afraid of Taft's anti-NATO stance. Taft's third and final run for president was fought to the bitter end. He was one of the first who maintained a firm belief that Southern Democrats could be persuaded to vote Republican.

Dick's first Republican convention ended up being one of the most contentious and vicious in history. It was a struggle for control of the national party between the conservatives of the South and Midwest against the establishment moderates from the eastern and coastal states. The ballots essentially tied on day one, with the Eisenhower campaign claiming that their delegates were being denied votes in several southern states. Though the accusations were not proven, the convention delegates nonetheless voted for the "fair play" proposal, which removed these Taft delegates and replaced them with Eisenhower delegates. The fair-play vote resulted in Taft's narrow defeat by Eisenhower. Taft later lamented that every Republican candidate for president since the 1930s had been "nominated by Chase Manhattan Bank," but he would eventually support Eisenhower.[19] Senator Taft died the following year on July 31st, 1953.

The contest remained the last dynamic primary on the national stage for quite some time. The conservatives had been defeated yet again. The battle would be the first of many between the conservative and moderate factions for the soul of the Republican Party, a division which can be seen to this day. The battle that took shape nationally would begin trickling down to the state and local levels.

The learning experience foreshadowed many tactics that Dick would later employ, like putting aside differences to work with a rival. The volatile, dramatic, and energetic convention was also the first to be televised nationally. It is no surprised that Dick would come home after that event energized and inspired to make politics a part of his future.

When the time came for Dick to choose a college, he didn't want to stay at home and go to Virginia Tech, where his father worked. His parents always encouraged their children to go to college somewhere different, outside of their comfort zone. In the months that followed, Dick enrolled as a freshman at Bridgewater College in Bridgewater, Virginia, a small, private liberal arts college founded in 1880. The reasons were many: Dick had been anxiously wanting to get off the farm, and it was a religious school—but more importantly, his best friend Rod Layman was also going to Bridgewater. He ended up rooming with Rod while at Bridgewater. Rod describe him as being very studious, just as he was in high school.[20] He studied economics and was

---

[19] Nichols, John. "The Nation: Why Do GOP Bosses Fear Ron Paul?" NPR. December 22, 2011. Accessed April 02, 2019. https://www.npr.org/2011/12/22/144122913/the-nation-why-do-gop-bosses-fear-ron-paul.

[20] Rodman Layman interview, August 17, 2011.

influenced by the ideas of conservative Austrian economists Ludwig Von Mises, Friedrich Hayek, Milton Friedman, Henry Hazlitt, and Wilhelm Roepke.[21] These great thinkers of the day also made an enormous impact on the mind of Ronald Reagan, who even appointed Milton Friedman as an advisor.

He continued to run cross-country track and was on a nationally ranked, undefeated debate team with his newfound friend Pasco "Bud" Bowman, who was one year ahead and became somewhat of a mentor to Dick. The two would remain on parallel life trajectories for quite some time and remained friends for years. First Bud became editor of the Bridgewater school paper, then Dick became editor. Bud became president of student council, then Dick succeeded him as president of student council the following year. "We had a lot of crossings. I liked him and admired him," Bud said of his old friend. Bud would eventually go on to be nominated by President Ronald Reagan as a judge for the United States 8th Circuit Court of Appeals.[22]

Every summer that Dick came back home, he would have to spend most of his time working on the farm while squeezing in a little bit of softball at the church every once in a while. There was always something that needed to be done on the farm. He spent his last summer vacation living at his aunt's house in Holland, Virginia, which is now a part of Suffolk. He took a summer job there at a Pepsi-Cola bottling plant and worked as a deliveryman, which he hated. The first week he had blisters everywhere, including all over his hands. Farming was hard, but these conditions were apparently worse. Unhappy and desiring to quit, he asked his father if he could come back home for the summer, but Dr. Obenshain refused to let him. Even Boyce Obenshain, who wasn't an "easy" man, thought Dr. Obenshain was being too hard on his grandson. Dick stuck it out, and the experience of hard work for little pay inspired him to continue his education beyond undergraduate studies.[23]

It wasn't until college that Dick began to even contemplate attending law school. There were no lawyers in the family at the time, but studying law

---

[21] Obenshain, Richard. "Biography" *Richmond News Leader*, July, 1964.
[22] Judge Pasco "Bud" Bowman interview, April 14, 2017.
[23] Betty interview, September 13, 2017.

seemed like a natural step if one had political ambitions. Several of his friends—Rod, Jay, and Tommy Clemens—became lawyers. But Dick had another passion as well.

Many are unaware as to how deeply devout of a Christian he was. In a biographical sketch, he once said that his theological inspirations were the existential theologians, Paul Tillich, and Soren Kierkegaard in particular.[24] Kierkegaard's ideas emphasized that individuals have a certain set of independent choices to make that defines his existence. His theological perspective perfectly coincided with his political beliefs in freedom and the responsibility of the individual.

Dick's impressive academic résumé resulted in an offer of a Rockefeller Fellowship to study divinity at Yale. The offer appealed to one of his earliest passions, which was that of his Christian faith. Simultaneously, he was offered a Root-Tilden scholarship at New York University Law School, arguably the most prestigious scholarship in the country, which his friend Bud Bowman had accepted a year earlier. Only twenty-four of these scholarships were granted annually.

Dick was now faced with his own choice of divine implications, a decision which would dictate the course of his life. His brother Joe recalled him mulling over this decision for quite a while. Letters of correspondence between Dick and his mother Josephine revealed that a spiritual leader at Bridgewater was trying to convince him to become a minister. In addition to that, his grandfather Dudley, who had been an inspiration to Dick's spiritual upbringing, had passed away during his time away at Bridgewater. The always reserved Josephine wrote a thoughtful response to her son, which impacted his decision more than anyone else could. In it, she emphasized the great responsibilities of being a minister and the expectations of being a perfect person. She delicately implied that she herself had a temper, although nobody in the home remembered ever seeing it. She continued that Dick had inherited certain traits from his parents, and asked whether his temperament was best suited for that

---

[24] Virkler, John S. "Richard Obenshain: Architect of the Republican Triumph in Virginia" Unpublished Thesis, Auburn University, 1987. p. 4.

type of career.[25] Dick could read between the lines in his mother's words and accepted the scholarship at NYU. Mr. and Mrs. Obenshain were both relieved.

Josephine was happy to visit Dick in her home state of New York. She and a few of Dick's aunts travelled to the city several times. His aunts, in true southern-women fashion, showed up with Queen Elizabeth pocketbooks and were seen wearing white gloves trying to hail down a cab. Despite being obvious tourists, they said the people of New York couldn't have been nicer, and they loved every visit.[26] After Dick's first year at NYU, his little brother Joe, in his early teen years at the time, took a train by himself to visit for a week. Joe looked up to his older brother and had an excellent time seeing the Bronx Zoo and Yankee Stadium. Dick was working for a law firm that summer, so Joe had to do a lot of activities on his own during the day. Once, he got lost after Dick accidentally put him on the wrong subway. It was the only hiccup during the visit.

Like many New Yorkers, Dick didn't have a car and had to walk everywhere. It was quite different than any place he had been before and afforded him opportunities that were simply not available in the Roanoke Valley. When he took a break from studying, he'd spend a lot of his time seeing Yankees games and Broadway shows. He got to witness Yankees pitcher Don Larsen's "perfect game" during the 1956 World Series. The time in New York gave him a new-found sense of sophistication that he enthusiastically brought home with him. It opened him up to a whole new world of theater, books, and music. His siblings said, "It expanded our horizons with him being in New York City and gave him a life-long love of music and theater." When he came home, he would bring records with him from Hal Holbrook's *Mark Twain*, *My Fair Lady*, *The Sound of Music*, and *Blackwatch*, a famous Scottish regiment band that paraded around Madison Square Garden. Beth recalled having to listen to the musical *The Music Man* repeatedly, which made its original appearance on Broadway in 1958 and won six awards that year.[27]

---

[25] Betty interview, July 20, 2011.
[26] Betty interview, September 13, 2017.
[27] Ibid.

Scott was now a college student, and when the two brothers were back for the holidays they would sit around the dinner table most nights providing entertainment for the family by having "rip and roaring political discussions, shouting at each other, then suddenly realizing a baseball game would be on".[28] They loved to discuss and argue politics for the sheer joy of intellectual stimulation. "It was lively whenever Dick and Scott were home. We'd sit around the table for hours after dinner and I'd listen to the guys argue back and forth. They'd find some difference, argue about it, and my parents enjoyed it and would just look on. My mother would bring in a book and read it. It was great family time," their sister Beth recalled. It was never personal, and they never got upset. They simply loved to debate, but it was clear that they were evolving into two different directions.[29]

The scholarship opened him up to a whole new world of friends as well, and he developed a wide range of contacts for a country boy from Blacksburg. Many of his friends were liberal, but Dick enjoyed the political give and take. His friend and fellow Root-Tilden scholarship colleague, Larry Dagenhart, recalled, "Dick had great strength of character and conviction. He was also very likeable and managed to be clear and forceful but never strident when he set forth his views. I think that made him unique." He could debate for hours on end and still be good friends with someone. That was one of the things that made him a charismatic figure: he never took things too personally. Larry and his wife Sarah remembered Dick as "a very pleasant southern boy," an assessment aided by a gap between his two front teeth and a strong Appalachian accent.[30]

One time, two of his closest friends in New York, Harvey and Murray, who were both from California, visited Dick for the holidays. They couldn't afford to go home, so Dick invited them to come back with him to his home in Blacksburg. Dick's mother and aunts "doted" over the boys and spoiled them for a couple of weeks. The boys got to experience a true southern Christmas, like a scene straight from a Norman Rockwell painting. They piled their plates

---

[28] Ibid.
[29] Ibid.
[30] Larry Dagenhart, e-mail message to author, December 4, 2009.

full of turkey, country ham, pecan pie, German chocolate cake, and the Obenshain specialty, ham biscuits. The boys had to reject the ham. They were even treated to a traditional Christmas Eve celebration at the Blacksburg Church. This made for an entertaining and culturally enriching experience for Harvey and Murray since they both were Jewish.

Dick took advantage of all the lights and glitter of New York, but he never got swept away by it. The hustle and bustle of New York was a culture shock and it gave him a new appreciation and nostalgia for his home life on the farm. In fact, he was actually homesick for Virginia. He never listened to country or bluegrass music prior to living in New York, but he became a fan and had a special fondness for Eddie Arnold's remake of "Cattle Call." It was his way of connecting with his roots.

Dick continued to be an earnest student and lived up to his scholarship's reputation. He worked for a law firm called Willkie Farr & Gallagher led by former presidential candidate Wendell Willkie. While at NYU, he and Bud Bowman remained friends and took several classes together with a tough professor by the name of Sylvester Petro. Petro was respected by his students but his ideals were out of the mainstream in legal academia. He was largely ahead of his time. Bowman recalled that if a student didn't agree with the professor's perspective, he assumed that they weren't too smart. Dick loved a good challenge, but Professor Petro did more to elevate the economic ideas that Dick already introduced himself to while at Bridgewater College.[31] Petro was a very conservative scholar who influenced many students during that time. He became a world-renowned intellectual in the school of Austrian Economics. With a particular expertise in labor policy, he wrote several works describing what he saw as growing power and corruption by labor unions and dismantled the current antitrust laws that existed in the United States. Eventually, he became a dean at Wake Forest. Like John the Baptist, Petro "baptized" both Dick and Bud to Austrian ideas concerning economics. Petro's influence took Dick from being just a casual, run of the mill conservative observer to becoming a die-hard believer in conservative ideology and the basic principles of free-markets and liberty.

---

[31] Bowman interview.

After graduation, Dick was faced with yet another fork in the road. He had a tremendous opportunity with the law firm he was working for while in school. New York itself provided many economic opportunities for a great mind such as his. His father argued that he should stay in New York and said there was no future in coming back to Virginia to build a Republican Party. But Dick was "determined that, by God, he was going to come back to Virginia to practice law, but mainly, to build a two-party system. At a time when nobody thought it was possible, Dick came back to do it".[32] He gave up the potential to earn lots of money, feeling that he now had the education and background to chase his dream. Although he loved New York, he loved his home state of Virginia more. The year was 1959 and Dick was 23 years old.

Meanwhile the power of the Byrd Machine was beginning to recede. It had faced a huge political defeat over Massive Resistance, a strategy invoked by Harry Byrd in response to the Brown versus the Board of Education decision in 1954. Attempts were made at preventing desegregation, and many public schools actually closed in 1958 and 1959. That same year, the judicial branch overturned these efforts and declared them unconstitutional. Dick, like most of the young emerging Republicans of his day, was racially progressive, believing that the founding ideas of freedom and opportunity belonged to all Americans.[33] While Republicans had made some small gains at the local level, they still barely existed as a formidable party statewide.

Upon his return, his siblings recalled that he had changed. He came home with a conviction in his heart that had not been there before, a consuming "fire" that he felt he needed to share with Virginia and the world.

---

[32] Joe interview, July 20, 2011.
[33] Wyatt Durrette interview, December 16, 2016.

Chapter 5:

The Young Republican

Dick had one more goal he wanted to accomplish before entering the workforce. Seemingly out of the blue, he entered into the Marine Corps. It was his own idea, a patriotic way of testing himself in a vastly different arena. It was also what many young men did to avoid being drafted: they would spend six months on active duty, followed by three to five years in the active reserves. The Korean War had been over for six years, but with the Cold War at its height there remained a strong possibility of sudden military intervention.

After graduating from NYU, he went through basic training at Parris Island, South Carolina in the summer of 1959. Dick was almost twenty-four years old and his master sergeant was only nineteen years of age. The age gap between him and most of the other recruits immediately made him the target for many "old man" jokes amongst his friends, but he was well-respected nonetheless, especially by his sergeant. He acted as a mentor to many of the recruits and was able to help a few of them get out of trouble, including one young recruit who stole a jar of peanut butter from the meal hall and was about to be court martialed for the incident. Later towards the end of his training he became severely ill and ended up in the infirmary for several weeks. He managed to pull through and still graduated. [1]

Dick was the only college graduate in his platoon to graduate as a private first class. After four years of college and three years of law school, he was very proud to have survived school, enlistment and illness. His mother and aunts made a trip for the ceremony. He described this time in his life to his brother Joe as being "challenging," but also incredibly rewarding. It was one of his proudest accomplishments, but, "I think it was the longest few months of his life," recalled Betty. He eventually became a lance corporal.[2]

Unfortunately, while serving six months on active duty in the Marine Corps Dick missed the wedding of his brother Scott, who wanted to have Dick as his best man. Scott's wife, who was affectionately called "Toots," was a very outspoken liberal and added to the fun discussions they would have at family get-togethers. Later in life, Betty also married someone on the other side of the political fence. The family joked that the two in-laws, Bill and Toots, would "nail down the left wing of the barn," during get-togethers.[3]

On February 15th, 1960, Dick started work at his first full-time legal position with a law firm in Richmond known as McGuire, Eggleston, Bocock, and Woods which is known today as McGuireWoods. It was just a small firm at the time, located in the Mutual Building on the corner of North and Main Street. Today they employ over eleven hundred attorneys. Dick was one of only ten attorneys when he joined. He began his work under a man named Carl Davis, who was a famous CPA and tax attorney at that time. The workload was steady, but it was a job he didn't really enjoy. Dick was an appellate attorney but didn't have a tax background. Therefore, he had to learn on the job. His main duty was to prepare and edit briefs. Ultimately, it wasn't a good fit for him.[4]

---

[1] Joe interview, September 1, 2017.

[2] Betty interview, September 13, 2017.

[3] Scott interview.

[4] George Hinnant interview, October 11, 2017.

Shortly after being hired, he went out and bought his first vehicle, a Dodge Dart in a "dashing bright colored red" said Betty, befitting an enthusiastic Republican. His new freedom was certainly welcomed, as he hadn't been able to drive in eight years while away at college and boot camp. His mother was also thrilled, but for different reasons. Now that he had his own car, she thought maybe Dick would finally find himself a girlfriend. It wasn't long before he did exactly that.[5]

It was during the fall of 1960 that a friend from the firm, Tom Newton, invited him to the annual Virginia State Fair held in Doswell, Virginia. Dick had been working a lot and pursuing his dreams, being heavily involved with the Young Republican group and various other campaigns. Tom thought he needed a break. Little did Dick realize that he was being set up on a blind date with a young teacher in the area named Helen Wilkins. Helen was born in Washington, D.C. and attended Mary Washington college, where she received a degree in psychology. In 1956, she moved to Richmond to teach third grade at Bellemeade Elementary School. Helen was about to move out of the city permanently when a friend named Effie Newton, who taught second grade across the hall, approached her one afternoon with an invitation she couldn't refuse. Effie invited Helen to the state fair to meet a handsome gentleman named Dick. "I should tell you," Effie said to Helen, "he is really interested in politics." That was fine by Helen. When she was a little girl one of Harry Byrd's associates was good friends with her parents. He had just returned from World War II and stayed at their home for a time. They spoke of "the senator" and politics frequently, and her parents, at that time, like most, were conservative Democrats. The thought of dating someone interested in politics was of no concern to her.

The blind date was set up at the fair. Helen's initial thought was that Dick was a very good-looking young man. She didn't find Dick to be shy at all, just a country boy who "had a dry sense of humor and was very serious." She found him to be a very interesting person. The two continued to see each other after that. Whenever she would visit him, she said, "He would have books open everywhere; he was always reading". He had half-read books opened and

---

[5] Betty interview.

stacked on top of one another, books turned over in between pages so he wouldn't lose his spot, books in the kitchen, books in the living room, books on the floor.[6]

The other members of the Obenshain family were excited to meet Helen when he brought her home for the first time a month after they had met. Joe and Betty were teenagers and were told by Mrs. Obenshain to be on their "best behavior." To them, that meant cleaning the cow manure off of their boots or leaving them in the barn. Mr. and Mrs. Obenshain were immediately fond of Helen. Dr. Obenshain and Helen particularly clicked the moment they met. Josephine thought she was perfect for Dick and hoped it would work out between the two of them. Dick brought her home again for Thanksgiving for the huge annual Obenshain family get-together, where Helen had to remember the names of more than thirty people, a useful skill she would have to invoke in the near future.[7]

It took less than a year for the two of them to get engaged. Dick proposed during a return trip from his brother Scott's home in North Carolina in the spring of 1961. Shortly after, Dick came down with a bad case of mononucleosis. Unable to work, he moved back home temporarily while he recuperated, which took six weeks. He used that time wisely though, going through magazines and planning a honeymoon with his future bride and getting ticket reservations. He also enjoyed getting to slow down for once and being waited on while at home.

The pair married on July 15th, 1961. Their wedding was held in Washington, D.C. at the National Episcopal Cathedral, which was Helen's family's church in D.C. Dick was getting ready to leave Richmond two days before the wedding. While waiting on his ride, he left his suitcase on the sidewalk outside of his apartment as they drove off. It took him until he reached D.C. to realize he didn't have his suitcase. Luckily, having many friends in Richmond, one of them was able to drive up and bring his stuff. He stayed at the home of one of Toot's (Scott's wife) relatives, who was a Presbyterian Minister at the Pilgrim Church in D.C. His friends found him the morning of

---

[6] Helen Obenshain interview, August 7, 2009.
[7] Betty interview.

the rehearsal, asleep at noon. According to Scott, one of his friends looked at him and said, "Well, he hasn't changed a bit." Scott continued, "[Dick] didn't like to get up. Once he left home and didn't have to get up and milk the cows, I think he was known for not wanting to get up in the morning, if he could get around it."[8]

For their honeymoon they traveled to New York and Montreal. *The Sound of Music* was still the big draw, and he made reservations for that. Upon returning home, they received a phone call from members of the local Young Republicans chapter. They wanted him to run for Chairman of the state club. "And it began from day one after the honeymoon," said Helen.[9]

They soon moved into a small apartment on Hanover Avenue called Gilmour Court. When Dick wasn't working grueling hours at the law firm, he spent a lot of his free time involved with a young republicans club known as the Young Republican Federation of Virginia (YRFV). A state chapter of the Young Republican National Federation (YRNF). The YRNF was founded in 1931 by George Olmstead with the goal of cultivating the next generation of republican leaders. It is both a social and political club in which members volunteer and help various campaigns. Dick's political activity started in 1960 as a precinct chairman for Richard Nixon. From there, he worked his way up and became vice chair of the YRFV. At their annual convention in August of 1961, he ran and became chairman of that organization. One of his supporters, Polly Campbell, who went on to have a decorated career with the party, knew of his family's history and shared similar experiences with the Byrd Machine as a child. Namely, "Growing up in a country community where most everyone was a Democrat as most were on the dole." Polly continued, "My parents were known Republicans, and I do recall the many times Dad would come home and say that he did not get the job he applied for as they knew he was a Republican. This would break my heart as I didn't understand it, but as I grew older and learned what the Byrd Machine was, I knew why Dad had such disdain for it. I remember we would attend all the Republican campaign speeches, even when they rarely won."

---

8 Scott interview.

9 Helen interview.

She recalled meeting Dick for the first time. "Dick was a little shy, but very dedicated to the party. He was charismatic and energized, plus he was a fantastic orator."[10] It was those qualities that helped him win this position with the Young Republicans. He showcased his organizational prowess during his time as chair by taking the club from 15 chapters with 700 members to 36 clubs with 2,000 members.[11]

Even as chair of the Young Republicans, he advocated for not just conservatism, but for realignment. He wrote, "The proper question for young Virginians is simply, 'How can the victory of conservative principles be assured?' The only realistic answer is for American conservatives to unite in the Republican Party, the only national party which can be returned to the basic tenets of constitutional government and individual freedom…Only if we Southerners will unite with conservative Republicans across this nation...can we attain the nationwide strength essential for political victory."[12]

In 1963 the Virginia delegation attended a National Young Republican Convention in Minneapolis, where Dick served on the resolutions board. Senator Goldwater was the keynote speaker. There was a candidate from Ohio running for National Chair named Donald "Buzz" Lukens. Lukens was also a member of Goldwater's air squadron and had Goldwater's endorsement. He was opposed by a man from New York who was supported by Nelson Rockefeller. On the surface, Lukens appeared to have all of the qualities that would have made him someone Dick would be happy to support, yet he didn't. His reasoning seemed insufficient, and fellow Young Republican Polly Campbell thought this was an odd move for Dick. "Dick was somewhat enigmatic, you just never knew which way he would jump. Dick told our group that we could not support Lukens (the conservative) as he was riding on Goldwater's coat-tails. This created a problem within our group, and some of the people did vote for Lukens. Years after that, every time I saw Buzz, he would shake his head about the fact that Virginia did not support him—he was elected, later became governor of Ohio, and then a congressman." In the 1990s

---

[10] Polly Campbell interview, July 31, 2011.
[11] Biographical Sketch, *Richmond News Leader*
[12] Atkinson, p. 268.

Governor Lukens was charged with contributing to the delinquency of a minor, and later convicted of accepting a bribe when he was a congressman.[13]

As the Young Republicans' chair, Dick was given an excuse to crisscross the state and build his network. He was reelected as state chairman in 1962, '63, and '64. Before resigning, he was able to persuade the group to endorse Barry Goldwater for President by a vote of 112-30. After he officially left, he remained active in supporting the YRFV, directly or indirectly, for the rest of his career.

Lots of things were unfolding nationally. The Civil Rights Movement was well underway, as was the Cold War. Eisenhower had left office in 1960, delivering his famous farewell address concerning the "misplaced power in the United States" and the military-industrial complex, a newly coined term. America had a new and unexpected president at the end of 1963 after John F. Kennedy was assassinated in Dallas, Texas. Lyndon Baines Johnson ascended to power in 1963 and rapidly increased military involvement in Vietnam while simultaneously helming massive new welfare programs such as "the Great Society" and the "War on Poverty." His actions as a very liberal president fractured the Democratic Party in Virginia and allowed an opening for criticism from Republicans—and an opportunity for them to win a statewide election.

Dick and Helen continued to reside in Richmond and had their first child, Mark, in June of 1962. Dick was working overtime at the law firm, now called McGuire, Woods, King, Davis, and Patterson. The firm had just lost several employees and had an enormous work-load conducting bond deals for major clients. He would handle the briefs and edit them to improve the language. Dick even made a new friend at the firm named George Hinnett. "Dick was always a gentleman. He was a very good speaker and writer and was very knowledgeable about history. He was a part of several history clubs which made him very formidable in a debate. He could give you 300 years [of reasons] as to why something was a bad idea," said George.[14]

---

[13] Campbell interview.

[14] Hinnant interview.

He was also beginning to make a name for himself within Republican circles. He resided in the 3rd Congressional District, which was made up of Henrico and Chesterfield Counties, Colonial Heights, and Richmond City and had not seen a Republican elected to Congress in the 20th century. Running for this seat as a Republican had, for years, been considered a suicide mission. However, the district had been looking more promising for Republicans in recent years. President Eisenhower had won it both times, while Nixon and Goldwater carried it during their presidential bids as well. The seat had been held by Democratic congressman Julian Vaughan Gary since 1946 after the resignation of Democrat David E. Satterfield, Jr.

Congressman Gary was a Byrd Democrat and World War I veteran, yet his popularity, like that of the Byrd Machine, was beginning to wane. After Gary's endorsement of John F. Kennedy exacerbated his problems, a write-in candidate had taken one-third of the votes in 1960 after merely placing a couple of newspaper ads presenting himself as a different option. In 1962, local obstetrician and prominent inner-circle member of the 3rd district Republicans Dr. Louis Williams would come within 350 votes of victory. Williams had the money, the ability, and desire needed to recruit people to the Republican Party on a statewide scale. He would become instrumental to the full realignment of the parties. In this race, Dr. Williams likely would have won if it had not been for a third-party spoiler candidate from the John Birch Society wing of the conservatives who managed to receive nearly 600 votes. The John Birch Society had gained rapid influence in the Republican Party in the 1950s, but the organization lost its influence after William F. Buckley, founder of the National Review, denounced the organization as a fringe group that same year. Nevertheless, the damage had been done and the 3rd district continued to be represented by a Byrd Democrat.

Dick had been actively involved with Dr. Williams' campaign, not just as chair of the Young Republicans, but as an informal advisor. Williams was able to garner much support from former patients, the district's black population, which was continuing in its struggle against Byrd-like candidates, and a huge following comprised of young workhorse volunteers brought in by Dick. Congressman Gary had further alienated the conservative base with his loyal support of presidential candidate John F. Kennedy and his legislative proposals. The 1962 race, while ending in disappointment, no doubt encouraged Republicans in the district that victory was a real possibility for the first time in recent memory.

The race took its toll on the victor, Congressman Gary. He knew he would be challenged again in 1964, and the pressure to mount yet another competitive campaign discouraged him from running again. Like many politicians, he decided to resign in order to go out on top. There were Democrats already lining up for the challenge to succeed him in 1964. Three Democrats entered the race for the Democratic primary. One of those who entered the race was David Satterfield III, son of former Congressman David Satterfield, Jr. This Satterfield was a former federal attorney and current member of the House of Delegates. He would make a formidable challenger to Dr. Williams if he chose to run again, but Williams decided that his role should no longer be that of a candidate.

Dr. Williams took much interest in Dick Obenshain. Dick undoubtedly impressed Dr. Williams, who had much clout in the 3rd district and shared the same vision as Dick regarding the need for conservatives to vote Republican and to shed the Democratic Party at all levels of the government. Dick had garnered his own following with the Young Republicans and within the 3rd district with his fiery rhetoric and his frequent editorials to the Richmond Times-Dispatch.

One afternoon while his family was visiting from Blacksburg, Dick was also visited by Dr. Lewis Williams and a group of people who were heavily involved in Dr. Williams' campaign. Since Dr. Williams now preferred to take a behind-the-scenes role within the party, the group asked Dick if he would run for the 3rd Congressional District seat that was open. Dick didn't provide an answer immediately. He loved politics, but he was working a lot, was a new father, and was still trying to discover what political role suited him the best. His parents were always supportive and had high expectations for their children. While Dr. Williams was pressing Dick to run, Dick decided to call his father one evening in the fall of 1963, whose opinion he always respected. Dick explained his dilemma to Dr. Obenshain and that he was thinking about running. It was an opportunity that Dr. Obenshain tried to discourage. "Papa was thinking more practical," Betty reflected, "because Dick hadn't been in Richmond that long, he was going to some churches, but he and Helen had not joined a church. Papa thought he should be more established in the community, he should pursue being a partner in the law firm, which was mostly Democrats, and he didn't want Dick hurting his position with the firm."[15]

It wasn't enough to deter Dick's decision. Dick "was pulled into running each time," said Helen. Thus, Dick Obenshain entered his first race for public office for the Virginia 3rd Congressional District to the United States House of Representatives.[16]

---

15 Betty interview.

16 Helen interview.

Chapter 6:

Mr. Conservative

Dick announced his decision to seek the nomination in early 1964. He had worked hard for the Young Republicans, for various candidates, and for Dr. Williams. Because of his efforts and the connections he made, he had momentum early on. Yet the young attorney later had another Republican vying for the same nomination: Joseph S. Bambacus. Bambacus was a United States attorney for the Eastern District of Virginia, appointed under President Eisenhower. While he had not been as politically active, he had credentials which made him a formidable opponent. Bambacus had most recently served as a special assistant to Attorney General Robert F. Kennedy. The 3rd Congressional district met for their own convention on May 22, 1964. It would be a nail biter, but Dick Obenshain would squeak out the win by eight votes, totaling 40 votes to 32.[1] Only twenty-eight years old, Dick was now his party's nominee for congress. Despite his victory, Dick had to overcome being

---

[1] Jones, Allan. "Obenshain is GOP Nominee For Congress in 3d District" *Richmond Times Dispatch.* May 23, 1964.

relatively unknown to the general public. This would be a reoccurring issue throughout his political career.

One of the many qualities he always had going for him was his ability to inspire those around him, which helped him recruit many volunteers for his campaign. He had another gift working for him as well, and that was his organizational skills. He gained a lot of experience with Dr. Williams, who had taken Dick under his wing, and he inherited much of the organization from the Williams campaign. Dick had a knack for taking what worked before and improving upon it. His campaign team consisted of many experienced staffers from the Williams race, and it was a finely tuned organization. The team consisted of several downtown Richmond elites who could potentially form an influential coalition, including Richard F. Banks, vice-president of the Bank of Virginia, as Dick's finance chair, Malcolm S. Underwood as chair of his budget committee, and H. Winston Holt III as his campaign treasurer. Other staffers close to Obenshain's own inner circle included campaign chair Arthur S. Brinkley, chairman of the Republican Third District Committee, and Bert Bradley. His events coordinator was Joseph B. Benedetti, William A. Forrest, Jr. served as the policy researcher. Public relations was headed by Hugh C. Newton, speech writing fell to E.D. Shriver, and Martha Smith was the head of women's activities. Lastly, as an effort to hold together the coalition that was created in 1962, Dr. Louis C. Williams and William C. Harris were appointed as special advisors.[2]

Obenshain had ideas which matched that of the district's constituency, he had the right skills, and now he had the right team assembled. Fortunately, having an early convention in May allowed Dick to get an earlier start on the general campaign. This was essential, as Dick had little name recognition within the 3rd Congressional District outside the inner circle of Republican politics. He immediately began speaking to local groups and attempted to define the campaign on ideological differences, exploiting what he saw as weaknesses within the Democratic Party and the three candidates vying for the nomination in July, which Dick claimed made for "strange bedfellows." Speaking at a South Richmond Rotary Club meeting, he got right to national issues and accused

---

[2] Virkler, p. 8-11.

Democrats, particularly President Johnson, of being a threat to individual liberty, and jokingly blasted President Johnson for his close relationship with Robert Baker, who was under investigation for political bribery.[3] Johnson's role in the investigation was dropped after he became president. The following week, to a smaller audience in Henrico he said, "The Democratic Party has lost the will to fight for constitutional principles."[4] Though Dick wasted no time attacking his opposition, it remained to be seen whether his hard-hitting approach would be enough to overcome the entrenched Democratic Party and its loyal voters.

Before Dick knew who his Democratic opponent would be, he flew out to Dale City, California, just south of San Francisco, as a delegate to the National Republican Party Convention. He brought Helen and their now two-year-old son, Mark, along with him. It was Helen's first convention, which she called "an experience I'll never forget."[5] The three-day event lasted from July 13th until July 16th, and like his first convention in 1952, it was a tense ordeal that brought out passionate conservative Republicans of the west and south, represented by "Mr. Conservative" Barry Goldwater, against the liberal and moderate Republicans of the "Eastern Establishment" faction represented by Nelson D. Rockefeller, now known as "Rockefeller Republicans."

Nelson Rockefeller was the son of famous financier John D. Rockefeller Jr. and Abby Greene Aldrich. His paternal grandfather founded Standard Oil, and his maternal grandfather was a U.S. Senator and architect of the Federal Reserve Act, a law despised by students of Austrian economics. Rockefeller strolled into the convention with the support of thirteen of the sixteen Republican governors at the time to oppose Goldwater. A few of these supporters were former presidential candidates themselves, including George Romney, whose son Mitt would one day run for president as well. Rockefeller had limited power within the party until 1960, when he met with then Vice-President Nixon and strong armed the Republican Party into altering its platform, an event which became known as the Treaty of Fifth Avenue.

---

3 "Obenshain Views GOP as Best Hope." *Richmond Times Dispatch.* June 19, 1964.
4 "Obenshain Says Foes Have Lost Will to Fight" *Richmond Times Dispatch.* June 28, 1964.
5 *Richmond Times Dispatch,* July 21, 1964.

Goldwater was the opposite of Rockefeller in almost every way. He had been critical of the Eisenhower administration, was staunchly anti-communist, and fiscally conservative. So intense were his positions that people were literally frightened at the prospect of nuclear war if he were to win the presidency.

While at the convention, Obenshain learned that his Democratic opponent was a man named David Satterfield, who refused to endorse President Johnson outright. Dick went on the attack again while on the other side of the country. He shined a light on a problem that southern Democrats were having everywhere, "This is one of the many differences between Satterfield and myself. I do not have to be urged to support the nominee of my party."[6] Obenshain tried to force the question for voters in the third district: do they choose to be good conservatives or good Democrats? Obenshain took every opportunity he could to exploit the constant conflict that plagued the Democratic Party.

The rise of Goldwater and Obenshain during this year was no coincidence. There was a new wave of conservatism with a libertarian tilt that was beginning to take shape, and Goldwater was its leader. Unfortunately, though Goldwater would still lose in Virginia, Dick was not able to ride any of Goldwater's coattails. While attending a conference for Republican candidates in D.C., Dick learned that Harry F. Byrd, Sr. had convinced Goldwater not to attend any events or campaign with any Republican candidates in Virginia. Instead, Goldwater provided a message to the voters of the third district by way of a letter which said, "Republicans have been gaining rapidly in the third...Richard D. Obenshain deserves the very best we can give him...Please help Dick."[7]

With Bambacus out of the way, Dick's next opponent, David E. Satterfield III, would be an even tougher challenge. Satterfield was the son of a well-liked former Democratic congressman of the same name who served the 3rd district twenty years earlier. The nomination for Satterfield seemed to be inevitable, as did a general election victory. He had the look, the name, and a well-funded campaign to match. One major obstacle however, was that Virginia

---

[6] "Obenshain Cites One Difference." *Richmond Times Dispatch*. July 21, 1964.
[7] *Richmond Times Dispatch*, September 17, 1964.

Democrats were deeply divided over support for President Lyndon B. Johnson. Despite having signed a loyalty pledge at the Democratic National Convention, Satterfield's strategy in his primary consisted of doing the opposite of the resigning Congressman Gary and his primary opponents by not stating whether or not he supported the new liberal president. The ambiguity gave conservatives the comfort they needed to continue supporting a Democrat. A few months after Dick's nomination, Satterfield won his primary on July 14, 1964 by an incredible 11,000 votes.

Satterfield was just about the most difficult opponent that Obenshain could have had. Dick made early attempts at portraying Satterfield as an accomplice to the more liberal Democratic agenda of LBJ, mainly big government programs and what was seen as communist appeasement. Satterfield focused on Obenshain's youth and lack of experience. One of Satterfield's first campaign strikes was to compare his life and work experience to Obenshain's. The Satterfield campaign unashamedly designed an advertisement which included a blank space of accomplishments for Obenshain. By making the campaign about accolades, Satterfield was able to effectively portray Obenshain as being too inexperienced for the job.

The problems were compounded immediately after a third candidate, Dr. Edward E. Haddock, entered the race as an independent. Haddock had developed a following of his own over the years, first by serving as the mayor of Richmond in the early 1950s. During his time as mayor, he made strides to improve Richmond's education system, and he was instrumental to upgrading Parker Stadium, which led to Richmond having its own Triple A baseball team known as the Richmond Virginians, which later became the Richmond Braves in 1966. He served two terms as a Democratic state senator and developed good relationships with the black community because he was one of the only moderate Democrat voices during the massive resistance error. Haddock began to easily wrestle away the support of black voters in the 3rd Congressional District who had supported the Republican Dr. Williams just two years prior. His hope was to win by a plurality.

Obenshain shifted his attacks away from Dr. Haddock directly. In a conservative district, Dr. Haddock was arguably considered more of a liberal than Satterfield, so Obenshain tried to isolate the Satterfield supporters by telling them that if they voted for Satterfield they were only helping to put the liberal Haddock in office.

While many general election voters outside of the Republican circles were still learning who Dick Obenshain was, Dick aggressively utilized another strength to improve his name recognition: his ability to connect with voters. When given the opportunity to speak to a crowd, Dick could win over the entire room. In order to greet voters with more personalized exposure, the campaign began holding "coffee" events. With the help of two local activists and Dr. Williams, Republican suburban housewives around the district would invite their friends and neighbors to their homes to meet the candidate. The small gatherings typically lasted little more than an hour, and they gave voters a chance to personally meet the candidate, hear him speak, and ask him questions. The events were helpful in making conservative Democrats feel comfortable voting for a Republican. Some of those voters would be voting Republican for the first time in their lives. Before the campaign was over, Obenshain held over 100 "coffees", which averaged around twenty people per event.

Author John Stanley Virkler attended one of these events and recalled a woman standing up, concerned about Barry Goldwater's statement, "Moderation in defense of liberty is no virtue, and extremism in the defense of liberty is no vice." In typical Obenshain fashion, he answered the question by pointing to his favorite founder, Patrick Henry, saying that Henry declaring independence from Britain was also an extreme act. He concluded by providing a parallel analogy that Virginians had ties to the Democratic Party that were similar to the ties they had held with England, but that the time for change and realignment—something he had firmly believed in since he was young —was now. According to the author, all in attendance were impressed with him and the delivery of his message.[8]

The coffee events also introduced Obenshain to many of his future campaign staffers, including Judy Peachee, who got involved after a volunteer for Obenshain's campaign knocked on her door. She became a precinct captain in the 3rd district and a member of the Republican Women's Club. "He blew everybody in the room away, a very good speaker, very dynamic, and a

---

[8] Virkler, p. 14.

visionary. The kind of speaker that could really get you excited. I got enthusiastic about Dick and it just kind of progressed from there."[9]

Satterfield, on the other hand, was not a gifted orator, but he continued to make the campaign about achievement and experience. Obenshain worked to define the campaign in his own way, boiling the choice down to "welfarism or freedom." He said that only a Republican majority could help Goldwater scale back the welfare state. Republicans needed forty new representatives in Congress in order to take the majority, which led to the rallying cry "forty more in '64." The Obenshain team motto became "Dick Obenshain and thirty-nine others." He continued to slam Satterfield and tied him to L.B.J, liberal policies, and encroaching big government, and exploited Satterfields refusal to reveal who he was supporting for president.[10]

With every speech, every coffee event, and every editorial, people in the 3rd Congressional District could sense that they were witnessing a rising star; that there was something special about Obenshain. It was in the way that he spoke, his passion, his ability to connect. He was a practical politician grounded by a deep sense of principle. One could envision him stepping into the halls of Congress and shouting the ideals of liberty with the passion of Patrick Henry, the eloquence of Thomas Jefferson, and the moderating respectfulness of James Madison. Those around him believed he could be the next Barry Goldwater, running for U.S. Senate and then for president years down the road. His inner circle, his loyal supporters, believed it. Obenshain believed it too, feeling confident that if he could win this race, he would be in position to achieve his dream of becoming a U.S. Senator. Many could see his rise coinciding with the rise of the Republican Party in Virginia and could see him challenging Senator Robertson in 1966 or in 1972 and becoming the first Republican senator from Virginia in 100 years.

Then a fourth candidate entered the race.

Unfortunately, no matter how competent a candidate may be, external factors cannot be controlled. When a race is close, a hiccup by another

---

[9] Judy Wason interview, March 3, 2010.
[10] Virkler, p. 11.

candidate or an outside event can shift the pendulum swing. Obenshain's coffee events made a lot of headway in suburban Chesterfield County, but a conservative by the name of Stanley Smith Jr. came out of nowhere and drew upon many of those connections. Between Smith trimming more of the conservative vote away and Haddock taking away the black vote, which had helped Dr. Lewis come within a few hundred votes, Obenshain's chances were looking slim once again.

The big day finally arrived on November 3rd, 1964. Obenshain made the customary visits at all of the major polls around the district. Future Obenshain staffer, Bob Hausenfluck, recalled meeting Obenshain for the first time at the polls that day in Henrico County and shared the same first impression that many others had of Obenshain, "I liked him, {there} was something about him I just liked, same as Goldwater too."[11]

Virginia voted for Johnson, but the 3rd District voted for Goldwater by nearly 57% in the presidential election. In the congressional race, last-minute candidate Stanley Smith received 939 votes all to his own. Haddock took away a 30% chunk of the vote with 39,223 and carried the city of Richmond. Nobody believed that these two candidates could win, but Haddock impressed many by putting up a good fight. The election came down to 43,226 votes for Obenshain, who carried Henrico, Chesterfield, and Colonial Heights, and 43,880 votes for Satterfield, coming in 2nd in all four of the localities. Despite having carried three of the four localities, Dick lost by a difference of 654 people.[12] Betty Obenshain recalled that, "at 2:00 a.m. they were sitting there, only 600 votes apart, and a judge from one of the precincts with more than that many votes had taken the ballot box home with him. We knew it probably wasn't enough to win...but still, there were enough votes that had not been counted and this (Democratic) judge had taken them home with him. It was a whole different world."[13] The next day it was first reported in the Richmond Times that Satterfield had accrued 43,459 votes to Obenshain's 43,212, only a

---

[11] Bob Hausenfluck interview, October 3, 2017.
[12] Guthrie, Benjamin J. "Statistics of the Presidential and Congressional Election of November 3, 1964." Http://clerk.house.gov/member_info/electionInfo/1964election.pdf. Accessed September 18, 2018.
[13] Betty interview, July 20, 2011.

247 vote difference, and the paper reported, "there was some indication of a foul-up in Richmond vote totals which might provide Satterfield with a slightly bigger win." Despite Haddock having carried Richmond, his vote totals were reduced from the original count of 39,910 to the final count of 39,223.[14]

Whatever the case, many would speculate in the aftermath as to the reason for his loss. It is likely that Haddock took more votes away from Satterfield than he did from Obenshain. Obenshain, while disappointed, had run an authentic campaign. Not only was he honest about his support for Goldwater, but he displayed it often and proudly. This undoubtedly turned off some of the black leaders who had previously supported Dr. Williams. It wasn't so much that they were highly supportive of Republicans, but their votes at this time were protest votes against the Byrd Machine. In 1961, 75% of blacks voted Republican, which gave Republicans hope that they could one day soon achieve victory statewide.

Instead, most of the black vote went to Dr. Haddock. According to Clarence Townes, a friend and black Republican leader in the Richmond area, Obenshain was given the advice to appeal to the black vote on non-ideological grounds, but it was something he could not do.[15] Some say that this was his downfall that year. But he would rather lose on principle than win by hiding or sugar coating his beliefs. And as Kenny Klinge put it, "Dick was just getting started."[16]

Satterfield would hold on to the 3rd Congressional District seat for sixteen years. Dick would not challenge him again. Despite Goldwater's loss, Obenshain maintained the belief that his ideas would eventually win the day. Soon after, he visited his old friend from law school, Larry Dagenhart, who recalled him being passionately optimistic and said,

> "Shortly after the 1964 election, when Johnson trounced Goldwater, a client of mine sold his business to A.H. Robins, a client of McGuireWoods. Dick came to Charlotte to handle the closing and

---

14 "Satterfield's Slim Win May Prompt Recount" *Richmond News Leader*. November 4, 1964.
15 Virkler, p. 17.
16 Klinge interview, March 3, 2010.

> stayed with Sarah and me. Sarah was very fond of Dick and would not have allowed him to stay in a hotel. After supper, Dick and I took a walk. He was suffering from his 600 vote loss in the congressional race in Richmond. He said that if Goldwater had met him at the airport he would have won, and if Goldwater had come downtown with him he would have won by a large margin, but that Byrd and Goldwater had agreed that Goldwater would not campaign in Virginia. I suggested that nominating Goldwater had been a big mistake. Dick stopped short, in the middle of the street, and disagreed. He said 'Larry, I was at the Cow Palace when Goldwater was nominated; it was almost a religious experience, and it was the right thing to do. You mark my words, it was not the suicide of the Republican Party, it was the making of the Republican Party, and we will eventually win because we are right."[17]

Ironically, this echoed Goldwater's slogan, "In Your Heart, You Know He's Right."

For the next several years Obenshain focused on raising his growing family, building his career, and building the Republican Party from the ground up. Dick and Helen had two more children, Anne in 1965, then Kate on the same day three years later in 1968. Helen became a full-time homemaker and they bought their first home near Toddsbury Road in the Westhampton area of Richmond.[18] During this time he became involved with the March of Dimes and was named chairman of the local Richmond chapter. In 1966 he visited his friend Pasco Bowman, who was teaching law in Georgia. Bowman recalled that Dick was seriously considering a faculty position with the University of Georgia, which isn't something he likely would have done if he had any serious thoughts of running for office again in Virginia. Around 1968 his law firm merged with William Battle's law firm and it became McGuireWoods and Battle. The Battle family were all active Democrats. William Battle's father John Battle was governor of Virginia between 1950 and1954. In spite of being a Republican, they all had respect for each other, and Dick would end up becoming a partner shortly after the merger. However, the merger would

---

[17] Dagenhart e-mail, December 4, 2009.
[18] Mark interview.

eventually prove not to be a good fit, and Dick became increasingly frustrated at the firm.[19]

Politically, while his aspirations had experienced a setback, he continued to be active with the Young Republicans and assisted with other campaigns. Republicans were making small gains in Virginia, but the particular ideological strand that Obenshain and Goldwater represented remained somewhat dormant in Virginia for the time. Obenshain was still dedicated and believed in realignment, and he continued to work to those ends.

In 1965 he was appointed as YRFV's campaign vice chairman in charge of election day activities in the 3rd Congressional District, the same district that he had lost the year before. While his political responsibilities were lighter in 1965 than they had previously been, he remained active in supporting and helping Republican candidates statewide, including a man named Linwood Holton.

---

[19] Bowman interview.

Chapter 7:

The Man of Opportunity

Gilbert Carlton Walker would be the last Republican to set foot in the Virginia governor's mansion as governor for nearly one hundred years. He left his post in 1873; however, he had changed parties when he left, and exited as a Democrat.[1]

Twenty years after Walker's departure, an economic panic forced fourteen-year-old Abner Linwood Holton to leave his family farm in Georgia and make his own way in the world. Abner educated himself and acquired the skills needed to ascend to vice president of the Interstate Railroad, which was later bought by Southern Railway.[2] He moved from Knoxville to Big Stone Gap and met Edith VanGorder, a stern Christian woman, to whom he was married in 1921. Located in Wise County, the farthest western county in Virginia, Big Stone Gap was a small, white-collar town. At one time its thriving mineral

---

1 "Walker, Gilbert Carlton" Accessed March 4, 2017.
http://bioguide.congress.gov/scripts/biodisplay.pl?index=W000054
2 Linwood Holton interview, September 29, 2017.

deposits promised it to be the "Pittsburgh of the South."[3] But its small population of roughly 3,000 people prevented it from ever becoming a large city, or even a small city, for that matter. It is no wonder that most of the folks living there often felt as though Richmond had forgotten about them. As a result of this isolation, the town produced many "Mountain Valley" Republicans that would eventually overthrow the Byrd Machine.

Two years later, on September 21st, Abner Linwood Holton, Jr., the man to break that Republican drought, was born. For as long as he could remember Lin Jr.'s goal was to become governor of Virginia, way before Obenshain conceived his lifelong dream of becoming a U.S. Senator. While attending school, Lin Jr. befriended all types of people, including several black students who were being bussed to a different school, which influenced his stance on integration years later—an issue that would become the cornerstone of his legacy. He began his quest as a fourth-grade student after he participated in Boys' State, a program sponsored by the American Legion that teaches youth about government. Lin Jr. cut his teeth in politics during the height of the depression in 1935. A local pharmacist by the name of Lewis McCormack, also a friend of the Holton family, was a candidate for town council. For weeks Lin helped his friend tirelessly by knocking on doors and handing out campaign literature. Although his efforts were ultimately futile and McCormack was defeated, the experience only heightened Lin's growing interest in politics.[4]

Lin graduated from Big Stone Gap High School and enrolled at Washington and Lee University, a private liberal arts college in Lexington. His family had no problem putting him through school as they were somewhat wealthy by most standards. Throughout these years he maintained his goal of becoming governor one day and this goal influenced nearly every life decision. In the spring of 1943, during his sophomore year at college, he was called to active duty in the United States Navy. Shortly after, he was commissioned to the Naval Reserve, where he served on the U.S.S. Beaver, a submarine in San Diego, and rose to the level of lieutenant. Lin preferred the Navy to other

[3] Clark, Amy D. "Appalachian Hope and Heartbreak." *New York Times.* August 2, 2013.
[4] Holton, Abner Linwood. *Opportunity Time.* Charlottesville, VA.: University of Virginia Press, 2008. p. 7-9.

military branches because of the near guarantee that every night one gets to eat and sleep in mild comfort. Meanwhile, college requirements were loosely enforced for those in the military. After his discharge, he returned to Washington and Lee to finish up his undergraduate studies and joined the Beta Pheta Phi fraternity. It was here that he met his lifelong friend John Warner. "It was apparent from the beginning of our friendship that John was as interested in a political career as I was," he reminisced.[5]

His next step in the path to becoming governor was to enroll in law school at Harvard University in the fall of 1946—but he was denied. Despite a subpar performance as an undergrad, a personal meeting with Dean Warren Abney Seavey led to his acceptance in the spring semester of 1947. Lin became what was called a "Seavey Estoppel" for the personal voucher. It was also Dean Seavey who encouraged Lin to stay in Virginia, arguing that the South needed more Ivy Leaguers getting into politics. Lin returned to Roanoke to work at a small firm known as Hunter and Fox.[6]

While in Roanoke, he was introduced to Jinks Rogers, the daughter of one of the partners at another local law firm called Woods, Rogers, Muse and Walker. Jinks was working for the Central Intelligence Agency at the time but had come home for the holidays. A blind date was later set up by a mutual friend, which led to a long-distance relationship between the two. Jinks was also a Democrat, however this did not prevent her from marrying him in 1953.[7]

He made an attempt at ousting the leadership within the Roanoke City Republican Committee. The reason for the coup was primarily ideological. The political battle for control over the Republican Party had been waging for years at the national level between Senator Robert Taft and Thomas Dewey and had begun to trickle down to local level politics with the campaign of Dwight D. Eisenhower. Robert Taft was the son of former President William Taft, a conservative and a non-interventionist. Dewey represented the moderate wing of the Republican Party dominated by the Eastern Establishment, in which Ike was considered an ally. Linwood Holton Jr. subscribed to the progressive ideas

---

[5] Holton, p. 185.
[6] Holton p. 27.
[7] Holton p. 36.

held by those in the Eastern Establishment, whereas most of this committee was dominated by conservatives who supported Robert Taft. Some technical missteps by the committee had forced another mass meeting in an attempt to elect a new party chairman. Almost 200 people attended the meeting at the Patrick Henry Hotel, where Holton won by five votes. This faction within the Republican Party gained even more momentum when Dick Poff was elected to Congress that year to represent the 6th Congressional District, which stretched up the Roanoke and Shenandoah Valley. Ike, who won the presidential primary, also won the Virginia delegation. Indeed, the Republican Party was beginning to win in Virginia, but it was the Eastern Establishment faction within the party who were making the gains.

Holton had been inspired to pursue his dreams after Democrat William Tuck was elected governor in 1946 after receiving just 6% of the vote from the entire voting age population in Virginia. This is how restricted the electorate was at the time. Building off of the Republican gains made by Ted Dalton's race for governor in 1953, and at the encouragement of Dalton himself, Holton ran for public office for the first time in 1955. At this time in Virginia, two delegates represented a single district in the House of Delegates. He, along with fellow Republican Hazel Barger, both lost to Democrats Julian Rutherford and Kossen Gregory in a race for the House of Delegates. Rutherford was ideologically similar to Holton but believed in changing the Democratic Party from the inside rather than building a mostly non-existent Republican Party. [8]

After the defeat, Holton continued to help grow the Republican Party at the local level while also growing his reputation as an attorney. During the time of massive resistance, he was very vocal about keeping schools open and joined the Republican chorus of allowing gradual integration. He and Hazel Barger again ran for the House of Delegates in 1957, this time on the same ticket with Ted Dalton, and again, they lost. In 1960, Holton became one of the delegates to the Republican National Convention. He made no admission about whether he would have supported Nelson Rockefeller instead of Nixon had Rockefeller entered the race that year, though he made his disdain for Barry Goldwater quite clear. For the next few years, Holton was limited in his political

---

[8] Holton, p. 51.

participation. The 1964 presidential year came and went. Holton was on the sidelines until, seemingly out of nowhere, he received a call from the National Republican Committee, which was eager to invest an insurmountable amount of funds into a young talent to run for governor of Virginia. Although it was his childhood dream, Holton didn't believe in the possibility of a Republican winning the governorship in Virginia any time soon. Once he received a guarantee that the campaign funds needed to mount a competitive race would be provided, he was convinced to try and run for the seat when it became open again in 1965.

Although Holton had no visions of grandeur in hopes of victory in 1965, he nonetheless saw it as an opportunity to build for the future. He thought he could get support from traditional Republicans from southwest Virginia, African Americans, labor unions, and moderate voters who were in favor of destroying the Byrd Machine once and for all. He had no real prospects of defeating his opponent, Mills Godwin. Godwin was a popular Democrat who successfully straddled both coalitions from the political center as well as those of the Byrd Machine. Holton's vision was more fixed on the possibility that he could win in 1969.[9]

Shortly after, a recent Democrat-turned-Republican convert from Emporia by the name of Dortch Warriner also entered the fray as the Republican candidate for attorney general. The lieutenant governor candidacy was yet to be filled until a man named Vince Callahan decided to make the attempt. It was always hard to talk a Republican into running for statewide office as it was essentially a political suicide mission.

Dortch Warriner, who played an important role in Obenshain's life, came from Brunswick County in southside Virginia. He grew up a Democrat by default, as there were absolutely no Republicans in the county. Warriner served as a page in the state Senate and met Ted Dalton, who taught him that Republicans could be good people and good Virginians. He didn't officially become a Republican until around the time he graduated from law school at the University of Virginia. When he started his own law practice in Emporia,

---

[9] Holton, p. 56.

he was urged to not let anyone know that he was a Republican, or else he might go out of business.[10]

During the campaign, Holton received help from his Washington and Lee friend, John Warner, who had just married into a family of great wealth, in the amount of $3,000 in 1965. Holton returned the favor by introducing him to some of his political contacts in the 7th Congressional District.

> "I realized that my 'pupil' had a lot to learn when he showed up at our scheduled rendezvous in the Shenandoah Valley (where John was thinking of running for Congress), in a two-engine private airplane, dressed in a dark blue pin-striped suit with a buttoned up vest—hardly suitable costume to create a favorable first impression on some of my Republican farmer friends in what was then a rural district."[11]

The mutually beneficial relationship would continue. Later, in 1968, Warner led the Volunteers for Nixon organization. After Nixon's victory, and after asking Linwood first (who may have also been interested in the same position), Warner expressed his desire to be appointed as Secretary of the Navy. Warner paid to fly Holton from Roanoke to New York to visit with President Nixon at the Pierre Hotel to discuss nominating Warner as Secretary. Nixon had already selected John Chafee, but Holton succeeded in convincing President Nixon to appoint John Warner as the Under Secretary.

Through Warner, Holton would continue to gain many D.C. contacts. Other D.C. socialites who supported Linwood Holton through the years included Secretary of Defense Mel Laird, Congressman Colgate Darden, who married into the wealthy DuPont family, and Lewis Strauss, who was also best friends with Harry Byrd, Sr.

Holton ran and lost handily to Democrat Mills Godwin by a vote of 47.79% to Holton's 37.71%. Dortch Warriner earned even less in his attorney general race, only receiving 29.8% of the vote. It may have seemed like a

---

[10] "Dortch Warriner" biographical sketch on file at Republican Party of Virginia.
[11] Holton, p. 182.

disappointing defeat, but Holton had performed better than previous Republican nominees.

Governor Godwin was perceived as a Byrd Democrat but received flak from his base for riding the "Lady Bird Special" with First Lady Bird Johnson during her husband's reelection campaign. Even Dick Obenshain, who had a position on the State Central Committee as a representative for the Young Republicans, received a standing ovation for a speech in which he called Godwin a conservative "turncloak" for his support of Johnson.[12]

Godwin vocally supported the Civil Rights Act and reached out to African Americans during his campaign. What was left of the older "Byrd Organization" type of conservatives formed the Virginia Conservative Party that year and only received 13% of the vote. They received even fewer votes in 1969, only achieving 1% of the vote. During Governor Godwin's tenure, he was the first governor to break away from the pay-as-you-go philosophy, and with the help of the General Assembly he established the Virginia Community College System his first year in office. During his second year he instituted a sales tax to help pay for public education. Godwin wasn't the kind of conservative governor that voters would have normally perceived as being associated with Byrd Democrats. His approach to governing was grounded more in problem solving and pragmatism: the kind of conservatism that had more closely reflected in the Virginia Republican Party for the past several decades.

For Holton, the Republican Party was now beginning to show early signs that it was becoming viable statewide, finally becoming less of a regional party limited to the western regions of the state. For Holton, it was an opportunity.

---

[12] Virkler, p. 49.

Chapter 8:

The Victory Ticket

The 1960's was a tumultuous decade in the United States. In the years that followed his 1960 loss to John F. Kennedy, Richard Nixon had reinvented himself and won the presidency, carrying Virginia by a plurality of 43%. A Goldwater-like conservative named Ronald Reagan became governor of California in 1967. At the height of the Vietnam War, the civil rights movement was winding down, and the anti-war movement was heating up. Along with that came rapid societal changes in the form of the sexual revolution, increased recreational drug use, and the hippie movement.

Shortly after retiring in 1965, in early 1966 Harry F. Byrd Sr. became ill and passed away. Byrd was actively involved in his organization until the day he died. This marked the end of an era and perhaps why Godwin was able to govern more moderately. Just before Godwin took office, Democrat Governor Albertis Harrison had appointed Harry Byrd Jr. to take his father's place in the U.S. Senate until a special election could occur the following year. Byrd, Jr. had no interest in running a political organization the way that his father had after winning the special election. That same year, Senator Willis Robertson, a staunch Byrd Organization man, was defeated in one of the biggest upsets in

Virginia history by William Spong, Jr. in the Democratic Primary. Spong had been recruited to run by President Johnson and represented the liberal faction of their party. The Robertson defeat resulted in bitter feelings by many conservative Democrats.

Most of the cultural change taking place was cultivated on college campuses around the country. There was an increase in campus riots, which put the issues of free speech and law and order into focus. In Virginia, national events were shaping the dialogue, and many student activist groups were united in their support of desegregation, but they were splintered when it came to methods of protesting. There were those who took a more militant approach under the umbrella group "The Radical Student Front." At the University of Virginia a group of 150 students protested on the lawn outside the Board of Visitors meeting on February 15th, 1969, calling for the board to be remade entirely in order to reflect the diversity of the student population. A few days later a coalition of hundreds of students held a softer protest outside the campus rotunda and called it the "Coat & Tie Rebellion."[1]

Obenshain attended a Young Republicans meeting on campus a few weeks later addressing the incident, but most of his speech revolved around his support for ending the pay-as-you-go method of financing the Commonwealth's budget, adding that state borrowing should be approved by a referendum. With regard to the protest incident on campus he took a principled yet measured approach to the ordeal, stating that it was "a perfectly justifiable exercise of free speech," but he didn't necessarily agree with all of the students demands. In a 2017 interview, friend Wyatt Durrette said, "Dick was progressive in that area" when it came to race relations, because it was consistent with the ideas of liberty which he championed. Later, as protests nationwide became more aggressive and violent, he took a harder stance when speaking to Young Republicans at the University of Richmond, saying, "It is not enough to just talk about vigorous enforcement of the law. It is time to go

---

[1] Gates, Ernie. "May Days, 1970: The week that would change UVA forever." *UVA Magazine*. March 7, 2018.

to the heart of the matter and begin to reestablish respect for authority in Virginia," while also attacking Democrats for taking no action.[2]

Meanwhile, Holton was looking to build off of his successes from the 1965 governor's race. Holton had presented himself as a progressive Republican in that race and lost to Mills Godwin, who had branded himself as a moderate Democrat. The next time however, in 1969, Holton positioned himself as more conservative than his Democratic opponent, William Battle.[3] Coincidentally, this was the same William Battle whom Dick worked with at McGuireWoods & Battle.

In order to win with this right-of-center position, Holton needed to have a diverse ticket that could draw votes from conservative Democrats and liberals alike for the lieutenant governor and attorney general positions. He met with his campaign team and went through the list. Publicly, Holton teased potential running mates such as state Senator J. Kenneth Robinson, James Turk, and Arthur Brinkley. Brinkley had been instrumental to Dick during his 1964 Congressional race. Holton's first selection as a running mate for lieutenant governor was H. Dunlop "Buz" Dawburn, a state senator from Waynesboro. The logic behind the choices was primarily geographical: they thought that Dawburn could draw in the mountain valley Republicans from the northwestern part of the state, while Holton could bring in the Republicans from the southwest and could again win the support of black and liberal Virginians who were as determined as he was to be rid of Byrd copy-cat candidates once and for all. There was one last piece; for the slot of attorney general Holton needed a strong conservative to help bring in the disaffected conservative Democrats and the conservative Richmond business crowd who were critical to funding campaigns. Obenshain, being a conservative from the 3rd Congressional District, which included Richmond, was the perfect fit. Holton stated, "I'm not sure who made the first overture, [but] I certainly was in favor of Dick being on the ticket. I approached him and asked him to do it."[4]

---

2 "Obenshain Says Respect Due the Law." *Richmond Times Dispatch*. May 6, 1969.

3 Atkinson, p. 213.

4 Holton interview.

"The Holton people thought it would be wise to have someone from the growing conservative wing of the party on the ticket, which is why they were open to Dick," said Virginia political operative Weldon Tuck, the 5th Congressional District Chairman who served as the liaison for this "victory ticket" idea of Holton's.[5]

Weldon Tuck had been familiar with Obenshain since 1962, when he was a student at Hampton-Sydney and a member of the Young Republicans while Dick was chairman of the group. Weldon wanted to get involved with the local committee in Halifax but found that the party was virtually defunct. It took him weeks to find out who the chairman of the party was, and when he finally did, the man gladly resigned his position to Weldon. One rainy evening, Weldon organized and held the first official meeting for the newly reassembled Halifax Republican Committee. While running for Congress, Dr. Lewis Williams came down for this event and brought Dick Obenshain with him. While the people there could not vote in the 3rd district, a few of them ended up hosting fundraisers for Dr. Williams as a result of the meeting. Weldon, Lewis, and Dick "hit it off" from the beginning. Weldon was also a fan of Goldwater and later attended the National Convention with Dick in 1964.[6] At this point in his career, Weldon was now friends with both Dick and Linwood and felt comfortable discussing the opportunity with Dick to be on the ticket in person at his home.

When Weldon approached Dick about the prospect of being on the ticket, he found that Dick wasn't enthusiastic about the idea. Dick had a lot of reasons to be reluctant. For one, he wasn't independently wealthy, and he had a family to support. Running a statewide race would require him to take a leave of absence from the law firm—a firm which held the name of the person on the opposite ticket—with no pay. The worst-case scenario would be if Linwood won and Dick lost and had to return to his position at the firm. In addition to all of this, the Democratic candidate for attorney general, Andrew P. Miller, was a formidable opponent and the odds of defeating him were 50/50 at best.

---

[5] Weldon Tuck interview, October 2, 2017.
[6] Weldon Tuck interview, September 26, 2017.

Weldon made several trips relaying messages between the Holton group and the Obenshain group. By this time Obenshain had made many more political friends and allies who were advising him on what to do. He had befriended Dortch Warriner, Holton's 1965 running mate, and Lawrence Lewis Jr., who was influential with the Richmond financial crowd. Dr. Williams, who had been Dick's mentor in 1964, had taken a step back as a public figure and worked behind the scenes advising as well. The group slowly became the foundational brain trust for things to come. They knew Dick's plan was to position himself to run for the U.S. Senate, possibly in 1972. Questions were frequently asked as to whether the attorney general role would stifle any future plans should he win. Dortch Warriner and Dr. Lewis Williams were perhaps his most influential advisors during this time.

The U.S. Senate was the elected position he had always sought. He was always politically to the right of Holton, which Holton needed to win, but Obenshain did not need Holton at this time. Helen and Dick had just had their third child in November of 1968, and Dick needed some kind of a guarantee that he would be able to take care of his family after the election, regardless of the results. Yet Tuck and Holton persisted. They were very persuasive and addressed many of Dick's concerns. In the event that Dick lost and Linwood won, Linwood assured him, "I will ask you to serve as an important member in my administration."[7] This assurance addressed another concern of Dick's: ensuring that conservatives had a permanent voice in the Republican Party and a voice within the administration. Once that promise was made by Holton, Dick was all-in.

The State Central Committee went with Holton's idea of having an early convention, so the Republicans held their convention on March 1, 1969 in Roanoke. This was close to Holton's neck of the woods. Governor Reagan gave the opening remarks to the convention delegates and got the delegation revved up. It was mostly an uneventful day, as all three of the nominees were unopposed.

Obenshain had already faced a tough opponent in Satterfield. Another defeat might damage his reputation, branding him an unelectable candidate.

---

[7] Holton, p. 66.

Andrew Miller was the son of Francis P. Miller, a Democrat who was the first to challenge the Byrd Organization from within its own ranks several decades earlier. Ironically, Francis Miller lost his race for governor against John Battle, William Battle's father. Andrew Miller was a likeable centrist candidate who had been involved in various youth organizations and could turn out the young vote.

Miller and his running mate for lieutenant governor, J. Sargeant Reynolds, were seemingly the surest bet for the Democrats in 1969. They both won their party's nomination with ease. The Democratic primary for governor, however, was a competitive endeavor. It consisted of a Byrd Organization man named Fred Pollard, moderate William (Bill) Battle, and liberal populist Henry Howell. Howell represented the growing liberal faction within the Democratic party at the state level. Pollard was easily knocked off, as the Byrd Organization was completely unpopular by this time. Battle ran a non-ideological campaign, and barely squeaked by with a victory after winning a run-off.[8]

Although Battle was able to win the nomination, it cost him in other ways, including time and money. The Howell supporters were very bitter after the primary, and Battle was depleted of his resources before the general election. Howell all but refused to help the victor afterwards. Howell said that his supporters, a group made up of black voters, labor unionists, farmers, and blue-collar workers were free to vote how they pleased in the general election; in other words, they could vote with their conscience. For Battle, this was the worst scenario, black voters especially had long supported Republicans as protest votes.

Once Dick made the decision to run, he was granted unpaid leave by his employer, McGuireWoods & Battle.

Dick came out strong as a "law and order" candidate and criticized Miller for his stance on crime, saying that he was "covering up his lack of any basic concept of why Virginia is undergoing a tremendous explosion of crime

---

[8] Virkler, p. 21.

and juvenile delinquency."[9] He also promoted prison and juvenile rehabilitation reform based on motivation and encouraging responsibility. "Teachers, psychiatrists, and prison officials should all work to motivate prison inmates and juvenile offenders to assume personal responsibility for their own lives," he opined.[10]

Miller and Obenshain never had a debate since there was very little notable difference between the two attorney general candidates. The attorney general position itself was not as political in the 1960's. Most of Obenshain's time was spent delivering conservative voters to Holton, particularly the conservatives from the important 3rd District, the Richmond area Republicans. This was no easy task as Holton had run as a progressive Republican in 1965, to the left of Mills Godwin. The challenge became a little easier a month before the election after the "victory" ticket received a financial boost. Lawrence Lewis was successful in converting 166 of Richmond's top businessmen to the Republican Party. The "New Republicans," as they called themselves, voted Republican at the national level, but were statewide and local Democrats. They agreed to vote Republican for the first time in a statewide election. This was a greenlight for many traditional Democrats to switch parties for this particular race. However, it angered and frustrated traditional Republicans that saw these new converts as opportunists, but they also realized the utility of this union. The conservative "main street" support was essential, because it provided the Republican ticket with the financial support that they needed to finish the final stretch of the race. It was the first time a Republican ticket outspent a Democrat ticket. Holton was also receiving substantial financial help through his friendship with the new Under Secretary of the Navy, John Warner.

Just days before, Holton had also been endorsed by the Crusade of Voters (COV), a group formed in response to massive resistance in order to mobilize black voters. The timing was impeccable. Had the former Byrd

---

9 "Miller Rapped on Crime Stand By Obenshain." *Richmond Times Dispatch*. September 10, 1969.
10 "Obenshain Asks Rehabilitation By Motivation." *Richmond Times Dispatch*. September 26, 1969.

Democrat Main-Street crowd endorsed Holton before the Crusade of Voters, the COV might have withheld their endorsement of any candidate.

The labor unions were also ready for a change in Richmond. They were not happy with the Godwin administration, and the Virginia AFL-CIO President Julian Carpenter saw a potential Holton administration as an opportunity to destroy the Byrd Machine once and for all. "We've been waiting a lifetime to kill the Byrd Machine, and this is our chance, and we're going to do it," he said.[11] The shock of a Republican governor would further catalyze a realignment in Virginia politics that would match that of the national political makeup. It was perhaps one of the only times in history where labor unions and the business community supported the same candidate. The COV and AFL-CIO, however, did not endorse the other two Republican candidates.

The stars were finally aligning for Holton in 1969. For Obenshain, however, they were not. As an outspoken supporter of Barry Goldwater, Dick had to fight the constant label that he was a right-wing extremist, or as many coined him, an "ultra" conservative. While Holton certainly enjoyed the fruits of his labor to rally conservatives, Obenshain didn't enjoy the benefits of having labor unions and black voters rally to his cause. Obenshain's message to Byrd Democrats was that "those who think alike should vote alike." His attempt to woo them to the Republican Party continued by painting the Virginia Democrat Party as becoming more like their national counterparts. He likened them to Washington Democrats by calling out the $83 million dollar surplus that Virginia had during the late 1960s that was entirely spent by the end of Godwin's term.

The Democrats were tasked with balancing their moderate and conservative wing with their emerging liberal wing. Andy Miller's strategy was to emphasize the difference in how he viewed the office of attorney general, as opposed to Obenshain. To Miller, the office was supposed to act as the primary state prosecutor. He also tried to stick to the issues solely concerning the office of the attorney general.[12] At the time much of the work was being outsourced to private firms, and Miller wanted to bring them in under his control. While

---

[11] Atkinson, p. 215-217.
[12] Andrew Miller interview, December 10, 2016.

Miller considered himself to be a moderate, his ideas resonated with voters who were left-leaning and simultaneously leaning toward Lin Holton in the governor's race. This was certainly a strange dynamic.

Holton and Obenshain had different styles of campaigning. Holton was slightly louder and more boisterous, while Obenshain was more subtle and personal in his technique, utilizing the power of the pen in the media. At the state fairgrounds, one of Holton's staff pulled out a giant bullhorn and shouted, "Meet Linwood Holton, the next governor of Virginia." When the bullhorn was handed off to a young Obenshain intern named Brad Cavedo, Obenshain rejected it and opted to continue shaking hands and quietly moving about through the fair crowd.[13]

The wives of all three of the Republican candidates were traveling around the commonwealth as well. They were doing a bus tour about three days a week and making roughly six stops a day for well over a month. The ladies were all dressed in similar blue and green fashion, the colors of Virginia's flag and Holton's campaign colors. Arguably, they were more presentable than their husbands. Holton was considered a sloppy dresser and often appeared disheveled, while Obenshain had a hard time finding suits to fit his smaller frame.[14] Betty recalled that Helen, in particular, took to the campaign endeavor well. "Helen unexpectedly had a knack for campaigning," Betty said. "She was quiet and dignified," but after travelling with Jinks Holton for several weeks, she was shaking hands with people everywhere, even at the gas stations. "When she shook your hand, she would look at you straight in the eyes and was totally focused on you. She was a wonderful campaigner," Betty declared. Helen had resigned her teaching job a few years earlier in order to take care of the children at home, but in order to be on the road, actively assisting with the campaign, someone had to help watch the kids. Dick's sister Betty stepped in to help. She took a semester off from college that fall to take care of Mark, who was seven, Anne, now almost four, and Kate, who was not even a year old.[15]

---

[13] Brad Cavedo interview, January 7, 2019.
[14] Tuck interview, September 26, 2017.
[15] Betty interview, September 13, 2017.

Scott also came to support Dick while he was on the campaign trail. The two were very different in terms of their politics, but Scott noted how his brother would listen. "I spent ten days traveling with Dick and we had an opportunity to talk about things; we talked about gun control. He looked at it through the lens of a legal issue, I saw it as a public health issue. He would listen, and my view was that it was nice to have a politician who would listen, and he did, not that we didn't have plenty of argument."[16]

Just like his congressional race, Obenshain managed an effectively organized group of loyalists, but financially, the campaign was struggling. Despite winning the support of Richmond's conservative elite, the Obenshain campaign didn't see a dime of the promised funds coming their way from the Holton campaign who had collected on it. At one point, things became so desperate that a Richmond financier offered to buy the Obenshain family farm in order to help Dick win his campaign. Dick's father rightly declined the offer. In order to help resuscitate his campaign, Dick's longtime friend and northern Virginia campaign manager, Bill Cummings, coordinated with a man named Kenny Klinge to hold a fundraiser at the home of Julie Crickenberger. Kenny was campaign manager for Vincent Callaghan and had access to many wealthy contacts in the northern Virginia area, including a man named Stetson Coleman. Coleman was a conservative bankroller who inherited a lot of money from the Quaker State oil business, and he was impressed with Dick Obenshain—so much so that he gave the Obenshain campaign $40,000.[17] The campaign raised a total of $150,000 that year, most of which was spent on media advertising and print. The Holton campaign coffers totaled close to half of a million.[18]

Unfortunately, shortly after relieving the financial pressure on his campaign, Dick was met with another distraction. In October he spent a considerable amount of time travelling to southwest Virginia. Two weeks before Election Day in Dickenson County, located in the southwest corner of Virginia, bordering West Virginia, nine Republican precinct judges were

---

[16] Scott interview.

[17] Klinge interview, February 2, 2010.

[18] "Obenshain Lists $150,000" *Richmond Times Dispatch*. December 4, 1969.

arrested on false accusations of intimidation after the judges refused to cast absentee ballots which were ""fraudulently and illegally" obtained by Democrats during the 1967 state elections. In the Richmond Times Dispatch Dick was quoted as saying:

> "We Virginians take our politics very seriously, but it is not our practice to fight political battles with criminal warrants and arrests in the dead of night. The arrest of nine Republican election judges and other citizens in Dickenson County is the type of act which most of us would not believe could happen in Virginia. To consider such honorable action (preventing ballot stuffing) a crime is an eloquent commentary on the Democratic machine in Dickenson county."[19]

The timing was peculiar, appearing to be meant to intimidate other precinct leaders and poll workers from challenging illegally mailed ballots in the upcoming election. Democrats in the county had acquired 1100 votes through absentee ballots through a process known as "black satchelling." A practice in which unverified votes seem to appear from nowhere. One voter applicant was found to be from a family that had moved from Dickenson to Knoxville a decade ago.

Obenshain cancelled several campaign appearances in order to visit and draw public attention in Dickenson County. He was able to skillfully turn it into a political issue and charged that Democrats in all of the southwestern Virginia had "five or ten thousand votes stashed away in a truck out there." Conveniently for Obenshain, Andrew Miller was a defense attorney for the Democratic leaders in the county and region. Obenshain remarked that if elected, he would strengthen absentee voter laws, and suggested that absentee voters, with the exception of military, the aged, or the infirm, be required to appear in person to obtain a ballot. Miller mocked Obenshain's lack of proof, saying, "I am still waiting for any word on these political arrests from my opponent."[20]

---

[19] "Obenshain Raps Arrests in Dickenson" *Richmond Times Dispatch*. October 19, 1969.
[20] "Obenshain Charges Votes 'Stashed Away'" *Richmond Times Dispatch*. October 20, 1969.

As it turned out, the chairman of the electoral board in Dickenson County was convicted in 1968 for the 1967 incident for pulling a gun on one of the Republican precinct judges who was being arrested. Obenshain urged that the chairman be removed from his post in order to ensure the integrity of the electoral process in Dickenson County. Dick ended up winning the case and defended the Republicans successfully. He never billed them for this service.

When the results came in on election night voter turnout was at an all-time high for a non-presidential election. To nobody's surprise, Buzz Dawbarn was far behind J. Sargeant Reynolds in the race for lieutenant governor, which he would lose 54% to 42% to the young Democrat. Obenshain successfully delivered every locality in the 3rd Congressional District to Holton. Holton's slew of endorsements and financing also paid off, and he defeated Battle 52% to 45%. Andy Miller had just arrived in Abingdon that night when he received word of his victory by a margin of 49.7% to Dick's 48.4%.[21] Each race had a spoiler candidate or two. Much of what was left of the racist elements of the Byrd Machine were voting for third party candidates. When he heard the results, Miller was not surprised, and Obenshain was not quite as disappointed as his first race. With Holton in office, Dick was given assurance that he would either find something in Holton's administration or in President Nixon's.

The assurances never materialized. Dick was interested in a position as head of the Virginia Department of Motor Vehicles, which Holton passed him on at the suggested of Rodger Provo who was in favor of a man named Vern Hill. Hill had worked for the Hertz Corporation in New York. Dick had the opportunity to become a judge in the 4th Circuit Federal Court, but he declined as it would have thwarted his desire to hold an elected office. Eventually, when Holton did offer him a position, it was more of an insult than anything. The only position offered to Dick after several months of waiting until early 1970 was a role as head of the ABC Board, an agency modeled after the Soviet Liquor Trust that Governor Harry F. Byrd established during the Prohibition era due to his hatred for alcohol. Dick could not run an agency that he was

---

[21] Virginia State Board of Elections. 1969 Report.
https://www.elections.virginia.gov/resultsreports/election-results/index.html

philosophically opposed to, and he turned down the offer. Instead, the position went to his best friend, Rod Layman. Holton would later lament in his memoirs that he wished he could have found something in his administration for Dick. In reality, Holton took little action to make that happen for his running mate.[22]

With a family to support and no income for almost a year, the worst possible scenario for Dick Obenshain had been realized. Holton had essentially broken his promise. The 1969 election would be the last time the liberal Holton and conservative Obenshain would find themselves as political allies and marked the beginning of their antagonism towards each other. To this day pundits argue the degree to which conservative Democrats helped the Republican win the governor's mansion, an office they hadn't held in nearly 100 years. Holton credited his victory to the Crusade of Voters endorsement, but a Nixon report showed that it was the conservative coalition that resulted in the win. Holton celebrated his historic victory that night, but the coalition that aided in that victory would soon rain on his parade.

[22] Holton, p. 97.

Chapter 9:

The Kitchen Cabinet Group

A few months after the election, George Hinnant was walking by the corner of Franklin and 8th street when he bumped into an old friend from the law firm, Dick Obenshain. George hadn't seen Dick in a few years since taking a job as a counsel to the Federal Reserve. He politely asked Dick what he was up to, even though he already knew. "I just lost the race," said Dick. He was still on a leave of absence at McGuireWoods & Battle, but it was clear that he did not want to go back. For nearly a year and throughout the campaign, he was anticipating leaving the firm one way or another but was now left without any prospects. George was also unenthusiastic about his job with the Fed. Instantly it became clear what they needed to do. "Let's starts a firm, and just do everything 50/50," said Dick. George also had a family and knew the risk they were taking but decided it would be worth it. "It was a great leap of faith," he knew. Within a few months, they set up their office at 1 North 5th Street in Richmond. Dick decorated his office with elephant statues and trinkets representing the Republican symbol, and a large portrait of Patrick Henry.

The early months were slow-going. They didn't have clients. George's father co-signed on a loan so that they could operate the business for six months until they could grow the practice. They were able to hire a secretary name Sandra, who passed the time by reading long novels at work. The phone wasn't ringing. After Sandra left at 5 p.m. Dick and George would look at how many pages she read to measure how little activity they had that day. George signed up to be a public defender for the City of Richmond, despite not having any experience or background in criminal law, just to bring in some income. After several months, they started to bring in some business. They added one more person to their now three-man team and became Obenshain, Hinnant, and Dolbeare. Over the course of several years, the firm took on a life of its own. They added names to their building and took names off, but the business slowly started to grow to a respectable size.

Occasionally, when times were good, the team would all go to the Bull and Bear Club downtown for a drink after work. Dick would enjoy a cigar and a martini, but never in excess. During one of their after-work socials, George recalled a conversation regarding several Texas oil companies that began offering retainers to their firm, but Dick would never accept them. He knew there would obviously be strings attached. The oil companies were looking to buy influence but even if that wasn't their intent, the optics of that would not bode well. "To his credit," George said, " he rejected that. I admired him for that, it was a part of his integrity." Still, Obenshain's political connections were beginning to help the firm gain name recognition.

As Dick grew older, he managed to reign in his temper. This quick temper had been his primary reason for not pursuing a career as a pastor. Although most attorneys work in a stressful work environment, George Hinnett said that Dick never seemed to get angry over much. Whenever he got mad about something, he'd simply slam his desk drawer and yell, "damn." "It was very short. And that would be the end of it," said George. This tended to happen with more frequency whenever he was working on a campaign. George described how he would listen in on what would be going on politically, "The news would always be inaccurate about who said what. I was privy to Dortch Warriner coming into the office, and together they'd be talking about one thing and the news would report something entirely false. I had no idea the news did that. I was naive about [it]."[1]

While building his new-found business venture, Dick stayed remarkably busy in other areas. People were moving into Virginia from all around the country, new businesses were coming in, and suburbia was growing along with new civic groups. Since Dick had the reputation for being an engaging speaker, he was always asked to address these new groups. Most of these speeches revolved around bringing like-minded people together.

Even though he lost his race for attorney general in 1969, the race made him a more recognizable figure in Virginia politics and a leader in the emerging conservative movement. His impressive campaign earned him significant appointments on various boards and added many accolades to his résumé. He was elected president of the Bridgewater College Alumni Association, and in the summer of 1970 he was appointed to the Board of Visitors at Virginia Commonwealth University. His service at the local March of Dimes chapter earned him a spot as the state chairman of the organization in 1970. Lastly, in late September, Richard Nixon appointed him to be a member of a 15-person delegation to the general assembly of NATO in the Hague, Netherlands. It was truly a remarkable honor and experience he never forgot, and his first time overseas.[2]

Meanwhile, at the Governor's mansion, Linwood Holton was burning bridges as quickly as he was building them. Dick was not the only Republican to have been slighted by the Holton administration. For decades Republicans had been prevented from holding any significant positions within the state. They were excited to finally have some representation when Holton took office, but this didn't materialize to the degree that they had hoped. Holton was working with a split government, as his lieutenant governor and attorney general were both Democrats. There was also a strong desire to retain many public servants who had the experience needed to run the administration smoothly. Ted Burr, who had helped on Holton's campaign and stayed on staff performing administrative duties during the transition, said, "Thousands of

---

[1] Hinnant interview.

[2] Helen interview.

letters came in of congratulations, and people wanting jobs, they hadn't been eligible before and thought now that there was a Republican in, they might be."[3]

He angered Republicans even more by raising income taxes and giving no credit for their assistance in getting him elected governor. For four years the debate raged among the Holton and Obenshain camps regarding the main reason for Holton's victory in 1969. Despite running further to the right of center than in 1965, Holton believed his win was due solely to the support of labor groups and black voters, thinking his moderate stances attracted the majority of voters to his campaign. Obenshain and his followers attributed the victory to Dick's ability to convince many Main Street Richmond Democrats to support Holton. Holton made no effort to convert this constituency during the campaign. A few years later, a leaked report to the Richmond News Leader coming from the Nixon administration suggested that the Obenshain perspective was, in fact, accurate. The report claimed that Holton won in 1969 because his opponent was not a conservative, as was the case in 1965 when he lost to Mills Godwin. Bill Battle was considered, by all accounts, to be a moderate. This created a political atmosphere in which conservatives felt comfortable switching to the Republican ticket, as they were made to feel welcomed by Dick Obenshain. Holton's victory numbers were also roughly the same as Nixon's totals the year before. While Holton enjoyed more support from black voters in 1969 than in 1965, overall, he only garnered 20% of the black vote statewide, which made up 2% of his total percentage. In the southern parts of Virginia, where Obenshain was the strongest, Holton saw an increase in his totals from 15% in 1965 to nearly 50% in 1969. The report concluded that the new conservative coalition would and should organize itself under the Republican Party in order to continue being victorious.[4] To make matters worse, Governor Holton cut off communication with Republicans almost entirely. "He wouldn't even talk to us," said Kenny Klinge.[5] Those Virginia Republicans looking in from the outside, especially the conservative

---

[3] Ted Burr interview, June 19, 2017.
[4] Virkler, p. 25.
[5] Kenny Klinge interview, September 8, 2017.

Republicans, felt used by Holton. Their relationships went from strained to cold.

If someone were to ask Holton about his time as governor, he would say it was a success. Others had contrary things to say, though tactfully. Various people in his administration also had grievances. Holton had certain habits, including taking things too personally, and was often prone to emotional outbursts, which made him difficult to work with. One of the few high points of his administration was the iconic moment in which he walked his daughter Ann to school, becoming the first governor to allow his children to attend an integrated public school. It was a meaningful and symbolic gesture that served to heal Virginia's past racial divisions. Holton made race relations the triumphant cornerstone of his tenure as governor. Aside from this important issue, he had little philosophical substance in other areas of governing.

Another point of contention occurred during his second year in office after the tragic death of Lieutenant Governor J. Sargeant Reynolds due to an inoperable brain tumor. A special election had been called for. Holton supported the moderate George Shafran, a wealthy real estate executive and freshman delegate in the General Assembly, to take Reynolds' place. With Shafran being independently wealthy, he could finance his own campaign. He also supported most, if not all, of Holton's agenda. Shafran looked to be the only option for a while, until the conservatives picked Delegate George Mason Green, a conservative true-believer like Obenshain. Both men were from Arlington. Since Dick didn't have a job in Holton's administration, he decided it would be acceptable to run Green's campaign. He was also tired of sitting on the sidelines and felt that Holton was taking the party in the wrong direction. It was the first contest that put Obenshain against Holton. A convention was called for by the RPV and Shafran was victorious. This proved that Holton, not Obenshain, was still in charge of the party.

On the Democrat side, the state central committee selected George J. Kostel as their candidate, avoiding both a primary and convention contest. The last nominating contest involving the liberal populist Henry Howell and the centrist Bill Battle had damaged the party in the general election. The Democrats wanted to avoid risking a repeat scenario. Perhaps out of spite, Henry Howell chose to run again anyway but this time as an independent. By not having a clear conservative in the race, the results were disastrous for both the Republican and Democrat parties. Shafran proved to be a disorganized candidate. As Holton's hand selected pick, he was seen as more liberal than Kostel, the Democrat. The split in the vote allowed Henry Howell to win by plurality.[6] The results drew much criticism of Holton, who had been insistent that Shafran was a winning candidate. Holton refused to take any responsibility for the loss. Shafran ran just to the right of center, which was Holton's strategy for winning, but the plan didn't account for an independent candidate. It had essentially split the conservative vote.

The situation forced many to contemplate whether Holton's election had merely been a fluke, rather than the beginning of a two-party system in Virginia. It made the conservative faction within the Republican Party even more certain that they needed to bring the conservative Democrats into the fold. "Many just didn't believe that the Democratic Party was no longer conservative," said Ted Burr.[7]

Another boost to this realignment could have occurred a year earlier in 1970, when Senator Harry Byrd, Jr. decided to run as an independent after protesting a change to the National Democrat Party rules. But Holton did not roll out the welcome mat for Byrd to switch parties. Instead, he convinced his friend, a moderate Republican from Roanoke named Ray Garland, to run for the U.S. Senate against Byrd. At that convention the liberal-moderate mountain valley wing of the party voted in favor of nominating a candidate contrary to the will of the "New Republicans," brought in by Obenshain, who desired to not run a candidate against Byrd, Jr.. The vote for nominating Garland was 635-419. It created a disastrous situation for conservatives in which a liberal Democrat almost won in the general election, foreshadowing the incident that occurred a year later with Henry Howell. The split in the Republican Party led to the formation of a "Republicans for Byrd" group. Garland was only able to raise $125,000, which was 20% of what Holton had raised for his Governor's race in 1969. On election day, Byrd Jr. edged out a win with 53.5% of the vote while his liberal Democrat opponent received 31.2%. Ray Garland only

[6] Atkinson, p. 258.
[7] Burr interview.

received 15% of the vote.[8] It was an embarrassment to Holton and to the Republicans.

The conservatives who were the majority voting bloc in the state, found themselves in a state of political purgatory. They didn't feel that they belonged in Holton's Republican Party, nor did they feel that they belong in the changing Democratic Party either. Obenshain, who was more concerned with the opportunity for realignment, said,

> "The Republicans could have joined hands with the conservatives and formed a practically unbeatable coalition in Virginia politics. But their pride was too much for them. They refused to keep their appointment with the conservatives at the altar and thereby invited their ignominious defeat," in an article aptly titled, "They Blew It."[9]

The origins of the Obenshain group, or, "the Kitchen Cabinet Group," as they were called to those in the inner circle, started somewhere between Dick's first race for Congress and his race for attorney general. "Some were there since day one, since his days as Young Republicans' Chair. They all had the same philosophy; it was essentially the foundation of the Reagan philosophy," Helen assessed.[10] The outer circle of the group would grow to become the conservative caucus.

Originally the kitchen group was informally built around four people: Weldon Tuck, Dick Obenshain, Dr. Lewis Williams, and Dortch Warriner. "We were just friends during that time, and the little informal group kept going," said Weldon. As he put it, Lewis was considered the "philosopher," Dick was the face of their movement, and Dortch and Weldon were essentially the conduits working behind the scenes. They didn't always agree, but at their core, they all believed in two things: that a conservative path was the right path, and that those who think alike should vote alike. They would come over to Dick's

---

[8] Virginia State Board of Elections website.
[9] "They Blew It" *Richmond News Leader.* June 29, 1970.
[10] Helen interview.

house every Sunday to plan while Helen would make a pot of coffee for everyone.[11]

Dortch Warriner, who was the 4th Congressional District Chairman, eventually received a judgeship appointment in 1974, and Weldon Tuck had taken a position at the Department of Commerce in 1972. Their new roles kept them out of politics for most of the 1970s. As some left, others were brought in. Dr. Lewis Williams and his twin brother Dr. Harold Williams remained involved and brought influential financiers Lawrence Lewis and J. "Smitty" Smith Ferebee. Ferebee was somewhat famous for winning a bet to play six hundred holes of golf in four days, in different locations around the country. He was a wealthy stockbroker prior to this endeavor. Judy Peachee, now chairwoman of the 3rd Congressional District, and Kenny Klinge became more central figures to the group as it expanded in the early 1970s. Besides Helen, Judy was the only woman in the group.

When it became clear that Holton's direction was leading to more losses and embarrassment, the informal group surrounding Obenshain began to expand. The larger version of the group tried to include at least one person in each congressional district around the state who were all conservatives and supported Dick Obenshain as a candidate. It took a while before many of them were able to obtain positions on the State Central Committee. Some of these people included Carl Crosdale and Jimmy Knight in the 1st district; Rod Layman, John Alderson, Don Huffman and Glen Williams of the 6th and 9th districts in western Virginia; Ray, Jade, and William Loginess, Bill Cummings, Bill Stanhagen, Hugh Mulligan of the 8th and 10th districts in northern Virginia; and Ted Burr and Gary Bengston of the 4th and 5th districts in south/central Virginia. Support always remained thin in the 2nd district near Virginia Beach and Norfolk. While the group formed around Obenshain, it eventually took on a life of its own. The group expanded, initially by word of mouth. Don Huffman said,

> "They put together an organization to help Dick. They didn't have anybody in the sixth, and that was Holton's territory. William Loginess had gotten in with Dick somehow, and he told Dick about me. They

---

[11] Tuck interview, September 26, 2017.

> were having meetings every two weeks in Richmond, and they were kind of shocked when I showed up; I was the only one from the sixth initially. We worked on making contacts and getting people to support Dick."[12]

Huffman would then bring in people of his own, including John Alderson, who remembers, "I got to know Dick in the spring of 1971. As time evolved there was a small network around Dick. I met him at one of the Sunday meetings. Don and I would leave here on Friday night and go to Richmond."[13]

When their numbers reached around seventeen, they moved their meetings from Dick's house to a conference room at the Virginia Inn, a hotel located off of Rt. 301 near the border of Henrico and Hanover Counties, owned by group member Smitty Ferebee. John Alderson recalled,

> "We had a congressional district chairman, a county chairman, and in some cases we even had it down to a precinct captain. We'd give a report on what was going on, what needed to be fixed, who could fix it, and how to fix it. All were principled men and women, our organization grew and grew, and the loyalty to Dick was incredible," said Alderson. "Dick didn't dominate the meetings, he was not a bully or vindictive but he would state would he thought. He was a genuine person—was a good listener. Before we went to the meetings we knew where we were and what needed to be accomplished. The camaraderie and spirit of collaboration was amazing. There was no squabbling—some differences, but we were able to work through those. It created lasting bonds. We wanted to make sure the party never embraced the ideas of creeping socialism, that was the impetus behind the whole thing."[14]

The core group stayed in almost constant contact with each other. "When the campaigns were underway the discipline within the ranks was pretty strong, and if you weren't serious and if you didn't have reports, Kenny would

---

[12] Don Huffman interview, June 18, 2017.
[13] John Alderson interview, September 19, 2017.
[14] Ibid.

be the one to come down on you." Alderson continued to describe, "people would call you at 2 a.m. and ask what you were doing. The phone was ever present. The thing that keeps a political organization alive, healthy, and intact is intelligence."[15]

After Green was defeated at the convention by Holton's man Shafron that year, Dick Obenshain found himself sidelined. It gave him a chance to ponder his next move, and he believed that now was the time for him to run for the U.S. Senate. The Democrat incumbent Senator Spong, was not shy about his liberalism and was becoming increasingly unpopular. This encouraged Dick's belief that the time to strike was now. Even after Republican Congressman Bill Scott indicated his intention to run, Obenshain did little to conceal his own intentions of running, saying, "I'm considering many possibilities—including the possibility of running myself...I do know that I have received a great deal of consideration around the state."[16]

Kenny Klinge and a few members of the group from northern Virginia were discussing what they were going to do about the Holton dilemma. They knew that they had to take back control of the party or else they would continue losing statewide elections. The only way to do that would be to win the party chair position with their own selection. Nobody had anything negative to say against the current party chair, Warren French. By all accounts he was a capable and well-liked guy, but he was a symbolic representation of Holton. Kenny suggested, "We ought to run Dick for chairman and take over the party; that's the only way you can deal with this son of a bitch Holton."[17] Thus the movement to nominate Dick Obenshain for party chair began in northern Virginia.

On December 5th, 1971, hundreds of conservative Republicans gathered at an annual retreat which was held that year at the John Marshall Hotel. This small group of Obenshain supporters from northern Virginia got him to join them in a hotel suite that evening after dinner. Dick assumed this

---

[15] Ibid.
[16] "Obenshain says GOP Needs Conservative Candidates" *Richmond Times Dispatch*. November 14, 1971.
[17] Klinge interview.

group was meeting for the purpose of discussing his planned Senate race. When the group was assembled at the suite, he opened by saying, "Well gang, I'm going for the U.S. Senate." The room became silent. Kenny Klinge approached him first, saying, "We wanted to talk to you about that." Dick slumped over in his chair with a long drawn out look on his face. "Don't you think I can win?" That wasn't the issue of course. Kenny had the privilege of telling Dick, "We can't win if you're not the party chair. We need someone with your stature, someone who can articulate the message as gracefully as you can, to lead the party." Disappointed was too soft of a word to describe Dick's reaction. Before leaving that evening, he told everyone in the room, "I'll let you know by the end of the year."[18]

Dick took his time deciding what path to take. The opportunity to run for the U.S. Senate, something he had dreamed of since his younger days, was right in front of him. But the words of Kenny Klinge and others were true: it would be difficult for any conservative Republican to win elected office with Holton in charge of the party. Dick called some of his close friends for counsel, including Rod Layman, Weldon Tuck, and Dortch Warriner. Weldon recalled, "Dortch was adamantly opposed to Dick running for state chairman. He thought it was the wrong thing to do, the wrong timing. He was very vocal at one point. I had to get them together at my house in Richmond and try to resolve it and be the peacemaker."[19] Dortch had good reason; he had been Dick's friend, but he also had some loyalty to Holton, as the two had run on the same ticket in 1965.

On January 15th, 1972, Dick called together several dozen conservative leaders from around the state, including members of his own close-knit group, for a meeting at the Golden Triangle Motel. "I'll run for chairman," he announced. Someone in the conference room full of people shouted, "What an asshole Holton is!" To which Dick replied, "I can't beat Holton; I'm running against French. Never say anything negative towards Holton ever again…"[20] In spite of their political antagonism towards each other, Dick and Linwood

---

[18] Ibid.
[19] Tuck interview.
[20] Kinge interview, February 9, 2010.

Holton actually got along well and never had any problems with each other on a face-to-face personal level.

On February 14th, 1972, Dick Obenshain, Holton's former running mate; Weldon Tuck, his former campaign liaison; and Dortch Warriner, his running mate from 1965, visited with Governor Holton to inform him of their intent to have Dick challenge Warren French for the chairmanship. After a friendly dinner at the Commonwealth Club, the men entered the governor's limousine when Dick decided to break the news that he intended to run. An overconfident Holton laughed at the move. After all, in his mind it was he, Holton, who had won the governorship, won his statewide election, and was leading the party, not Obenshain. Holton thought of himself and his particular ideological brand, which resembled that of the Eastern Establishment, as the future of the party. Holton did not try to talk Dick out of running but told him that victory over French would never happen. Obenshain's good nature prevented this meeting from being one of intense awkwardness, but that didn't stop Holton from instructing his driver to "pick up the speed" as the vehicle flew through multiple red lights, racing over speed bumps. When they arrived back at the governor's mansion everyone exited without saying a word. "Holton could not have gotten out of there faster," said Obenshain intern Brad Cavedo.[21]

[21] Cavedo interview.

Chapter 10:

A Coup d'etat

Dick shared the same frustrations as many in the Republican Party and within he conservative ranks over Linwood Holton. Running for chairman would be a service to his party. He formally announced his intent to do so on February 22, 1972. Although he alluded to them, he didn't attack Holton and French directly, remaining focused on positive change instead. He said, "We have failed to capture the allegiance of the vast majority of our citizens—an allegiance we once had...I intend to lead the way in creating a change. I am not interested in raking over past mistakes." He was accompanied to the announcement by several other Republican delegates, including the recent unsuccessful candidate for lieutenant governor, George Mason Green. The goal would be "to lead the way in creating an unbeatable coalition of Republicans, Independents, and independently minded Democrats who have lost a home in their own party...wandering around in limbo...sick of the Democratic party." [1]

---

[1] Latimer, James. "Obenshain." *Richmond Times Dispatch.* February 23, 1972.

The larger group that had formed around Obenshain began meeting every two weeks at the Virginia Inn, while the smaller group continued to meet every week. As the group branched out to over 50 informal members, Kenny Klinge noted, "the interesting thing is that ones in the group didn't know who all of the ones in the group were". It became a very compartmentalized grassroots takeover of the State Central Committee, as well as various committee units around the state. Kenny continued, "We operated by congressional district. We started from the bottom, going through the whole process, and wiped [Holton supporters] out. It was a war."[2] John Alderson from Roanoke said, "We learned to get commitments from the convention attendees early on, we stayed in contact with them frequently. Our job was to vote count and produce an accurate count. It had better be accurate, or you won't be in the group long."[3]

Kenny Klinge was in charge of Dick's campaign, but publicly a young man named Ted Burr was chosen as the face of the operation for a time. Ted Burr had recently worked for Governor Holton during his campaign. Like many, he had been a Democrat his entire life before that campaign but now saw himself as an independent conservative. He was still politically "green" and not seen as controversial to anyone. He currently worked for Dick's friend Dortch Warriner, who suggested his employee, Ted. "They wanted a person to be his campaign chairman. Most people within the party didn't want to take on a sitting governor, except for the hardcore conservatives. They wanted someone who wasn't really known to anybody. That nobody could get too upset with. I didn't know a thing about running a campaign; Kenny was the real operation, they just needed someone to hold the title." Dick had come down to ask Ted directly, to which Ted replied, "You got to be kidding me. You have to understand, I don't know anything about anything." Dick responded, "You don't need to, don't worry about it. Everything's taken care of, we just need someone to put their name out there." Ted reflected later on, "I guess at that point, I became a Republican."[4]

---

[2] Klinge interview, February 9, 2019.

[3] Alderson interview.

[4] Burr interview.

Ted then became a part of the Obenshain group. “I
Dortch all the time. We met at the Virginia Inn. We were plott
the party at this hotel,” he said. Ted was eventually talked into running for GOP chairman of his hometown in Emporia. He remained the chairman of the campaign for several months until Obenshain named Delegate Jerry Geisler of Carroll County and John Marlow of Warren County as the new co-chairs. Dick wanted to gain more influence at the last minute in those areas located in the west. French was from the Shenandoah Valley, and Holton of course had much influence in Southwest Virginia.

During the chairmanship race he focused much of his time building relationships with Republican youth. He knew that young people were the key to the future of the party. Most of the Young Republicans now shared his vision for the future of the party and were open to change. An outdated political alignment would do nothing but damage future elections for conservatives in the commonwealth. His efforts paid off quickly in his bid for chairman, as the College Republican Federation of Virginia was the first group to announce their endorsement of Obenshain in March. They said in a statement that Obenshain would bring “fresh and dynamic leadership at the highest level.”[5] Like his mentor Ted Dalton, Dick was always interested in giving young people opportunities. It was something he always advocated for in his speeches as well. Listening to the youth and giving attention to their ideas and concerns is what solidified and preserved Dick’s legacy well into the future.

Bill Hurd, a member of the College Republicans, recalled, “There was talk among some in the party that Dick was too conservative and would scare away young people from the party. I was an officer in the College Republicans. Our board wanted to endorse [him]. The fact that we came out so strongly was a big plus.”[6] The College Republican Board voted 17-1 for Obenshain. The chairman of the organization, Carlisle Gregory, said, “French had not been helpful to us; he was pretty dismissive of us. For a certain number of people Dick was their favorite guy. We figured we’d get a better shake with Obenshain.” Thus a group formed called “Youth for Obenshain,” which

---

5 “College GOP Board Backs Obenshain” *Richmond Times Dispatch*. March 28, 1972.
6 Bill Hurd interview, October 3, 2017.

worked hard at helping the candidate during the convention scheduled for June 2nd and 3rd.[7]

At the suggestion of Judy Peachee, Obenshain brought in another young man to be his driver, and a new member of the group by the name of Steve Maupin. Maupin, a recent graduate of UVA, recalled the intensity of Dick's travel schedule:

> "On a typical day, we might leave his home early in the morning, visit a country chairman in Tidewater, drive to the northern neck for a lunch meeting with the leaders of a small county, and then drive to northern Virginia for a reception at Fairfax or another urban county or city. At the end of the last meeting, we would return to Richmond. On some days, our trip would be by airplane. These private 'charters' would usually be on a small single engine plane owned by one of Dick's supporters who contributed it to the campaign. Sometimes we would drive one-way to a meeting and a plane would be arranged to take Dick back to get more rest. On return trips, I was often very tired, and I remembered thinking, 'please don't let me go to sleep and hurt Dick.' I was always relieved when I could put 'the candidate' as we called him on a plane."[8]

The two got to travel together a lot during his race for chair. From March to June, Stan would drive Dick from place to place, visiting 125 different localities around the state. Stan got to see a side of Mr. Obenshain that many didn't get to see. "He was a man of faith, and each day when we were in a hotel he would open the Gideon Bible and pick a quote from a random page he would select by letting the bible fall open. He would use the quote to make a point during his speeches that day"[9]. Dick didn't wear his religion on his sleeve, but most were inspired by his devout faith. He went to church, but didn't intermingle politics with his faith, although he would use spiritual analogies to make a point from time to time.

---

[7] Carlisle Gregory interview, July 12, 2017.
[8] Maupin, Stan "Driving Dick Obenshain" personal papers.
[9] Ibid.

"We got to talk a lot, but he never talked about religion," Maupin remembered. The two would listen to country music along the way—"Loretta Lynn type of stuff," said Maupin. "We'd be going to Mathews County and he'd ask me to look up what was going on in that area and we'd talk about that on the way. I'd call somebody who knew somebody who knew somebody." When they weren't chatting, Dick always had a book with him and was always reading.[10]

At the last minute, when the two would approach their destination, Dick would say to Stan, "I guess I better write my speech." He'd then proceed to take an envelope and write a dozen words and points he'd like to make on the back of it. He'd usually talk for a half an hour, allowing the words to flow, speaking entirely on instinct. Stan said, "no two speeches were ever alike, and none were formulaic. I never once sensed he was being insincere; he'd never shake your hand and smile and then say something about you. He never talked bad about people."

At a lunch stop in Fredericksburg one afternoon, Stan and Dick approached the hostess, who looked surprised and said, "Aren't you Dick Obenshain? I read about you in the paper." Dick was surprised that he was becoming a recognizable face around the commonwealth. When the pair sat down, Maupin said Dick was amused and told him that it was the first time a stranger had ever recognized him.

Another characteristic Stan observed was Obenshain's quick deliberation. After a lunch stop in Orange County, Stan informed Dick about someone he needed to meet: a wealthy individual who was a Democrat. When Stan arrived to pick up Dick the next day, he was amazed when Dick told him that he had already reached out to the person and "won him over."

A historic memory for Stan was when the idea for the TV show "Little House on the Prairie" was conceived following one of Dick's meetings around the state. Meeting at a mutual location, a donor from New York happened to arrive early and decided to stop at a used bookstore, where he was appalled that he couldn't find any books by Laura Ingalls Wilder. When this donor returned

---

[10] Stan Maupin interview, September 14, 2017.

home after his meeting with Dick, he called Roger McBride, a prominent libertarian, to inform him about Dick Obenshain but to also express his concern that "Little House on the Prairie" was becoming a lost piece of art. Two years later a movie and TV show based off of the books was produced.

Among the numerous impression-making moments during that time, the one Stan Maupin remembered most fondly occurred when they had returned to a two-room suite they had rented for the evening in Newport News for a meeting with several potential financial supporters. It was late, and the pair were exhausted. Maupin recalled, "Dick slumped on the sofa and began talking politics with these influential Republicans. He realized he had left his briefcase in the car and asked me to retrieve it for him." Without hesitation, Stan stepped outside and brought the briefcase back to Dick. Dick took the case and paused in mid-sentence, looked at Stan and said, "Stan, you're not my servant. We're friends. I should not have asked you to do that for me. The next time you need something, I want to get it for you." He then returned to his meeting. Stan remembered sitting in the room, stunned by Dick's level of consideration.[11]

Obenshain himself was still a young man, only 36 years old. In a short time, he had run for Congress and statewide office and had proven himself as an articulate, principled conservative with an understanding of practical politics. He was years ahead in seeing the cracks among the ranks of Virginia Democrats, and he knew those cracks had to be exploited if Republicans were to continue winning in the years ahead.

> Dick said, "With George Rawlings and the McGovern crowd in control, only the hardcore liberals still feel at home in the Democratic party. What we must do is to use the next six months to dramatically increase the strength of the Republican Party in Virginia. For 20 years Virginia has been voting for Republican presidents and Republican congressmen, only to drop back into the Democratic Party for four more years. It's time to get the politics of Virginia straightened out."[12]

---

[11] Ibid.
[12] "Opportunity Seen for GOP" *Richmond News Leader.* April 28, 1972.

Over the next several weeks Obenshain advocated strongly for unity within the party and argued that the GOP needed to elicit strong emotions in order to motivate people to volunteer and vote for the party again.

Sensing that the tides were going against him, Warren French resorted to attacking any way that he could during the month of May, 1972. French, who had a business of his own as the founder of Shentel, couldn't fathom how Obenshain was able to find the time to campaign full-time. He assumed that Obenshain's campaign must be heavily financed, suggesting that Stetson Coleman was behind it. The Obenshain campaign had only spent a very modest amount, around $8,000, during the chairmanship race. Obenshain charged that French was not campaigning as hard, not because he was a working man, but because he had just spent the past two weeks vacationing in Rome.[13] This was true and Dick was simply campaigning harder. He was splitting part of his time during the day practicing law and campaigning in the evenings.

Dick continued to run a positive campaign and focused on party unity while deflecting the negative attacks from French. At a 7th District Committee meeting he repeated that he had "done everything in the world to preserve unity ... I have not run against Warren French or the governor. I just feel that we must have aggressive leadership if we are to bring in independents and conservative Democrats into the party."[14]

A reporter had asked him whether he was running out of resentment towards Holton, to which he again insisted, "[this] is not an ideological fight. No basic anger or antagonism. It is a difference in viewpoints on how to build the party."[15]

Many Republicans were excited to have the opportunity to elect Dick Obenshain as chairman. After 1969, he had become the de facto leader of the growing conservative wing of the party. John Paul Woodley described how many felt, "Dick had the vision and seemed to be just an absolutely committed

---

[13] "Obenshain calls Foe Desperate." *Richmond Times Dispatch*. May 12, 1972.
[14] "Obenshain Confident Of Election." *Richmond News Leader*. May 31, 1972.
[15] "Close to 537 Votes Obenshain Says." *Richmond Times Dispatch*. May 23, 1972.

advocate for the principles of limited government, strong national defense, and reasonable taxation. All of the values that are my values."[16]

As the convention on June 2nd and 3rd approached, Obenshain was confident in his chances. Others knew that he was a natural fit for this position. He never speculated on his chances in previous races, but this time he allowed himself to humbly state, "I think I'm getting reasonably close to the 537 delegate votes needed to assure election as Republican state party chairman."[17]

He had a broad range of support among all parts of the state, but especially in the power centers of Richmond. Fifteen out of the twenty-four Republican members of the House of Delegates shared Dick's worldview. Dick also had 300 committed delegates going into the convention. He only needed 257 more. Despite the numbers clearly tilting in Obenshain's favor, Holton nonetheless believed his ally, French, would emerge victorious. After all, French was handpicked by the historic sitting governor. It wasn't until the night before the nomination, that Holton seemingly accepted the possibility of defeat. At a dinner with the convention delegation he gave a speech in which he said, "You do what you want to do about the party leadership. Whatever you do, when we come out of this convention, I'm going to be with you."[18] An effort to save face, perhaps, as his handpicked candidate faced an inevitable defeat.

The convention was attended by about a thousand people and was in Holton's territory again: Roanoke. The votes were divided fractionally according to the Republican voting power of the previous statewide election. The magic number needed to win was 537. Dick's confidence allowed him to stay focused on the issue at hand and to avoid getting dragged into the mud of negative politics. He again asserted that the race was about different viewpoints regarding how to build the Republican Party of Virginia. Holton and Warren French viewed the state party similarly to that of their leadership counterparts at the national level. The RNC leadership believed they should be a moderate counterweight to the increasing liberal tendencies within the Democratic Party.

---

[16] John Paul Woodley interview, July 10, 2017.
[17] *Richmond Times Dispatch*, May 23, 1972.
[18] Atkinson, p. 284

A moderate approach, they felt, would attract non-ideologues, and conservatives would naturally toe the line out of fear of liberalism.

There was much excitement at the 1972 convention. The first sitting Republican governor in one hundred years was being challenged by a group of rebels within the party. Bob Dole gave the keynote address, followed by Linwood Holton and Dortch Warriner.

Holton publicly said that he would not get involved by trying to sway delegate votes. Yet Holton's henchmen attempted to influence the convention by having a rule change that would have affected the number of committed delegates. The French supporters didn't have the votes to do this. The party allowed "directed" votes in which a chairman of a local unit could instruct his delegates how to vote; it was a form of block voting. Holton was trying to force individual delegate votes within each "unit" as a last-ditched effort to possibly save French. The results would have been close to the same, except the vote counting would have taken much longer. The Obenshain people had their own signals for instructing their supporters on how to vote on these procedural decisions, which they delivered from a control area high in the Civic Center. The role of the state chairman is to maintain neutrality, even when he is the person up for re-election. So, when Dortch Warriner accused Warren French of running the convention by fiat during his speech to nominate Obenshain, it had a powerful effect on the delegation. Party Secretary Polly Campbell reflected, "This race was the first ever 'down and dirty' one I had been involved in."

The 1st district, which had four members of the Obenshain group overseeing it, heavily support Obenshain, as did the northern Virginia and Richmond delegations. The Roanoke area had remained difficult for Dick, but before the votes could even be announced, Warren French motioned to have the committee unanimously nominate Dick Obenshain as their new chair. Four months after Governor Holton told Dick that he couldn't win, his victory was a landslide 769 to 288. Moderate Republican Delegate Vince Callaghan moved to nominate Obenshain, while Delegate Wyatt Durrette, a new face in the party who was on the party steering committee, gave the seconding speech.

The Republican delegates also continued to nominate a chairman for the Republican delegation to the national convention in Miami. They elected

Governor Holton as chairman for that delegation, perhaps softening the blow that occurred to him on that day. The next order of business was for the party to nominate Congressman Bill Scott for the U.S. Senate. Scott was unopposed. Had Obenshain run against him, it may also have been an ugly contest. While Obenshain was deciding on whether to run, Scott made it clear that he did not intend to step aside. As Bill Scott took to the podium to accept his nomination after being uncontested, many thought "that could've been Dick." The thought certainly must have crossed the mind of Dick Obenshain. Instead, there was now harmony.

It would have been a less exciting day had it not been for the frenzy surrounding an Obenshain chairmanship. This meant many things for those who had waited for a political realignment to happen for nearly two decades. "This is a great day for Virginia's conservative majority…and we have Dick Obenshain to thank for it," said the Richmond News Leader's editorial board.[19]

In the years leading up to this moment, the remnants of the conservative Democrats had suffered a blow when Harry Byrd had died. Conservative Congressman Howard Smith was defeated in his primary by the considerably more far-left George Rawlings, Jr. who was in turn defeated by the same Republican Bill Scott in the 8th Congressional District, which comprised most of northern Virginia. The political realignment was then hastened after the liberal Joseph T. Fitzpatrick was elected as the Democratic state party chairman in a landslide victory comparable to Obenshain's. Former governor, Mills Godwin, was denied a delegate seat at his own party's state convention, as were many other moderate Democrats. At their national convention, the Virginia Democrats helped to nominate George McGovern for President in 1972. Even the liberal U.S. Senator Spong himself considered the tactics employed by liberal activists who were trying to take over the party to be similar to that of the old Byrd Machine. The exclusion of moderates and conservatives was even worse at the local level. Progressives such as Henry Howell, thought the moment for realignment was long overdue but ultimately these series of events alienated many lifelong Democrats who were no longer welcomed in their own party.

---

[19] *Richmond News Leader*, June 3, 1972.

Obenshain got to work immediately on inviting those disaffected conservative Democrats into the party. His election as party chair was largely symbolic of the Republican Party's full embrace of the conservative electorate. "To Dick's credit, in a very short time after he was chairman it became apparent that he was really building the party and working very hard to bring the various factions in," said executive director Arlen Rains.[20] He kept Arlen on for a time before bringing in Kenny Klinge less than a year later. Having a full-time executive director position was new for the party and showed that they were acquiring the ability to fund themselves. They established a headquarters at the Heritage building in downtown Richmond. While electing Bill Scott to the Senate was the top priority, Obenshain began teasing the goal of convincing Mills Godwin to switch parties. "Holton was irrelevant after that," said Kenny Klinge. "We did things to embarrass the governor." Dick, however, wanted "peace in the valley."[21]

At the first post-convention State Central Committee meeting, Dick and Kenny looked around the room and found it was now almost entirely Obenshain group members—almost. The coup had created some antagonism from former friends. The party's secretary, Polly Campbell, who supported French but supported Dick during their days as Young Republicans reflected, "He set out to get rid of me as an officer, but he could find no one who would run against me, so I retained my secretaryship. He would tell me perhaps it would be better if I sat at the other end of the table."[22] After the slights and failures of Holton, the Obenshain group approached things with a "take no prisoners" attitude from that point on.

As chairman, Dick had an elevating impact on the group. "Nobody could get too far out of line," said John Alderson. Outside of state central, the informal Obenshain group continued to meet after 1972, though not as frequently. It continued to stay in place and function. Alderson continued, "We all got to know one another, there were no defections and few surprises for a

---

[20] Atkinson, p. 285.
[21] Klinge interview.
[22] Campbell interview.

long time. It became a tight-knit group, and that was what gave great strength to the Republican Party."[23]

After his election, Obenshain continued to be involved with the Young Republicans and the College Republicans. "He took the College Republicans very seriously. He would come and speak to our gatherings and help us," said college student John Paul Woodley.[24] CRFV Chairman Carlisle Gregory reflected,

> "The College Republicans had their own seat on State Central, so I had some interactions with him [Dick]. A guy named Tom Davis, who was roommates with Richard Nixon's son-in-law, became the youth arm for the presidential re-election campaign, and he gets put in charge of Virginia. So there was some turf war. The president thought all College Republicans should work for him, and we thought we should work with them, not for them. We had a confrontational meeting in Richmond between their side and ours when Dick Obenshain walked into the room. He came and sat down on my side of the table. That was the end of the discussion. I was a fan of Dick Obenshain's anyway, but I became an even bigger fan after that."[25]

That moment exemplified the clout that Dick Obenshain had. Dick continued to make strong impressions on many young people during his time as chair. Bill Hurd, a college Republican at the time, reflected, "The first time I met Dick was at a dinner meeting with Jim Gilmore, when Dick came to a Virginia Young Republicans meeting." Like the descriptions of others, Hurd said, "He treated everyone as if they were a friend. That's how he would introduce you. If I'm the guy driving the car down to southwest Virginia, he wouldn't say, 'this is Bill, my driver' he'd say 'this is my friend Bill.'"[26] Another Young Republican, Jim Gilmore, was also captivated by the Republican leader. "In the fullness of life I've had the opportunity to see hundreds of people give speeches. While you cannot always tell the difference, you can often tell when

---

[23] Alderson interview.
[24] Woodley interview.
[25] Gregory interview.
[26] Hurd interview.

people are just not sincere. Dick was sincere. That was what was so inspirational about him: the fact that he was authentic in his views and what he thought was right for the country," he remembered. Gilmore recalled looking to Obenshain for guidance. Obenshain actually made time for him and would take him to lunch from time to time at the John Marshall building a few blocks away from his law firm. "Instead of pushing me away as an irrelevant kid, he actually embraced me."[27] Gilmore eventually became the sixty-eighth Governor of Virginia.

Dick never slowed down in building the party at the grassroots level either. Dick once received a call from someone in Charlotte County who wanted to start a local party chapter and wanted Dick to come speak. Dick told Wyatte Durrette, "I don't know if it's going to be just Ed and his law partner or whether it'll be 5 or 15 people," but he went down anyway. "That's what he did. He'd go every time. He knew that's what you had to do to build a political party. You weren't going to win elections unless you did," said Durrette.[28]

Dick shocked his inner-circle shortly after the convention by declaring his intent to ensure the election of Bill Scott to the U.S. Senate. It wasn't so much his desire to see that happen that had shocked his friends, but by his enthusiasm to be closely involved with a campaign that was viewed as a sinking ship. Nobody believed that the Scott campaign could win. Scott was known to be eccentric, lacked a competent campaign organization, and was incapable of raising the funds needed to mount a competitive race against Senator Spong. Obenshain believed that a Republican triumph in November was required in order to convince Mills Godwin to switch sides next year. The Obenshain group decided that they needed to take charge of the Scott campaign in order to achieve victory.

Congressman Bill Scott soon appointed Dick as his campaign manager in August. Scott had a name recognition problem; a problem which he hoped Obenshain would help him with. As predicted Scott was also struggling to raise money and needed to utilize Dick's personal connections. Finances became a contentious point between the two men. At one point, Dick was able to acquire

---

[27] Jim Gilmore interview, October 3, 2017.
[28] Durrette interview.

200,000 from Stets Colemon for the Scott campaign, but Scott felt that Colemon was trying to buy himself influence and nearly refused the money. Helen recalled Dick wanting to quit almost every day during this campaign.[29]

Now with a large amount of funds, Dick chaired the independent group "Virginians for Scott" which allowed him to experiment with phone banking and television advertising. Like the "coffee" idea from his 1964 race, Obenshain continued to find innovative and creative new ways of messaging. The commercial advertisements led by Obenshain were said to have transformed Virginia politics. The ideas and technology were new, and Dick used the Virginians for Scott group as a way to explore the effectiveness of these new tactics. Scott himself ran a traditional campaign that utilized radio, newspaper advertising, and public stump speeches and visits, while Obenshain provided the ideas for new advertising and financing. It was considered by political scientists to be the first "modern" campaign in Virginia. As the race was coming down to the wire, John Warner came up with several hundred thousand dollars to support a massive radio ad campaign to aid in victory. "Scott was not a good campaigner. But he was good on the radio...he had a good voice," Warner said.[30]

His robustness as party chairman even caught the attention of the new Democratic chairman, Joseph Fitzpatrick, who said, "Dick was a master organizer. He was the best in the country. He was good at raising funds to get a computerized list of voters, and he was also good at getting affluent Virginians to contribute to the Republican Party. Obenshain moved the Republican Party ahead of the Democrats in fundraising. He knew that Republicans had to outspend Democrats to elect statewide candidates to overcome the tendency of voters to follow their natural inclination to vote Democratic."[31]

Senator Spong had already destroyed himself with the Virginia electorate by supporting gun control measures and coming out in support of presidential candidate George McGovern. Obenshain did most of the dirty work for Scott, attacking Spong publicly. When Spong went after Scott for "riding Nixon's coattails," Obenshain responded, "Spong's voting record has

---

[29] Atkinson p. 288-289.
[30] John Warner interview, April 30, 2012.
[31] Virkler, p. 134

not represented the people of Virginia and his radical party represents only a small minority of people in Virginia. Spong is trying to divert attention from his own associations."[32] Obenshain then went after Senator Spong for his support of the controversial 1968 Gun Control Act, saying, "The mass majority of Virginians oppose gun control legislation. As on so many other votes, Spong deserted his constituents in supporting this broad firearms legislation."[33] According to Attorney General Andy Miller, who tried to help Spong during his race, "Spong was old school, very laid back, and he was not very organized for that campaign. I did everything I could to support him."[34]

There were some hiccups during the race. Stetson Coleman gave a huge amount of money to Bill Scott's campaign: $200,000 to be exact. As Scott had feared, the media's perception of this gift was very negative, so Obenshain decided that there needed to be a press conference at the John Marshall Hotel to address the issue. Colemon, known for his dry humor and timing, observed quietly in the audience as Obenshain presented the reasons for the generous donation. Immediately a reporter interjected, "Don't you think that is a pretty big gift to give from a single person?" Stetson Coleman himself happened to be sitting in front of this reporter at the press conference. He turned around, lowered his face with his glasses resting on his nose and said, "It may be for you, young man." This tongue and cheek reply caused a room full of serious reporters to erupt with laughter. That was the end of the press conference and for some reason, the end of that news story as well.

While grudgingly trying to work through Bill Scott's personality and senate race, Obenshain was also working diligently with a reluctant candidate from the 4th Congressional District named Robert "Bob" Daniel, who had grown up as a Democrat but left the party and became a Republican during the 1960s. As a first-time congressional candidate, it may not have been his idea to run in the first place. Staffers found it difficult to get Daniel to do the work required of him in order to win. All of the typical campaign work that candidates sometimes struggle with doing; attending events, shakings hands but

---

32 "Obenshain Charges Diversion by Spong" Richmond Times Dispatch. September 29, 1972.
33 "Obenshain Chides Spong on Gun Vote" *Richmond News Leader*. September 14, 1972.
34 A. Miller interview.

mostly, making fundraising calls. Reportedly, Daniel kept wanting to quit the race, what seemed like every other week. Dick Obenshain had to keep making special trips to visit him and talk him back into running. [35]

It was the first time that citizens the age of 18 could vote. On election night Nixon easily carried Virginia, and Scott defeated the incumbent Senator Spong by almost 100,000 votes, receiving 53% of the total. Despite devastating losses the previous year, Obenshain utilized his new position as chairman to help a little-known congressman become the first Republican U.S. Senator from Virginia since Reconstruction—a seat that could potentially have gone to Dick Obenshain, had he made a different decision in November of 1971. With Dick Obenshain's leadership, the GOP maintained two open congressional seats and picked up an additional seat with the election of Bob Daniel, who succeeded retiring Democrat Watkins Abbitt. The Republicans possessed 7 of the 10 Congressional seats, the governorship, and now had someone in the Senate along with the Independent Senator Byrd.

Much like Holton, Scott's time in the U.S. Senate was shaky and somewhat of an embarrassment to the GOP. While Scott seemed smooth on the campaign trail, his tenure as a U.S. Senator was littered with gaffes, faux pas, and downright offensive statements. Some say the problem was that Scott actually had a personality and he didn't change it for the sake of his public office. Many of his statements were in jest, not meant to be taken literally, but his humor came across through media outlets as horrifyingly ignorant. Reportedly he confused missile silos with grain silos while being briefed on Soviet military capabilities, saying, "Wait a Minute! I'm not interested in agriculture." In a 1974 New York Times article, Scott was named the Dumbest Member of Congress.[36]

Many knew that Scott's time in the Senate would likely be one term, if he could even survive public office until then. But that didn't stop Republicans from basking in another historic victory for the time. The breather between November and January was a short one, as all eyes would soon turn to the upcoming governor's race of 1973, to decide who would succeed the historic

---

[35] Klinge interview, March 3, 2010.
[36] Totenberg, Nina. "The Ten Dumbest Members of Congress." *New York Times.* 1974

governorship of Linwood Holton. Meanwhile, Holton was trying to stir up fear amongst mountain-valley Republicans that Dick's emphasis on "philosophy over party"[37] would lead to the destruction of the stable two-party system they worked so hard to build in Virginia. Obenshain countered this at an annual Robert A. Taft banquet by saying that conservatives "will not impose a Byrd-style organization on the state Republican party…the Byrd organization is dead…and it's a new time in politics for Virginia."[38]

---

[37] Atkinson, p. 282.
[38] "Democrats Welcome GOP Says" *Richmond Times Dispatch*. June 27, 1972.

Chapter 11:

Principle Before Party

Towards the end of his administration, Governor Holton befriended New York governor and former Goldwater foe Nelson Rockefeller. They were first introduced through Winthrop Rockefeller, who was the Governor of Arkansas and head of the Governors' Association. "Before the end of my term, I had developed a very friendly relationship with Nelson Rockefeller, then governor of New York, and I respected him enormously as a dedicated public servant. I admired him and we became very close friends." Governor Rockefeller was seriously considering running for President again in 1976, to which Governor Holton gleefully responded, "I have made no commitments for the period between January 1974 and the presidential campaign in 1976. I'm available for whatever you might like me to do to help your campaign for the nomination, and, hopefully, the election." [1]

---

[1] Holton, p. 173-174.

Once, while travelling together, they ran into Holton's rival, Dick Obenshain. Holton recalled, "Once when he happened to be in the same area of National Airport at the same time as Nelson and I were, I tried to get him to come over and speak to Governor Rockefeller. Dick and I always got along, although we were ideologically at opposite poles, so he grinned at me when I said, 'Come on over and speak to Governor Rockefeller.' He replied, 'Governor, you're trying to get me in trouble.' And he didn't come over." Dick was one of those pesky ideological "rascals," despised by elites, that Professor Carl Quigley talked about.

Rockefeller was fond of Holton as well. Instead of making him a part of his preliminary campaign staff, and as an example of the kind of power he wielded in Washington, he suggested something else. "He reflected on that offer for a short period, then suggested that I take the position of Assistant Secretary of State for Congressional Relations on Henry Kissinger's staff, which would be vacant in early 1974 (I assumed he would find a way for me to be considered for the nomination to that position). A phone call came from Henry Kissinger exactly at the end of my term as governor, who said he wanted me for that position."[2]

Holton was a bit concerned by Kissinger's reputation for secrecy, but after he voiced this concern Kissinger responded, "Of course you'll be kept informed. I wouldn't want you running around like an unguided missile!" [3] Holton accepted the position. Although Holton claimed to have enjoyed it, he only held the post for a year, garnering many D.C. contacts during the time.

While Holton rubbed elbows with D.C. elites, the Chairman of the Republican Party of Virginia, Dick Obenshain, oversaw many victories and substantial growth of the party. In just his first year, he helped elect an unknown candidate as the first Republican to the U.S. Senate in a century and helped the party pick up an extra seat in Congress. Obenshain proved that he could win and that he was a sharp political tactician. His focus was wholeheartedly about the "visible expression of enthusiasm for former conservative Democrats and

---

[2] Holton, p. 175.
[3] Ibid.

Independents," [4] a plan that had to be pursued with care lest it offend the longtime Republican faithful. Chief among those he wanted to avoid offending was former Governor Mills Godwin.

The plan for realignment continued to make immense strides for both sides during the 1972 election. Mills Godwin, the former Democratic governor who ran against Holton and won in 1965, had chaired "Virginians for Nixon." This was after Dick Obenshain had convinced him to chair the group as way of getting comfortable with the idea of supporting a Republican. According to Godwin it was the first time that he supported a Republican for president. Nixon's rival, George McGovern, was too liberal for even the most ardent conservative Democrat. Godwin was perhaps the most prominent conservative Democrat that had not yet fully crossed over to the Republican Party. Byrd, Jr. had remained an independent. After Godwin left office in 1969, he remained loyal to many of his friends who were still Democrats. He supported Holton's opponent, Bill Battle, and was obviously still emotionally attached to his party. But in just a few short years, by 1973, the Democratic Party had officially come to be dominated by its liberal faction and had aligned almost fully with national Democratic Party. This led to the progressive Lt. Governor Henry Howell throwing his hat in the race to become Virginia's next governor in 1973. As a left-wing populist, Henry Howell was essentially the Huey Long of Virginia.

It would be an understatement to say that Godwin disliked Howell and the direction that the Virginia Democrats were taking. Godwin was contemplating running for governor for the second time, something that had not been done in Virginia in the 20th Century. In Virginia, a governor is constitutionally prevented from serving consecutive terms. It does not say, however, that a governor can't run again four years after his term ended. For weeks, Godwin teased the possibility of running again. Unfortunately for Godwin, he couldn't oust the emerging populist power of Henry Howell. When the year of decision came, considering the state of the Virginia Democratic Party compared to the absurdity of running as a Republican, he thought it best to run as an independent. Senator Harry Byrd Jr. had recently won re-election as an independent, and Henry Howell became lieutenant governor as an

---

[4] Richmond Times Dispatch, May, 23, 1972.

independent as well. To Godwin, winning as an independent seemed like good odds, especially since he had already been a sitting governor once before.

The Republicans, now led by Obenshain, were short-handed in their list of potential candidates. However, they were determined to run their own candidate in 1973, no matter the odds. They first considered two sitting congressmen, J. Kenneth Robinson of Winchester and G. William Whitehurst of Hampton Roads, then added Paul Trible, a prosecutor from the 1st District, as a third possibility. It was important for the growth of the party, Obenshain knew, that the Republicans run their own candidate no matter what Godwin decided to do. Still, they weren't ignorant of the fact that if Godwin jumped in as an independent candidate it would definitely split the conservative vote and result in a Governor Henry Howell. The only answer was to attempt the impossible and convince Mills Godwin to run as a Republican.

The first meeting occurred in October of 1972 and was met with a flat-out rejection. Godwin gave Obenshain and Dortch Warriner, who were leading the attempt, a simple "no" answer. They were encouraged, however, by what still seemed like a warm and receptive meeting. Godwin's primary goal was to protect Virginia from Henry Howell, something he thought he could do successfully as an independent. Obenshain and Warriner were focused on building the party and knew that if Godwin switched, he would bring with him the entire old remnants of the conservative majority who still voted Democrat, and with them, more funding and more votes. After the first meeting, they realized that they all needed to work together to some extent and agreed to meet again.

Warriner met with Godwin by himself a few times, and Obenshain met with Godwin several more times at the Virginia Inn. The former continued to make the case for running as a Republican, while the latter discussed issues concerning the convention and what the logistics would look like should a switch occur.

Warriner and Godwin were both from the 4th Congressional District, a district covering the southern part of Virginia. All of south-central Virginia was dominated by older Democrats. During the 1960s the district had held a history of "dispensing patronage" and making sure Republicans voted for the Byrd Organization. A Godwin switch would potentially bring a large portion of that area into the Republican fold.[5] Some voters farther down south were still stuck on racial issues. They found it hard to switch because Republicans were not in step with them on past racial issues which were still important to them. Republicans were not hospitable to the racial politics of the past, which effectively died with Harry Byrd, Sr. Wyatt Durrette, a Republican delegate from northern Virginia, was also actively working at getting some of his conservative colleagues to switch. He tried to emphasize that "the Democratic Party was changing, it was not their party anymore; they needed to recognize that."[6]

Dick Obenshain made the prospect of running as a Republican seem as appealing as possible to Godwin, but Godwin still did not indicate his intent either way. Godwin was a senior Virginia statesman and had a presence about him that commanded respect. Dick had to tread lightly, but he had to make sure Godwin understood the consequences of not running as a Republican. If he pushed Godwin too hard, he could run as an independent out of spite. If Godwin already knew what he had to do in order to win—or rather, to save the commonwealth from Henry Howell, he wasn't letting on just yet.

Dick and Dortch teamed up again to attempt to persuade Governor Godwin one last time. Financial giant Smith Ferebee was also making his case before the former governor to switch parties, utilizing a Virginia Beach real estate mogul named Dick Short as a go-between. Meanwhile, Dick Obenshain and Dortch devised a "good-cop, bad-cop" scheme. Dick had taken a softer approach to Godwin, but Dortch was "the iron fist in the velvet glove."[7]

The back and forth went on for months, into February of 1973. Godwin had advisors continuing to whisper in his ear who felt that he should follow the path of Senator Byrd and run as an independent. Clearly worried, Godwin was coming up with every excuse he could to avoid a switch. Most of his friends had been lifelong Democrats along with him. Godwin was even worried that Democrats would feel so slighted by a switch that they might even

---

[5] Archives, Republican Party of Virginia.
[6] Durrette interview.
[7] Joe interview, July 20, 2011.

support Howell. Warriner became angry at the absurdity of that suggestion. Obenshain began to feel like a ping pong ball between the two men.

They headed down south to Godwin's home in Chuckatuck (now part of the city of Suffolk), holding their breath to make their final appeal. Godwin was "getting short" with the pair, which brought Warriner to a boiling point. In anger, he said "If you don't run, I will!" clearly relaying the message that Godwin would not receive a Republican endorsement if he did not run as a Republican. In order to win, Godwin had to be endorsed by the Republicans or be nominated by them. One of those options was now off the table, which left Godwin with only one choice.

Dick was scheduled to represent a case in Atlanta around the time of Godwin's scheduled announcement, so he made one last ditch effort to persuade Godwin. He sent him a simple letter dubbed "The Road Damascus." In typical Obenshain fashion, he used a biblical analogy to describe the situation Godwin was in. He invoked the story of Saul and his conversion to Christianity after having spent his whole life executing Christians. After Saul's conversion, many in the church had a difficult time accepting him, but eventually they did. After which Dick sent another note, this one to his Republican pals describing that he had done all that could and ended by simply saying, "good luck."[8]

A few days went by, and there was still no word on what Godwin would decide. "Godwin didn't tell anybody," said his friend George McMath, a recent Republican convert. The press was anticipating a Godwin announcement sometime in February, and they remained on their heels. Without indicating his decision prior, he called for a press conference on March 4th, 1973 at the John Marshall Hotel. At Dick's request, Dortch and Weldon attended, "So that Godwin would know that the people that had been a part of all of this were there listening." Warriner stood ready to announce his candidacy if he needed to.[9] When the two arrived they lingered in the back of the conference room, switching between leaning against the wall or pacing back and forth. Dortch nervously anticipated that he was going to have to make good on his promise

---

[8] Archives, Republican Party of Virginia.
[9] Tuck interview, October 2, 2017.

and run for governor against Godwin should Godwin choose to run as an independent candidate.

While he waited, he ran into Smitty Ferebee, who had also been an important part of the Godwin negotiations. Smitty revealed that he was able to acquire a copy of Godwin's prepared statement, which read, "I welcome their support, and I will accept their nomination or endorsement if tendered to me at their convention next June." The "they" Godwin was referring to was Republican voters. Nowhere in the transcript did Godwin mention that he would run as a Republican. Warriner was fuming mad.

Godwin made his appearance before the sea of press and in his southern drawl made his remarks exactly how they were written. Then he looked up at Smitty Ferebee, Dortch Warriner, and Weldon Tuck. Straying from his notes, he closed his announcement with, "and of course, having accepted that nomination, if it is forthcoming, I intend to run as a Republican in the campaign next fall for governor." Out of pure joy and forgetting about the press in the room, Warriner yelled at the top of his lungs and embraced Ferebee. The commotion caused all the reporters to stop and turn around, perplexed. None of them were aware that one of the two men responsible for the decision had just witnessed the fruits of his labor come to pass. Of course, he was also probably excited that he didn't have to eat his words and run himself.[10] When word reached Dick Obenshain, he was also quite relieved.

"For Godwin it was a hard pill to swallow. He likened us to being a bar of soap," said Kenny Klinge.[11] Yet Obenshain was confident in the prospect throughout the process and didn't appear surprised at all that Godwin "saw the light," as he put it.[12] All seemed to be going according to plan. Godwin would seek to run as a Republican.

Republicans still struggled to find other viable candidates to fill the void of running for lieutenant governor and attorney general. A month after Godwin's announcement, a grassroots "Draft Obenshain" movement formed.

---

[10] Atkinson, p. 302.

[11] Kinge interview, February 10, 2010.

[12] Helen interview.

It was allegedly started by the industrialist from northern Virginia, Stetson Colemon. Conservatives wanted Obenshain to run on the ticket for lieutenant governor. John Dalton, son of Ted Dalton, who had helped introduce Dick to the national political scene and the thrill of a convention, was also contemplating a run. Many viewed Dalton as a moderate, and an Obenshain run would have angered the mountain-valley Republicans who were already upset with the fact that Obenshain was bringing in a swarm of former Democrats to their party. In order to hold this precarious coalition together, Obenshain decided against running, which kept the mountain-valley moderate Republicans happy and willing to support the entire statewide ticket. Two weeks later, on April 6th, Obenshain formally announced he would not run.[13]

Obenshain was now tasked with fusing the factions together to successfully win Godwin the nomination and put him back in the governor's mansion. Godwin did not make things easy for him. Obenshain was exhausted with Godwin's constant attempts to be an "at arms-length" Republican. His reluctance, like that of many Democratic converts, began to fuel animosity between the old Republicans and the new, the conservative wing, and the moderate wing of the party. Obenshain was trying to hold all of these factions together. What made matters worse was Godwin frequently referring to Republicans as "you people" at every event and district meeting he attended. It wasn't necessarily a good strategy for winning people over.[14] Furthermore, the Watergate scandal was looking worse, and Godwin told reporters that he might have to "reassess" whether he would accept a nomination as a Republican. Obenshain wasn't overly concerned, but he responded with "It is not a state issue, its real threat is, as Senator Goldwater said the other day, to the Republican ability to pick up a large number of congressional seats in 1974." [15]

While Dick was juggling Godwin, he continued to take light-hearted jabs at Henry Howell, sending him a telegraph that thanked him for his "interest in helping to grow our party." Further down the telegraph read, "We especially appreciate what you did for us last year when you nominated George Rawlings

---

[13] Latimer, James. "Obenshain Will Not Run." *Richmond Times Dispatch.* April 7, 1973.
[14] Klinge interview.
[15] "Obenshain Not Alarmed At Godwin's Statement." *Richmond Times Dispatch.* April 16, 1973.

and Joe Fitzpatrick; it helped to give us the opportunity to run against George McGovern. Further, your lukewarm support of Bill Battle in 1969 was a big help in our election of the first Republican Governor of Virginia. While I know you must feel a keen sense of pride in the Republican growth you have stimulated, our party is strong and yours is somewhat weak."[16] Howell was running as an independent again, but was considered a Democrat as the Democrat Party chose not to run a candidate for governor that year.

Howell may have perhaps been the first to use the term "Republicrats," which he used to describe Mills Godwin's situation. Obenshain was definitely the first to use the term "zippiecrat," which he used to deflect Howell's attacks. Howell had held a rally that spring and had several rock bands playing at the event. Obenshain, in his cleverness, came up with the term by combining Zippo lighters which are used at rock concerts, with the word "hippie" and of course, "democrats". He insulted Howell further by saying that Howell lashing out was "the result of the fact that Henry Howell killed the Democratic Party in Virginia."[17] Years later, Howell reflected on Obenshain in saying that,

> "Obenshain had an instinct for the jugular. He convinced a lot of people that I was going to bus students from Northern Virginia into Washington, D.C. Godwin put Carter Lyons and Pat Paschal in charge of his 1973 campaign. They were fine men, but they were in their sixties. They didn't know anything about modern campaigning. Godwin would have lost if he hadn't replaced them with Obenshain. Obenshain turned defeated into victory for Godwin by his last-minute attacks on me in 1973."[18]

Godwin was running an old-style Democratic campaign. His manager, Carter Lyons, had been his chief of staff during his first tenure as governor. They ran a "pass the word along" type of campaign that had worked for the Byrd Machine for so many years but it was not going over well with the more individualistic Republicans.

---

16 "Obenshain 'Thanks' Howell for Interest." *Richmond Times Dispatch*. February 19, 1973.
17 "Howell Described As 'Zippiecrat'." *Richmond News Leader*. April 11, 1973.
18 Virkler, p. 72.

Finding a candidate to run as attorney general was the most difficult task; nobody wanted to be the sacrificial lamb to the popular General Andrew Miller, who had defeated Obenshain and was running for his second consecutive term as attorney general. Dick and Kenny eventually recruited a state senator from Arlington named Marion Patton "Pat" Echols, Jr..

Right up to the hour before the 1973 Republican convention, Dick Obenshain, Wyatt Durrette, Judy Peachee, Mills Godwin, and the driver made several rounds circling the John Marshall Grand Hall before getting out of the car. Inside the vehicle, the three Republican leaders were desperately trying to convince the former governor that he must clearly state to the convention delegates that he was a Republican. "This is going to be bare knuckles; if you don't have the enthusiastic backing of the Republican Party, you're not going to win," said Durrette. They exited the car with bated breath that morning.

At the convention, unexpected procedural battles ensued similar to the battles that had taken place in recent years. An anti-Godwin faction led by Ed Trotman of Chesapeake, attempted to thwart the nomination, a move that if successful, might have resulted in a similar coup like the one led by Obenshain just a year before, this time by the moderate factions. Ed Trotman was a Holton insurgent, bitter from last year's results. But the Obenshain people had the votes by an enormity and prevailed again. Wyatt Durrette summarized that most, "seemed to believe in the concept of a conservative coalition and realignment of the parties in Virginia."[19]

Godwin's frequent reference to Republicans as "you people" became a coined catchphrase. Those unhappy with Godwin brought signs that said, "We are not 'your people.'" Those who supported him wore buttons which said, "I'm proud to be one of 'you people.'"

An all-out insurgency was probably prevented due to the nomination of John Dalton for lieutenant governor. He was a Holton ally from the Valley and had announced his plan to run before the "Draft Obenshain" group could gain any traction. The Daltons and Obenshains, of course, were family friends.

---

[19] Durrette interview.

Dalton's political move gave Dick the excuse he needed not to run, while also preventing another tense convention fight.

Godwin was nominated by a convention vote of 1253-208. The building was silent anticipating the slow-moving arrival of Godwin to the podium. He adjusted his microphone, paused, and began his acceptance speech with, "As one of you" to which the crowd erupted with a standing ovation for several minutes. It was the closest he could come to calling himself a Republican, but it was a step in the right direction. It worked.

Henry Howell was able to quickly gain traction amongst poor white voters and was able to portray Godwin early on as a representative of big business. Howell was an excellent campaigner himself and the Godwin campaign strategy of old was clearly not working. Godwin needed someone with the right public relation skills and an organizational mastermind who could offset Howell's political prowess. Things began to turn around after he named Obenshain as his acting campaign chairman, a honorary position that he held for all three statewide candidates on August 4, 1973.[20] Except even before this appointment, Dick had already been working behind the scenes.

Dick was hard at work employing modern strategies during this campaign much as he had done a year before with Bill Scott. He implemented phone banks, polls, and letters, and spent heavily on television advertising. Godwin campaign consultant Edward DeBolt noted "that phone bank, more than anything else gave birth to the legend of Dick Obenshain as the consummate party mechanic." [21] Obenshain didn't invent these strategies; in fact, it was a man named Buddy Bishop, who worked at the National Headquarters, that came up with the idea for phone "banking," which revolutionized political campaigns. After a campaign meeting in Arlington, Dick and Kenny decided that an auxiliary Godwin campaign should operate out of the Richmond GOP Headquarters in the Heritage building. With the

---

[20] Latimer, James. "Obenshain Is Named By Godwin." *Richmond Times Dispatch*. August 5, 1973.
[21] Atkinson, p. 312.

help of Kenny Klinge, they were able utilize phone banks from computerized voting lists by the third week in September.[22]

Obtaining voter lists were finally made possible by the 1971 state legislature, which established a central voter registration database with the state Board of Elections. Before, the only way to acquire a voter list was through the local registrar's office, most of which were stacked with loyal Democrats.[23] Once the lists were acquired, Obenshain had established a secret phone banking operation for Godwin. It was the first time the party had ever used phone banking as a method of campaigning.

They were able to acquire 65% of statewide registered voter information for around $700. While time restrictions prevented them from calling every voter, they micro-targeted heavily in Republican precincts. Obenshain himself categorized all 1,832 precincts in order of most to least-leaning Republican. The entire phone bank operation ending up costing $35,000.[24] Obenshain had created an independent organization outside of Godwin's campaign to experiment with the endeavor. The reason the operation was secret was because Godwin was an old school politician and didn't want to do it. Godwin thought this kind of campaigning was too personal and beneath him. Whatever the case may be, it proved successful in that race, and the party was able to estimate the election results with decent accuracy. The phone bank system became so efficient that for every special election, the party would roll out the same phones, connected to one universal outlet, and start the process over again.

The phone banks were just one aspect of the entire "Get-Out-The-Vote" effort the Republicans employed that year. Once a Republican voter was identified, they would receive another phone call the day before the election, as well as a letter in the mail reminding them to vote. It's hard to imagine, but Virginians had never seen this type of focused effort by a campaign before.[25]

---

22 Klinge interview.
23 Hurd interview.
24 Virkler, p. 66.
25 Virkler, p. 67.

One volunteer was kept at the headquarters on election day while the rest of the volunteer "army" were out getting people to the polls. Despite the election happening only a couple of weeks after Nixon's "Saturday Night Massacre," (which had Mills Godwin questioning his decision to become a Republican) Godwin still managed to squeak by with 51% of the vote. Thus, Virginia had been "rescued" once again from Henry Howell. John Dalton became lieutenant governor with roughly 53%. The incumbent Democrat, Attorney General Andrew Miller, however, dominated the night in his bid for re-election, taking almost 71% of the vote, proving that a centrist Democrat could still win statewide. In just two years Obenshain was now two for two when it came to statewide races that he personally managed: Bill Scott and Mills Godwin.

Republicans won, but the party didn't receive much funding after the Godwin race. There was hope though, that they could now grow. Godwin's nomination brought a lot of animosity from some Republicans for bringing former Byrd Democrats into the party, something Holton would have never done. Some of the reasoning was due to pride—a mentality of, "We've labored in the vineyards and now they are going to come in and pick all of the fruit." Older lifelong Republicans bore some resentment that lasted months, years, even decades for a small few. The atmosphere was contentious at the state central meetings at that time, but the Obenshain position maintained that, "We always thought the goal of a party was to convince the people in the other party to correct posture and come over and join. That's what campaigns are about. Our candidate is right and is right on the issues."[26]

In the aftermath, Washington Star Reporter Brian Kelly wrote, "Governor Godwin may be remembered as the man who marked a change in Virginia's political structure—the man who signaled the transition from a domination by conservative Democrats to a powerful alliance of their heirs and the resurgent G.O.P. But history should also note that Obenshain was the G.O.P's chief negotiator, its most tireless worker, in the delicate, time consuming decisions that finally resulted in Godwin's conversion."[27]

---

[26] Alderson interview.

[27] Kelly, Brian. *Washington Star*. November 7, 1973.

Chapter 12:

Spreading "The Gospel"

On August 9th, 1974, President Nixon resigned. When President Ford selected Nelson Rockefeller to be his vice president on August 20th, 1974, it angered a lot of conservatives, including Dick Obenshain, who was "losing his shit" over Rockefeller.[1] For weeks Dick had been advocating for President Ford to nominate Barry Goldwater. While visiting the Cape Charles Rotary Club he said, "Nothing could show more clearly the President's commitment to the highest standards of moral integrity." He continued, "Most Americans want this country to move toward what Barry Goldwater symbolizes: a reduction of massive government power and reckless government spending."[2]

A week after the selection, thirteen southern Republican State Chairs were then invited to Washington D.C. for a brief discussion with White House aides and Rockefeller himself. All of them were opposed to his nomination, with Obenshain being the most vocal. Ford's staff assured GOP leaders that

[1] Klinge interview, September 8, 2017.
[2] "Obenshain endorses Goldwater." *Richmond Times Dispatch*. August 16, 1973.

Rockefeller would campaign for southern Republican candidates in the fall, and that the White House would counsel with them on issues. Dick left the meeting saying that despite ideological differences, they could potentially have a good relationship with Rockefeller. Whether he truly believed it or if it was just superficial political theater remains a mystery.

While this may have appeased Obenshain temporarily, he continued to hammer inflationary spending as a critical policy issue. In 1973 the U.S. inflation rate was a high 6.2%; in 1974, it had soured to 11.04%. "Unless inflation is checked, clearly and unmistakably, this country will not have a stable foundation for its domestic life. And unless inflation is checked, I do not believe the Republican party can retain the presidency in 1976."[3] His astute prediction in 1974 proved to be correct a few years later, when the Republicans lost the White House to Jimmy Carter. Throughout August of 1974, Dick continued pester President Ford while serving as chairman of the Republican Party of Virginia. At one point, Obenshain lost his temper at a press conference, again publicly blasting the president's decision regarding Rockefeller.

The loud and fiery rhetoric caught the attention of Jack Marsh, a former congressman from the Shenandoah Valley, now a counselor to President Ford. Ford had just selected Mary Louis Smith as the first woman chairman of the national Republican Party, a post previously held by George H.W. Bush. Bush had stepped down to become U.S. ambassador to China. The chair position had traditionally been held by a man, while the co-chair position was typically held by a woman. Ford's selection of Smith was historic. The conservative wing of the party was again red-hot about another Ford selection. It was not because she was a woman but because Smith was considered to be too much of a moderate, a "Rockefeller Republican" more inclined towards the liberal wing of the party. Until this point, the Rockefeller faction had been losing ground within the party. Being from Iowa, she was a good choice for winning over midwestern Republicans who tended to mistrust the Eastern Establishment.

Marsh had been the one to suggest to Ford that the conservative Richard Obenshain of Virginia would make a great co-chair: one that could

---

[3] Ibid.

represent conservatives and southerners alike at the national level. Ford agreed and directed Marsh to make the call.

Kenny Klinge, who was still working as the executive director for the Republican Party of Virginia, recalled Dick dialing him up one hot summer day and asking, "I just got a call from Jack Marsh, and they want me to be co-chair of the RNC, what do you think?" Kenny's response was to the point.

"Do you plan on retiring from politics?"

"No," said Dick.

"Then your answer is yes," Kenny simply replied.[4]

However, Dick had his reservations. The co-chair role was sometimes seen as an afterthought position. There were lingering doubts about how he would be treated by Smith and Rockefeller. The President requested a meeting with him at the White House at 10 a.m. on Labor Day in 1974. Dick asked Kenny to drive him up to D.C. so the two could talk about it along the way. Dick was as much a brother to Kenny as his two biological brothers, and the two were often very candid with each other. Kenny drove up to the front door, which people were still allowed to do in those days and dropped Dick off at the box. Dick waited inside for 45 minutes before being seen while Kenny waited in a parking lot nearby. The meeting itself only lasted about 15 minutes, and when Dick returned, he was quiet for a time, until Kenny finally broke the silence. "Well?" he said. Dick responded unenthusiastically, "Yeah, I'm co-chair." Kenny remembered, "Dick and I both knew he got the job in order to shut his ass up."[5]

Dick found a way to make his new role work to his advantage. His job would be to travel to different parts of the country, giving speeches to grassroots training seminars and acting as a voice for the Republican Party on the national scene. This aspect of the job is what Dick found attractive. He thought he could do some good, and he saw the job as an excellent vehicle for

---

[4] Klinge interview, February 10, 2010.
[5] Ibid.

"spreading the gospel," as he put it.[6] He was known to use religious allegory when describing political concepts from time to time.

The announcement of Dick's appointment was made on September 4th, 1974 and was seen as an encouraging move by Ford for conservatives. Obenshain held a press conference and said he would be focusing on "building morale...hastening a realignment in the South...building the party." Ending his speech with, "It's exciting." The official swearing in of Obenshain and Smith took place on September 15th. Together the pair would make grassroots development a core focus for the party.[7]

When asked whether he would support another nominee for vice president in 1976, Dick merely responded, "I'm not going to be in a position to push in any direction."[8] While his role required him to be neutral in any primary contest, little did the reporter know that Dick sought not just a new vice president, but a different president as well. The co-chairmanship gave him the opportunity to encourage and visit with a rising conservative star from California: Governor Ronald Reagan. Reagan, Dick thought, should run for President in 1976. If he did, Dick resolved to do everything he could to see him win. He viewed Reagan as a philosophical successor to Goldwater. These interactions with Reagan were kept quiet.

The time between the announcement and the first day on the job was spent searching for a replacement chairman for the Republican Party of Virginia, as Dick could not occupy both positions at once. In the two short years that Dick had been state party chairman, he had converted Godwin and led his campaign to a historic, nonconsecutive second term and elected Bill Scott in another historic election. The Virginia GOP held seven of ten congressional seats, a senate seat, the governorship, and the lieutenant governorship. Virginia laid claim to having the strongest Republican Party among the southern states. In order to continue having this level of success the party had to stay the course by inviting former conservative Democrats into the

---

[6] Helen Interview.
[7] McDowell, Charles. "Obenshain Gets No. 2 Post on National Committee." *Richmond Times Dispatch*. September 5, 1974.
[8] Ibid.

party. The best person to do this, they felt, was Governor Godwin's friend and fellow convert, Delegate George McMath.

McMath was in the newspaper business and had served his first term in the House of Delegates in 1963. He had been a Democrat until 1973, when he ran as an independent, and then finally became a Republican in the middle of 1974. The presidential race of George McGovern and Henry Howell's new status as "the Kingpin" for the Democrats in Virginia were the final straws which broke the camel's back for McMath.

The idea for a McMath chairmanship came from John Dalton and Mills Godwin. They thought that as a former conservative Democrat he could bring in more former Democrats like himself. He was known for his organizational prowess and was very likeable and non-controversial. A fresh face for the party, unstained by some of the intraparty fights that had taken place in recent years. But McMath had to be talked into it. "I've only been a Republican for a little while," he responded to them. He didn't think the traditional Republicans would accept it. After a long conversation with Kenny Klinge, McMath decided it'd be a great opportunity to revitalize his party. He crisscrossed the state with the message "Think Big," and reminded everyone that, "We are still the party that elected the philosophy of Richard Nixon, even though he isn't around."[9]

To the surprise of Dalton and Godwin, McMath was correct in his assessment that some long-time Republicans on the State Central Committee would not respond well to his nomination, but he was unopposed, so it wasn't likely that they would refuse. While he waited at a nearby hotel room, the committee met and debated. One member stood up and held a brochure from McMath's most recent election which did not have the word "Republican" anywhere on it. His lack of acknowledgement created a long discussion, but it wasn't enough to sway the majority of the committee, and McMath was nominated.[10] He proved to be the right kind of successor to Obenshain's

---

[9] George McMath interview, November 14, 2017.
[10] Ibid.

leadership, which Kenny described as being "a benevolent dictatorship" during 1972-1974.[11]

McMath described his five-year term as chairman as being primarily "pragmatic." He wanted to create a large umbrella for anyone who wanted to join the party. He appointed a "blue ribbon committee" throughout the commonwealth to come up with a code for the party's platform. He liked what they came up with, however, he noticed that they didn't reference God anywhere in the platform, so he had that one tenet added.

Regarding Obenshain and his followers, he said, "They let me lead on my own. There was no effort made to control my actions as chairman. I was a Dick Obenshain supporter and had Obenshain people working with me, but I didn't let that control my actions. I did what was best for the party. I was there to expand the party under this new code we had adopted. No faction objected under my umbrella." Kenny stayed at the headquarters for several months after, but would resign his post on Christmas Eve, 1974.[12]

Meanwhile, as RNC co-chair, Dick ran a series of training sessions all around the country. "I traveled with him on those, what we used to call 'the dog and pony show.' Dick would go to attract the crowd and the RNC staff would get these communication workshops for candidates and state parties," said Bill Royal, who was working in the communications department at the RNC during the time under Buddy Bishop and Mary Louise Smith.[13] Many of the attendees were also Republican activists inspired by his message. Republicans from all over the country were beginning to take notice of Dick Obenshain. "I'd get calls all the time saying that he gave a 'heck of a speech,'" said Kenny.[14] "We flew from town to town. He was the big motivational speaker at the events and talked more about strategies, and the rest of us talked about tactics," said Bill Royal. Royal was also amazed at how Obenshain could

---

[11] Klinge interview, March 3, 2010.
[12] McMath interview.
[13] Bill Royal interview, September 15, 2017.
[14] Kenny interview, September 8, 2017.

be a "competent speaker without notes; he always knew the material."[15] The staff at the RNC loved working with him.

While in D.C., Dick still stayed abreast of Virginia politics. He also kept the pressure on Harry Byrd Jr. to change his status from independent to Republican, although the switch he hoped for never occurred.

The law practice that he and his partner George Hinnett founded together still remained a part of his busy schedule. He managed to split his time equally between the firm and his responsibilities at the RNC by getting up at 4 a.m. to drive to D.C. and getting back in time to practice in the evenings, but George admitted, "We saw less of him, but he was still coming to work."[16]

At the RNC office in D.C. a young activist who Mary Louise Smith had "inherited" from her predecessor was working in the training division. When Dick entered into his role, other staffers at the RNC recommended this young man to him, and he became Dick's executive assistant. The staffer's name was Karl Rove. Describing his working relationship with Dick, Karl said, "this guy was young, intense, very gentlemanly, courteous, and direct. He was just a wonderful guy to be around, and well-read. He recommended books I ought to read as a young conservative. I was 23, but you would have thought we were peers; he was that kind of guy, just treated everybody with respect and as an equal."[17]

Madame Chairman Mary Louis Smith treated Dick with respect and openness, despite her opposing philosophy. Dick reciprocated by remaining loyal and providing constructive ideas to advance the party's agenda. Dick had a way of commanding respect even from those who disagreed with him. As Karl said, "He had a quiet way of talking, which made people listen to him. He didn't pound at the table. When he spoke, he thought about it, and when he spoke, you paid attention."[18] Indeed, his time at the RNC perhaps turned out to be better and more cordial than what he could have expected. Smith said of

---

15 Royal interview.

16 Hinnant interview.

17 Karl Rove interview, December 9, 2016.

18 Ibid.

Obenshain, "Dick Obenshain brought a spirit of enthusiasm and vitality, plus a vast amount of knowledge and experience to the Republican Party, at whatever level he served."[19]

Dick Lobb, who was on the communications staff at the RNC, worked on a TV program called "Republicans are People Too," intended to get Republicans out of the doldrums post-Nixon and Watergate. Dick was chosen as the right guy to give the motivational pitch to activists on the show. His message was, "Nixon might be gone, but the ideas that got him elected live on." Dick had fun working on the project (it was the only way to reach a mass audience), but the show didn't enjoy great ratings.[20]

Eventually the frequent travel began to take its toll on him. Two of his children were teens and pre-teens, and the overnight trips became difficult for his family. They saw far less of him during this time. "It just sort of became the norm," said his daughter Anne. Helen had returned to teaching, and the stress of juggling work and three kids was taxing on her as well.[21]

After a meeting between Obenshain and Reagan, towards the end of 1975, Karl Rove unexpectedly received a call from Bill Royal, who had taken a job at the Republican Party of Virginia as the executive director. He offered Karl a job as finance director with the state party apparatus. Not having any experience in raising money or financing, Karl turned him down. He was enjoying working for Obenshain which is why it came as quite a shock when Bill said that it was Dick who told him to offer the opportunity. Stunned and confused by this, he went to Dick's office soon afterwards and told him about what happened. "Dick was signing papers. Without looking up he said, 'I think you ought to seriously look at the job.'" Karl was "devastated." The message seemed clear: "It's time for you to move on." So, Karl agreed to an interview and was offered the job. "I drove back from Richmond and Dick was in his office. 'Well, they made me an offer.' Dick replied, 'you're going to take it.'" Karl didn't know what to do except call Bill Royal and accept the job. The following Monday, Dick announced his resignation as the RNC co-chair. Karl

---

19 Virkler, p. 290.
20 Dick Lobb interview, November 8, 2017.
21 Anne Obenshain Zumbro, October 15, 2018.

then understood that Dick was trying to take care of him, placing him in a position where he could build contacts and experience, and perhaps work on his campaign for U.S. Senate. But Dick didn't want to burden Karl with that much information at one time. To this day, Karl Rove remains extraordinarily grateful to Dick Obenshain for making certain that he had a place to land.[22][23]

When Obenshain announced he was leaving his post, the reason cited was because he wanted to spend more time with his family, which indeed he did. He was also eyeing the U.S. Senate seat which was likely to be left open after Senator Scott, who was not enjoying the post and had little prospect of holding the seat if he chose to run again. If the opportunity came, another statewide campaign would mean evenings away from his family again. During the years 1976-1977 he would try spending more time with them. In his letter to Chairwoman Smith, he said, "Although my activity on behalf of the committee has been extremely challenging for me, the time away from Richmond has been very difficult for my family. My children are at an age where the heaviest burden of these continued absences falls on them." Obenshain's resignation was made official on February 11, 1976.[24]

There was another reason for his resignation, and it happened after his meeting with Ronald Reagan in the fall of 1975. Reagan gave assurances that a primary challenge to Ford would be "conducted in a calm and reasonable way."[25] Dick wanted to be free to support Reagan as a delegate to the national convention in 1976. He didn't he feel it would be appropriate to continue serving at the RNC as a Ford appointee if he wouldn't be supporting Ford. Dick had much respect for the Office of the Presidency and informed President Ford of his decision in person. Although he was making outstanding contributions to expanding the Republican Party nationwide, he chose to take an opportunity to expand conservatism within the national party by leaving. It was classic Dick Obenshain: putting principle before party.

---

22 Rove interview.

23 Rove, Karl. *Courage and Consequences: My Life as a Conservative in the Fight.* Threshold Editions. New York, NY. 2010 p. 42-43.

24 "Obenshain To Leave GOP Job." *Richmond Times Dispatch.* January 27, 1976.

25 "Obenshain Sees Reagan as 'Calm.'" *Richmond Times Dispatch.* October 15, 1975.

The Republican National Convention was in Kansas City, Missouri that year. Heading in, the convention had a massive block of uncommitted delegates, most of which were from Illinois and Mississippi. Ford had used his position as president to impress many of the uncommitted delegates and win them over to his side, but Reagan had a much larger number of committed delegates supporting him. This gave Reagan a very promising chance of winning.

Dick was elected as a national delegate but remained uncommitted publicly out of respect for President Ford. Still, everyone knew he was voting Reagan. Kenny Klinge was working for the Reagan campaign in Iowa that year but was with Dick at the convention. He noted that, "the Ford people thought they had it all locked up." The event ended up being a four-day convention. Ford didn't have enough votes to meet the 1,130 that were needed. It was the most contested race in the twelve years since Goldwater defeated Rockefeller. Klinge recalled, "We had one of the biggest splits in 1976 that you could have. They let the Ford delegation stay in hotels in Kansas City; they (the RNC) put all of the Reagan delegates as far away as they could. One delegate was 60 miles away. They were in charge of all of that. That's another reason why Dick got the hell out of there in January." Dick gave one of the speeches at that convention, speaking out against talks of the U.S. giving back the Panama Canal, which was seen as a strategic mistake during the Cold War and didn't actually occur until 1999. [26]

An awkward situation had developed throughout the presidential primary. Dick had called George McMath prior to the convention and asked him to be a delegate for Reagan. Godwin was sitting next to McMath in that moment and shook his head "no." Godwin was for Ford, and on the day of the vote, Godwin was flexing his political clout. Reagan had 2/3rds of the Virginia delegation, but five people had switched from Reagan to Ford. Obenshain suggested that the delegation be polled publicly to find out who was switching. The Virginia delegation were in the "cheap seats," so Dick called his friend Kenny, who was working the convention for Reagan, to "get it done." Dick didn't want to do it—since he was about to run for Senate, he didn't want

---

[26] Klinge interview, September 8, 2017.

to directly cross ways with one of his biggest allies, Mills Godwin. Kenny eventually found a delegate willing to request the public poll named Herb Martin. Martin boldly grabbed the microphone from Governor Godwin and said, "I'm Herb Martin from Virginia and I'm asking that we poll the Virginia delegation."[27] The poll took around twenty minutes. The Virginia delegation still voted for Reagan over Ford by 35-16, but Ford came out as the overall victor after about 2:00 a.m. on August 19th. In a dramatic moment, Obenshain could be seen throwing a huge stack of paper ballots over his head in utter despair. He had worked hard and put a lot on the line for Reagan.[28] The final vote tally was 1187 to 1070. Despite defeat, "It was a new spirit in the Republican Party that was opposed by some of the regulars. His contribution to Reagan in 1976 should not be minimized. People like Dick, who were the young enthusiasts, paved the way for the group in 1980," said Ed Meese, a former advisor to President Reagan.[29]

After Reagan's disappointing loss to Ford, the Virginia Republicans supported Ford every step of the way. Ford named Obenshain as chair of his Virginia campaign. Again, Obenshain did his due diligence and Virginia once again proved to be a strong Republican foothold by being the only southern state to choose Ford over Carter. Despite winning the nomination, Ford lost the general election to Jimmy Carter.

Ford's loss stalled the career progress of another ambitious Virginian by the name of John Warner.

---

[27] Klinge interview, September 8, 2017.
[28] Kate Obenshain interview, September 19, 2018.
[29] Edwin Meese interview, November 12, 2018.

Chapter 13:

The Man of the Sea

A people of strong and sturdy stock, the Warner line stretches back to Ipswich, Massachusetts, and even further back to a small town in England. John Warner's maternal line can be traced back to Scotland, where they were famous contractors who owned many granite quarry mines. His ancestors were also responsible for building many huge structures all throughout England and Scotland, including the Balmoral Castle, which became a Scottish holiday home for the Royal family.

John Warner's grandfather, who was also named John, moved from Amherst, Virginia with his wife Mary Susan Tinsley to Baltimore, Maryland shortly after the Civil War. It remains unknown how or why the family moved, as the Tinsley family was a wealthy and well-established family in Amherst. They were significant landowners—not the biggest, but significant. John and Mary had two sons. One became an Episcopal minister in D.C. at a church affiliated with the Washington D.C. Cathedral. The other son, John William (W.), went on to become a medical doctor.

After graduating from Washington & Lee University, John W. became a school teacher in a one room school on the Virginia and West Virginia border, close to Winchester—near Harry F. Byrd's stomping grounds. He boarded with a doctor and was headmaster of a small boys' school between 1903-1905. He also drove this unknown doctor's horse and buggy, until one day while the doctor was with a patient he asked John, "Will you help me?" From that point on, John W. would assist with more serious tasks, such as holding patients down during amputations, etc.—the type of thing that a typical country doctor in those days would have to do. Eventually this country doctor said to his would-be apprentice, "John, you know how to do everything I do, why don't you go and get your license and practice?"[1]

The experience proved invaluable as John W. was offered a scholarship to New York University Medical School, where he studied for four years. He practiced in New York for a short time until the United States entered World War I, where he served on the front line and in the trenches as a doctor. He was also an intern on one of the last horse ambulances before they became motorized. He was wounded while in France and became a decorated war veteran. The army sent him back to a hospital in New York where he met a nurse named Martha Budd. Martha was helping to take care of wounded soldiers at various hospitals in New York at the time. They quickly married and moved south to Washington D.C., where Dr. Warner became a gynecologist and set up his practice while they raised their children. Martha became a full-time stay-at-home mother while being active with the Washington Cathedral and with various charities in D.C.

Few have lived as colorful a life as John William Warner. Born on February 18th, 1927, John was the first of two sons to Dr. John W and Martha Warner, and had fond memories of his childhood growing up in Washington D.C. The family did well enough financially that they were able to send John to an elite boarding school in D.C. called St. Albans.

In January of 1945, a month before his 18th birthday, John eagerly enlisted in the United States Navy as a petty officer. As soon as the war was over, he ended his service as a third-class electronics technician. Warner followed in his father's footsteps and went straight to Washington and Lee University for undergraduate studies, a time he looks back on with "great gratitude." While at Washington and Lee he was introduced to Linwood Holton. They joined the same fraternity and became good friends but parted ways at graduation, only to be reunited two decades later to enjoy another 50

[1] John Warner interview, April 13, 2017.

years of friendship, weaving an entanglement of lives the likes of which Warner doubts history had ever seen. Both were members of Beta Theta Pi. Holton was three years older than Warner and was a pledge master in the fraternity. As part of the initiation, Warner had to walk through a series of whacks with hard wooden paddles. He recalled that Lin "whacked my fanny with a wooden paddle so hard that it broke the paddle. Since then we've been the closest friends to this day, even though his political orientation...I don't know what it is."[2]

After graduating, he applied for law school at the University of Virginia. In 1950 Warner paused his studies at UVA and enlisted as a marine to fight in Korea. He continued to serve in the reserves after the war ended, and eventually made the rank of captain. Once he had graduated from law school in 1953 he obtained a clerkship with Judge E. Barrett Prettyman in the United States Court of Appeals. He remained in this position for three years before becoming a United States attorney in 1956. Many years later he joined the private law firm known as Hogan and Hartson.

Warner maintained close relationships with influencers at the U.S. attorneys' office. One afternoon while in his office, Attorney General William P. Rogers met with him to inform him that, "The vice president would like to meet you." Warner responded with, "What? Why? "I am just an obscure guy, what would the vice president want with me?" Rogers responded, "I'm not kidding you, your name has come up out of a hopper." The vice president at the time was Richard Nixon. He was preparing for his first run at the presidency and was putting together a team of young men who could stand on their own feet and were feisty, and he had a fondness for prosecutors, as he had been one himself. Enamored with Nixon, Warner was convinced to work at the White House for President Eisenhower in their public relations department. His job was to review all of the speeches of cabinet members and to clear those speeches with the White House. Nixon later offered Warner the opportunity to travel with him on the road and become an "advance" man, which meant going ahead of him to an event. He did that for Nixon for one year, until Nixon lost his first presidential election. They stayed in touch afterwards and Warner

---

[2] John Warner interview, April 30, 2012.

helped Nixon with his governor's race in California in 1962. In 1968, Nixon decided to have two campaign headquarters for his second attempt at the presidency: one in New York and one in Washington D.C. Warner was asked to run the Washington headquarters, which they operated from the Willard Hotel and was able to cultivate an army of 1,800 volunteers nationwide to help Nixon win in 1968. He was rewarded for his efforts and for his service in the Navy. With the help of his friend Linwood Holton, Warner was appointed by President Nixon as Under Secretary of the Navy in 1969. It was Nixon who first planted the idea in Warner's head for him to run for the United States Senate, as he said, "You've got the makings of a senator." Before his appointment, Nixon suggested to Warner that while he thought Warner should soon run for the United States Senate, he should work for the government in the administration first in order to get some time and space between himself and the unpopular Vietnam War. Warner did just that, and in three years, he succeeded Secretary John Chafee as Secretary of the Navy. Warner stayed in this appointed position until 1974. After years of grooming, later Nixon told him, "Now you're ready to run for the U.S. Senate."[3]

Also helping Warner during this time was Gerald Ford, who replaced Nixon as president after his resignation on August 9th, 1974. Ford appointed Warner to participate in the "Law of the Sea" talks, which were a series of meetings that eventually established rules and guidelines for nations to follow with respect to world's oceans. Later he participated in the U.S-Soviet Incidents at Sea Agreement, which aimed to prevent any incident or accident between the two nations at sea. Finally, Ford swore him in as administer for the American Bicentennial, an event commemorating the nation's 200th birthday, which Warner described as one of the most fascinating jobs he ever had the privilege of having. He traveled extensively to each state in the country as well as 22 foreign countries as a guest of the United States, claiming it was like a "crash course" in American history. He had endless speaking events, press conferences, and television appearances. The job raised Warner's name recognition substantially, more than any position he held prior and prepared

[3] Ibid.

him for his next goal and adventure: running for the United States Senate in Virginia.[4]

Another interesting aspect of John Warner's life was his selection of spouses. In 1957, after his appointment to U.S. attorney, he married Catherine Mellon, the granddaughter of Paul Mellon.[5] The Mellon family were wealthy financiers who dabbled in financing the growth of various industries in the United States. At one point the Mellon Bank of Pittsburgh was the largest financial institution outside of the New York circle of financiers. With that, Warner suddenly found himself with an access to wealth he never dreamed of. The marriage lasted sixteen years, ending in 1973. Three years later, on December 4th, 1976, he married actress Elizabeth Taylor at the Second Presbyterian Church in Richmond. While his first marriage brought wealth, his second brought fame. Warner was known mostly in D.C. circles prior to the second marriage, which raised his name recognition outside of those who followed politics closely. His marriage to Liz made him a celebrity to the general public.

Elizabeth Taylor was a British-American who had been an actress since she was a child. Her family connections helped her land a small role in her first film, "There's One Born Every Minute," but her fame took off after she officially signed with MGM Studio.[6] She would end up starring in thirty-five films with her most well-known film being "Cleopatra." Her career began to decline in the 60s and 70s. By the time she married John Warner she was more committed to helping him with his career than her own.[7] After their marriage ended in 1981, she gained an interest in public service and began a long philanthropic career.

One afternoon in 1969 Warner received a call from an old fraternity brother and Navy colleague, Linwood Holton. Holton certainly knew of

---

[4] Ibid.

[5]Mewbar, Mary K. "Real Estate News." The Washington Life Magazine. May 2005. http://www.washingtonlife.com/issues/2005-05/realestate/

[6] Kashner, Sam; Shoenberger, Nancy. *Furious Love: Elizabeth Taylor, Richard Burton, and the Marriage of the Century*. p. 37. HarperCollins Publisher 2010.

[7] Kashner & Shoenberger, p. 389.

Warner's successes in life and his wealthy connections. Holton asked for his help in raising money for a second attempt at campaigning for governor. Warner agreed and served as a co-chair on Holton's fundraising committee, and he worked at it diligently. He didn't have an official title necessarily, but Warner was an ardent supporter of his friend Holton. He was an integral part of Holton's success that year.[8]

Warner also helped Senator Bill Scott on his campaign in 1972. This was when he first encountered Dick Obenshain. Dick was serving as chairman of the state party at this time. He recalled, "He was party chairman. I was a financial contributor to the party. He struck me first as a sort of quiet political intellectual. You got to capture his mind, he was light years ahead in thinking in conservatism."[9]

Warner stepped down from his position at the Bicentennial Committee after Independence Day in 1976. He spent the next several months crisscrossing the state on behalf of Gerald Ford, as did Dick Obenshain. This put Karl Rove in an awkward position. Although his official role was as the finance director for the RPV, he was acting as a scheduler for both Obenshain and Warner for a short time during this period. It was clear that both men would soon be vying for a run at the U.S. Senate, and Karl's loyalties were to Dick, who told him "Look, your job is to help carry Ford in Virginia. Don't worry about it, make us both look good."[10]

Warner was also making attempts at wrestling potential staffers away from Obenshain. He offered a young man of rising influence from Virginia Beach named Gary Byler one thousand dollars a month to come work for him. Byler turned him down at the prospect of working on Obenshain's nomination for free.[11] In late 1976 Warner was invited to speak at VMI, and he asked Karl to come along and help him draft the speech. Karl visited Dick at his law firm, in agony over the invitation. "Dick rarely laughed, but I remember he laughed

---

[8] Warner interview, April 30, 2012.
[9] Ibid.
[10] Rove interview.
[11] Byler interview.

that day and said, 'go ahead and help him; he asked you to do it. I'm not worried about it and tell me anything you find out!'"[12]

What he found out ended up being a story that made Dick laugh even harder. The president of VMI held a party the night before graduation. While at the event, Warner asked Karl to visit him the next morning to go over the speech. "I show up at 7:30 and Liz Taylor opens the door in her revealing nightgown. Warner comes walking down the stairs wearing his black tie from the night before. Liz makes fun of him and says, 'you're not going to go give that speech in a black tie, go put on your dark blue suit.'" While waiting, Liz cooked Karl some breakfast, obliviously still in her revealing nightgown. When Karl got back to Richmond he told Dick the story. "He could tell how embarrassed I was. I told him the story and he howled with laughter."[13]

Warner was still keeping in touch with both Nixon and Ford by 1977. Both "said they wanted me to run for [US Senate] because they know me and I've worked with them. They said I performed exceedingly well. They were always plotting. Mills Godwin thought I wasn't conservative enough, but we got to be good friends later."[14]

In early December of 1977, he finally announced his run for the U.S. Senate.

---

[12] Rove interview.
[13] Ibid.
[14] Warner interview, April 30, 2012.

Chapter 14:

Down, Not Out

1977 would be a pivotal year for Obenshain. Towards the end of that year, he was determined to announce his bid to replace the retiring Bill Scott in the United States Senate. It was an opportunity to finally chase his long-awaited dream. After a few years on the national scene at the RNC, and after Ford's loss, Obenshain refocused his efforts again on Virginia and began to prepare the conservative coalition for the upcoming governor's race to succeed Mills Godwin. It also gave him a chance to be home and slow down.

After Dick's resignation from the RNC, the Obenshain family moved to a bigger home in a wealthier neighborhood in Salisbury, a location the family would later say was never a "good fit."[1] They were only there for two years. Within a few months after the move, Dick found himself close to another newsworthy incident. His neighbor, Willie Lanier, a Richmond native who was a linebacker for the Kansas City Chiefs football team just moved his family to

---

[1] Kate interview.

Salisbury as he was preparing to retire from football. Another family nearby, the Wrights, had also moved into the neighborhood recently. One of the perks to living in the neighborhood was access to the Salisbury Country Club. The club had never rejected an applicant until the summer of 1976 when the board rejected both the Laniers and the Wrights on the basis of race. Obenshain objected to the club's clearly racist decision and wrote a letter condemning the board, as did the acting Attorney General Anthony F. Troy. Obenshain said in his letter that he wished to "voice his objection and ask the board of directors to reconsider their decision." The story caught national attention over its absurdity. It resulted in a lawsuit which battled in court for several years while a substantial number of families renounced their own membership with the club.[2] One of the Wright children, Crystal, grew up to be a conservative political author and commentator.

While Obenshain remained busy and focused on his next endeavor, being home more often again gave him much needed time with his family. The Obenshain children recalled their home life structure being very traditional, accompanying that with a very traditional mother and father distribution of labor. "He was super strict. Even if he had been gone for a while, his role was to administer discipline," said his daughter Kate. "Pop," as they called him, was very serious about telling the truth. It was an important rule in the Obenshain household. Kate also recalled, "We could watch virtually no TV. I was allowed to watch 'The Waltons' and that was it." For a while the Obenshain kids were allowed to watch a show called "Electric Company." Kate remembered watching an episode when she was around seven years old which concluded that it was okay to tell a white lie, sometimes. That happened to be the moment Dick Obenshain walked through the room. "He flew over to that TV and slammed it off, saying 'You will never watch that show again.' I'll never forget that moment, there was never justification for not telling the truth."[3]

Philosophical conversations around the dinner table were the norm in the Obenshain household. For a while each of the kids were expected to come

---

[2] Wright, Crystal. *Con Job: How Democrats Gave Us Crime, Santuary Cities, Abortion Profiteering and Racial Division.* p. 217-219. Regnery Publishing, New Jersey, 2016.
[3] Kate interview.

to the dinner table prepared to discuss one particular topic going on in the news. The Obenshain kids learned that any disagreements were based on high-minded ideals and were nothing personal. They learned to constructively argue their points and return to being a family again afterwards, just as the Obenshain household did in Blacksburg.

Mark, the oldest child, was considered the leader of the three siblings and he crossed-ways with his father the most. Since Mark was also a teenager, he was often the more rebellious of the three children. Anne, the middle child, was the peace-maker, more shy and quiet. Kate, the youngest, was nine years old and was captivated by her father's endeavors, although she may not have fully understood them at the time.[4]

Dick and Helen maintained a very loving relationship. Kate recalled, "Every single day when he got home, he and my mother would have this long sweet kiss and embrace; they adored each other. They'd have their evening cocktail and couch time and we would leave them alone. We weren't instructed not to, we just knew that that was their time."[5]

With all that was going on in his life, it was always hard for Dick to relax. "He was very thoughtful but distracted in some ways by everything; he didn't totally disengage at home," said Anne. But when he did, he usually enjoyed a cigar or a pipe while watching a football game in the living room. On Sundays he refused to actively campaign, whether it be his own race or another candidate's. The only time he would ever fully "turn-off" would be at his in-laws' beach house, Anne recalled,

> "I remember when we did go to the beach, that was the one place where I can remember him being totally relaxed and disengaged and not distracted. That I could sense. My mom's dad had bought a place and we would see her parents down there. It was a getaway location. He was also relaxed in Blacksburg, but even with his family in

---

[4] Anne interview.
[5] Kate interview.

> Blacksburg there was more engagement and discussion around the dinner table."[6]

Others remembered visiting him at his oasis on the eastern shore. John Paul Woodley recalled a time he and Karl Rove visited Dick,

> "Karl must have called ahead and we went up and spent the whole afternoon at this beach cabin. We got to visit him and it was kind of shocking because he was always very well-dressed, very formal, but he was in a polo shirt, shorts, and no socks. It was wonderful to see him in that state, as he was often dealing with very serious things."[7]

George McMath didn't get the chance to spend much time with Dick outside of formal functions, but one Sunday Dick asked him and his wife to come and visit them at the shore. They spent the whole day with the family, having a pleasant time.[8] It was a peaceful setting that created a lot of memories for many different people.

As 1977 approached, Dick's friend Delegate Wyatt Durrette approached him about his interest in running for attorney general, a position Dick had once sought nearly a decade ago. Durrette had long been a supporter and friend of Dick's and gave a speech supporting Dick when he became chairman of the party in 1972. Durrette first ran for the House of Delegates in 1971 and was a part of an emerging new class of ambitious young Republicans, many of whom were first inspired by Obenshain himself. Dick agreed to help his friend and was instrumental in his campaign. Durrette's primary opponent was also a young blood in the party, a mountain-valley Republican by the name of J. Marshall Coleman.

John Dalton had announced his candidacy for governor and was unopposed. Dalton was also a longtime friend of Dick's, and it was his father, Ted Dalton, who took Dick and his friend Rod to the 1952 convention when they had both just finished high school. John was just a few years older than Dick, and though his politics were slightly more liberal the two remained friends

---

[6] Anne interview.
[7] Woodley interview.
[8] McMath interview.

throughout the years and their paths crossed often. John, like Dick, was considered a very likeable guy, and Dick was said to have "never lost a friend."[9]

For lieutenant governor, some were again trying to recruit Obenshain for the job, but he of course, was interested in the Senate race the following year. The Republicans struggled for a while to find a viable candidate until they decided on a Richmond investor named Walter Craigie. "We thought in 1977 that we had to replicate the 1973 formula. We had Dalton at the head of the ticket, we needed someone in the middle to be from the older crowd. They went through the process and Craigie emerged as that guy. But Walter didn't have the connections in the party."[10] Dalton and others also felt that Craigie could finance his own campaign. Obenshain was convinced to support Craigie for this reason, and also because of his friendship with John Dalton. Since Obenshain was better known in the party, he agreed to help convince the party regulars to get behind Craigie.

Shortly after, a state senator from Virginia Beach who had worked for the Reagan '76 campaign named Joe Canada was about to announce his intentions to run. He felt that he had waited long enough, and nobody else in the party was stepping up. But when he arranged a meeting with Governor Godwin to inform him first of his intent, the response was, "Mainstreet people don't want you. They want Craigie," to which Canada responded, "I already put 25,000 in the bank, Governor. I wish you had told me that earlier. If I had known I would have never gotten in to begin with."[11]

Canada was a charismatic leader and had an advantage in that the Obenshain group had little influence in the 2nd Congressional District. Meanwhile, Craigie spent his time raising money and bragging about selling his first bond at the age of seven. Walter Craigie was an investment banker, former Secretary of the Department of Finance under Governor Holton's administration, and a Ford supporter. Craigie had what Canada did not, and

---

[9] Durrette interview.
[10] Hurd interview.
[11] Joe Canada interview, December 16, 2016.

that was the support of the Richmond activists, former Byrd Democrats, and main street business crowd that dominated much of Virginia politics.

Some of Dick's closest allies, including Republican financiers such as Lawrence Lewis Jr. and Smith Ferebee, were adamantly opposed to Canada for various reasons. Primarily, they did not believe that he had the fundraising capabilities needed to mount a competitive campaign against the Democratic candidate for lieutenant governor, Chuck Robb, the son-in-law of President Lyndon B. Johnson. Dick did not want to support Craigie to the extent that he did, but because Dick was at the center of the coalition and never supported anyone half-heartedly, he went all in. [12]

Dick was thus pulled into supporting Craigie, doing what he thought was best for the party as he had always done. "Dick was about building a coalition around him. They maybe didn't agree with everything he stood for, but they really respected him for his commitment to the party," recalled Judy Peachee.[13] Some of his most loyal supporters could not support Craigie, including Bill Stanhagen, an important Obenshain supporter and National Committeeman from the 10th Congressional District. Ted Burr explained, "Dick was holding a coalition from all over the state. We supported Wyatt, who had a lot of integrity. Part of the battle was that they were worried that the party would be taken over by a lot of the financial people; old-line Republicans didn't like the fact that they saw these financial backers trying to take over the party with their money. New people versus the old."[14] It was uncharacteristic of Dick to support this kind of a candidate. Dick once said to John Alderson that, "You have to be careful of who you endorse in the political world because people will let you down, but your principles never will."[15]

On the night of the convention, Craigie staffers slipped brown paper bags containing voting instructions for the next day underneath the hotel doors where the delegates were staying. That morning, Wyatt Durrette entered the Roanoke Civic Center with a 100 vote lead over Coleman. Not a substantial

---

[12] Canada interview.

[13] Wason interview.

[14] Burr interview.

[15] Alderson interview.

amount, but enough to feel comfortable. "Convention politics is a different breed of cat; it was vicious, you have slighting and instructions—it's brutal. When you have multiple contests, it adds to the confusion and chaos."[16]

The chairman of the convention, a different role than that of the chairman of the party, was a rising star from the Shenandoah Valley, a state senator named Nathan Miller. As Nathan approached the podium in front of a large crowd of three thousand people, he knew it was going to be an unforgettably close convention race, but he didn't realize the passion and the importance this convention would have. The convention crowd in 1977 were a fiercely contentious bunch. The atmosphere was electric and intense. Nathan had not attended many political conventions in his lifetime, but this one was unique and unlike any he had been to before. He remained neutral, as someone in his position should (he couldn't cast a vote anyway). He liked all five candidates and tried to be as fair as he could to all sides.[17]

Dalton, unopposed, was the first to be nominated so that the convention quickly moved on to the competitive races. After a speech by Obenshain, the Canada versus Craigie nomination for lieutenant governor was next. Before he took to the stage, Canada had his own bluegrass band accompany his intro. Bob Hausenfluck, who was working on Dalton's staff, remembered, "That race was tight; they had me running all over the civic center trying to find this guy and that guy. It was old style politics. Joe Canada had a bluegrass country southwest band with him. It was so different than any convention I had ever seen. Joe was the skinny cat running against the big fat cats." Part of what was going on was regional. Coleman was from the western valley region, Canada from eastern Virginia Beach. Both of their opponents represented areas along I-95. The 2nd congressional delegation hadn't elected someone statewide from their region before. The eastern shore Republicans were entirely for Canada.[18]

Canada, worried that the Republican establishment would not allow time for him to speak, took to the stage early after another speaker had

---

[16] Durrette interview.
[17] Nathan Miller interview, June 29, 2011.
[18] Hausenfluck interview.

conceded his time. "I gave my own nominating speech, which had never been done at a Republican convention in Virginia," said Canada. It began with, 'A lot of you got something under your doors last night on a brown paper bag and what did it say? It said who to vote for. Who runs this party? Is it Main Street people who run it? Who runs it? We run it!' Canada fondly reflected how he, "had them going!" Some said it was one of the best convention speeches they had ever heard.[19]

A rousing speech led to a surprise upset victory for Canada. Although close, the race was over after one ballot. The astonishing results created an even more contentious atmosphere, one that particularly frightened the Durrette campaign, who were also backed by Obenshain and his new "establishment" label. After the first race, Dick now sensed that Durrette's voters were swaying. When he saw his friend Kenny walking through a line to the convention coordinators, he shouted, "We've got to whip the troops together," to which Kenny responded, "I got news for you, we ain't in charge."[20] Regarding Craigie, Judy Peachee said, "We all wanted what Dick wanted, and we [also] knew that we were falling on our swords."[21]

Next was the nomination for attorney general. While convention chairman Nathan Miller remained on stage managing the second race, the Wyatt Durrette supporters were clamoring on one side of the podium, vying for more time to vote. J. Marshall Coleman's delegates were on the other side, and in between there were undecided voters getting worked over the entire evening. Each committee unit had almost a quarter of its members switching back and forth between candidates.[22] Durrette remembers, "I got John Warner's support, he switched and voted for me." Both Durrette and Coleman were rising political stars, representing a bigger split within the Republican Party, and both were working the floor hard. Dalton was all over the place, making his case for Durrette, while former Governor Holton was fighting hard

---

[19] Canada interview.
[20] Klinge interview, March 10, 2010.
[21] Wason interview.
[22] N. Miller interview.

for Coleman. The crowd was similar to that of a mob; so loud that Chairman Miller had to bang his gavel multiple times to get people to settle in.[23]

Throughout the chaos, Nathan Miller kept his composure and tried to maintain order. Unit chairmen were crawling onto the stage, trying to get him to hold the vote so that they could re-caucus again and again. The non-committed group of voters kept shifting. The ballots were recounted several times, dragging well into the evening. Because the race was so tight, a committee would re-caucus for as little as two or three people. Unit chairs would look at the tally board on the stage as other votes were being counted to see how close it was, then re-caucus. The way the conventional system works is that every time a congressional district would be forced to caucus, individual units would have to tally their votes and report back to the congressional district. This whole process could take up to an hour each time. Miller recalled constantly hearing the reply, "We're not ready Mr. Chairman, we are still caucusing." The chairman would be forced to run-down the list again. On the fifth vote, Chairman Miller got to the 8th Congressional District (out of 10) with what looked like a potential finish to a long evening. Suddenly, "Mr. Chairman! Mr. Chairman!" exclaimed yet another unit chair, "We'd like to re-caucus." With each new roll call, the crowd became more impatient, more unruly.[24] Bob Hausenfluck noted, "they had a lady up on stage with a calculator. They were trying to do fractions and percentages; unless it was lopsided you were in real trouble. They reported by congressional district; under parliamentary rules, if you get a certain number of county chairs to demand it, then they have to count it by counties. Its procedure to protest the rights of those counties, which slowed things down even more."[25]

Obenshain could be seen walking through the crowd, pleading his case for Durrette. He was betting his political future on Craigie and Durrette. With one already defeated, he could not risk losing the other. Durrette lamented, "The problem was most of the people supporting Craigie were supporting me.

---

[23] Durrette interview.

[24] N. Miller interview.

[25] Hausenfluck interview.

Craigie and Canada were locked in a tough race. They did a lot of work on undecideds for Craigie, and weren't able to do any for me."[26]

Each recount would potentially result in a loss for either candidate. Chairman Miller didn't know what the vote count would finally conclude but he knew that at the end of the night, nobody would go home happy with the results. "I'm not going to make any friends here today," he thought. He knew he had to make a decision as soon as all ten congressional districts reported or else the entire process might break down. If that were to happen it would be devastating and embarrassing to the party, a result which they might not recover from going into the general election cycle. When the last district reported, he looked up and saw a few unit chairmen clamoring to get his attention. To his right, another was climbing onto the stage to be recognized. This was the only point in the evening at which all district votes were in. Earlier in the evening he had granted re-caucusing requests, but he now realized that if he didn't make a decision at this precise moment he might not get the opportunity again. He didn't consult with anybody, he just slammed the gavel down and said, "done." Once the results came in, J. Marshall Coleman was declared the victor by only .45 fraction of the vote.[27]

It was not one, but two losses that Dick suffered that night. "I remember people saying that Obenshain's future was defeated," recalled Bob Hausenfluck.[28]

Obenshain wasn't one to sit back after a defeat. He went out and campaigned heavily for Dalton, Canada, and Coleman. In regards to his relationship with Obenshain after the convention, Canada stated, "It was fine. He supported Craigie because him and Dalton were close. I understood that. We did some campaign events after that. He was an outstanding patriot. No animosity. He came out and supported me and campaigned for me after the

---

26 Durrette interview.
27 N. Miller interview.
28 Hausenfluck interview.

convention. He was that kind of guy. Even if he didn't support you he'd help you after you won."[29]

Dalton, on the other hand, was not quite as helpful. At the start, he pledged to give 25% of the money he raised to the general ticket. But after Henry Howell demanded that the Republican candidates release their tax returns—and Coleman actually released his—Dalton was infuriated. He thus told his running mates to "raise your own damn money."

Canada had an uphill battle and learned that even in 1977, there were still those who voted Democrat out of habit, whether it made sense or not. Once, on the campaign trail Canada explained, "this guy came up and I introduced myself and he asked 'I'm going to vote for you now. You are a Democrat, aren't ya?' 'No,' I responded. 'Well, I'm going to have to vote for the other guy then. I don't care if he's from Mars.'" He spent a lot of time meeting everyday people; tradesmen, truck drivers, and other blue-collar workers.[30]

That summer, while Obenshain was helping the statewide candidates, he was also visited by many friends of his own who were trying to keep his dream alive. He was already being talked about publicly as a possible Senate candidate for weeks, but Obenshain himself "alternated between moods and ambition and introversion." [31] The disastrous results of the 1977 convention gave him doubts about whether the coalition he helped to build would support him. In addition to that, he had just spent much of the last decade on the road campaigning for himself and other candidates and wondered, now that he was home, if this was where he belonged for the time being. It was uncertain whether he would have the opportunity again. If a Republican won the 1978 Senate race, they would likely serve for several terms and no conservative would dare challenge Harry Byrd Jr. while he was in office. It took some effort and time, but his friends helped him regain his resolve. Once he did, they began to

---

[29] Canada interview.
[30] Ibid.
[31] Atkinson, p. 394.

make plans and work towards fixing the relationships that were damaged earlier in the year.

The Republican State Central Committee had just voted 50-14 in favor of a convention for the following year. Since Holton had much less clout within the party, he proposed a primary for the next year's U.S. Senate nomination, believing he would have a better chance with the general public than the party faithful. The Obenshain forces favored a convention because they had more influence working within the system and Obenshain's strength was in the party structure now. A convention increased his odds at a successful run if he chose to do so.

Several weeks before the 1977 general election, Obenshain's old foe Linwood Holton stopped by his office. "I conferred with Dick Obenshain in his Virginia office, optimistically and rather naïvely thinking he would stand aside if he knew I was going to enter the race. Dick made it clear he was going to make an all-out effort to win the nomination himself."[32]

On election day, John Dalton successfully defeated Henry Howell with 55.9% of the vote, becoming the third consecutive Republican governor. J. Marshall Coleman was also successful in his race, defeating Ed Lane with 53.6% of the vote. Only Joe Canada came up short on the ticket, receiving 45.8% of the vote in his loss to LBJ's son-in-law, Chuck Robb.

Dick decided to waste no time in announcing his decision to run for the U.S. Senate. He decided he would make a public statement three days after election day. He hoped an early announcement would dissuade any other potential candidates, as he was seen as the frontrunner. However, before he could make an announcement, he was blindsided by state Senator Nathan Miller, who had chaired the recent convention, announcing that he too, would be seeking the nomination for the U.S. Senate. With that, an entire block of would-be Obenshain supporters in the Shenandoah Valley were taken away. Although few outside of the valley knew who Nathan Miller was.

---

[32] Holton, p. 185.

Chapter 15:

The Man of the Hour

Raised in the heartland of the Shenandoah Valley on a farm just outside the small town of Bridgewater, Nathan Miller did not grow up in an active political household. His mother, Edith Huff, was a rare Republican to be found in the area at that time. Her support for Republicans was due to her father having been appointed to postmaster at Fort Defiance by a Republican president: Herbert Hoover. The Huff family was grateful that he had a job throughout the 1930s when many in the country did not.

His father, Garland F. Miller, was a poultry and cattle farmer. He later became a businessman and owned his own manufacturing company. Like many businessmen during that time, he was a Byrd Democrat and supported other conservative Democrats in the area, such as John (Jack) Marsh.[1]

Marsh, a native of Winchester, had previously served as a judge in Strasburg and was a member of the Virginia General Assembly at that time. He

---

[1] N. Miller interview.

would eventually be elected to Congress in 1963, the year of the Kennedy assassination, and served his freshman term with another notable congressman elected that year: Donald H. Rumsfeld. Under the Ford administration, Marsh gained more accolades serving as Assistant Secretary of Defense, National Security Advisor, and Counselor to the President. With the election of Ronald Reagan, he would serve as Secretary of the Army, and maintained close ties with Vice President Dick Cheney toward the end of his career.[2]

Nathan's earliest encounter in the realm of politics happened to be a quick and embarrassing meeting with Jack Marsh himself on the front steps of his parents' home. Mr. Marsh had approached the home while campaigning door-to-door, a task some politicians were inclined to do. Nathan, his father, and the family dog, Tuxie, greeted him at the door. Tuxie immediately dashed at Mr. Marsh and covered his nice coat with the dirty prints of his two front paws. While Mr. Miller was annoyed, Jack Marsh, known for being a relaxed southern gentleman, laughed off the incident.[3]

Handsome and intelligent, Nathan had a storybook childhood growing up in rural Virginia. He was even born on Independence Day in 1943. In high school he played football, ran track, performed well in school, and was active in his church. As a lover of history, one of his favorite "characters" was Teddy Roosevelt—not so much for his politics, but for his vast array of interests. When he was 18, his parents insisted that he get his voter registration, and he voted in every election thereafter.

Destined for great things, the all-American boy would go on to graduate from Turner Ashby High School, and from there enrolled at Bridgewater College. He continued to flourish in academics and extracurricular activities. He was nominated to the American Colleges and Universities' "Who's Who," became chairman of the Honor Council, and was Senior Class President. He also continued to play football for Bridgewater as a middle linebacker. Dick Obenshain, a Bridgewater graduate himself, was the inspiration that motivated

---

[2] Spoehr, Thomas. "Remembering Reagan's Army Secretary, John O. Marsh, Jr." *The Daily Signal.* February 4, 2019. https://www.dailysignal.com/2019/02/04/remembering-reagans-army-secretary-john-o-marsh-jr/ Accessed February 10, 2019.
[3] N. Miller interview.

Nathan to join the Young Americans for Freedom organization. He graduated from Bridgewater in 1965 with a B.A. in economics. With a similar political promise looming on the horizon, he received the same degree over a decade after that of his eventual friend and rival, Richard Obenshain. Passionate about his degree of study, he contemplated pursuing a Ph.D in the same subject. It wasn't until he took and performed well in an elective undergraduate course on law that he discovered he might want to attend law school instead. Late into his last semester at college, he was unable to choose between his two passions and unsure about his future.

Finally deciding on a path in the spring of 1965, he took the Law School Admission Test and applied to different schools in Virginia for the fall semester but was a little late on the application process. After waiting anxiously for an acceptance letter, the first letter came…and he was waitlisted. He received a second letter from another school and was waitlisted again, and yet again upon receiving the third letter. Finally, he received a letter from his top choice, the University of Richmond, and was told that he had applied too late. Disappointed, he decided it would be best to enter the working world and took a job as a social studies teacher at Ladd Middle School in Augusta County. He signed a teaching contract with the school for one year, rented a farmhouse from his grandmother, and helped raise 5,000 turkeys while teaching. However, the ups and downs of applying to law school were not yet over.

William Taylor Muse was a tort law professor from the University of Richmond, most known for his work on the famous Palsgraf case of 1928. Later in his career he served as dean of the school from 1947-1970. Upon his appointment, he resolved to enact a number of reforms to make the University of Richmond one of the top law schools in the country, which it remains today. He raised admission standards, expanded the curriculum, and improved facilities. Many referred to him as "the dean of deans." Late in the summer of 1965, Dean Muse called Nathan personally to inform him that there was an opening at the school and that he was number two on the list. This put the young college graduate in a grueling position a week later when he became the top person to fill in the spot, having just signed a teaching contract with Ladd Middle School, a commitment he did not want to break. Nathan was forced to turn down the offer. Dean Muse respected him even more for his decision and told him there would be a spot available to him next year if he applied again.[4]

The year proved to be a blessing in disguise for Nathan. He was able to save up some money and gained valuable life and work experience in the meantime. As Dean Muse had promised, there was a spot open for him the following year, and Nathan eventually graduated from the University of Richmond in the spring of 1969.

He returned home that same year to practice general law. His involvement in politics had been minimal at best, but he quickly made contacts and developed relationships with many in local Republican Party circles through his law practice. The sharp young man caught the attention of a local attorney and Republican activist, John Abbott Paul. The Paul family had been well-established in the area for centuries and were well connected. Previous generations of Pauls served in nearly every major American war. John Paul himself served as a captain during the Vietnam War. He returned to Rockingham County to run for Commonwealth's Attorney but his bid was unsuccessful. He continued to be an active member of the local Republican Party and later, he became the first Republican to be appointed as a lower court judge since the Readjuster period after the Civil War.

The 1970 Republican State Convention was to be held in Norfolk that year. The party had gathered to nominate Ray Garland to take on the now Independent Senator Harry Byrd Jr. John Paul asked Nathan if he was interested in riding with him to the event. Although he was a conservative, Nathan came from a split party household and had not identified himself as either a Republican or a Democrat at this point in his life. Still, he agreed to go with Paul to his first political convention. Paul proudly introduced him to many of the party leaders. Whether he was aware of it or not, it was clear to see that Nathan Miller was being groomed for something more.

The following year, the House of Delegates 16th District seat opened when the incumbent resigned. The district included Harrisonburg City, Shenandoah, Page, and Rockingham County. Virginia, at that time, elected two

---

[4] Ibid.

delegates per house seat, another institutional remnant of the old Byrd Machine, designed to ensure party control. The Republicans had elected Clinton Miller from Woodstock and Grant Rush of McGaheysville. John Paul made a case for Nathan, but nothing formal. The "McGaheysville Mafia," as they were called, were adamant about nominating Rush for the seat. Later on, Rush's father was suddenly stricken with an illness and injured in a fall. The incident forced Rush to reduce his workload as a teacher and it prevented him from continuing his political run.[5] The Republicans were forced to caucus again in what was a classic "smoke-filled room" meeting. Those in the room included Rockingham County Republican Chairman Leonard Estep and Harrisonburg City Republican Chairman M.B. "Pete" Markey Jr. Markey had the ear of the Paul family, who advocated for Nathan Miller, who nobody else in the room knew much about. Other names were tossed around that evening. Dee Floyd, who had entered the contest for nomination just before the local convention in August, was the first to be considered. Ironically, he was no longer interested in the nomination, which upset Leonard and Pete. Recent redistricting had already confused the nominating process, but it was agreed that whoever was selected as the candidate should be from either Harrisonburg or Rockingham since the two localities made up well over half of the district's population. With the general election only four weeks away, Nathan received a call from Paul himself, asking him to run. Since many respected Paul's wisdom, more calls would come. The state party leader, Warren French, followed by Governor Linwood Holton himself, called to say, "You need to run; we need to fill that slot." Republicans barely existed as a formidable minority in the House. Eager to potentially have more of them, Holton told Nathan he wanted an answer within twelve hours. Becoming a politician was not in Nathan's life plan at the moment, but that was all about to change.

Just four weeks before the election, in October of 1971, the nominating process took place at the MD's Restaurant in New Market. It was attended by roughly twenty-five people. The original candidate, Grant Rush became Miller's

---

[5] John Paul interview, December 7, 2016.

treasurer that evening. Miller's fast-assembled campaign pamphlet simply read, "I Need Your Help and Support."[6]

The Democratic opponents were Lewis F. Jolly of Harrisonburg and Perry Sarver of Strasburg. The Democratic machine was beginning to bust, and Nathan won handily. At 28 years old he was the second youngest member of the House, with the youngest being the 27-year-old Richard W. Elliott, a Democrat from Rustburg. Upon his victory, humble and banking on his youth, Delegate-Elect Miller would say, "I am not so foolish as to believe that I can solve the problems of this state and area or even assist in their solution any better than others. What I hope I can do is bring a fresh and energetic approach to government."[7] Soon he felt the weight of responsibility on his shoulders and what it meant to be a representative who had to make tough decisions. As a former teacher he prioritized education and vocational training over everything. His other interests included reorganizing the Governor's Committee, and he did not take a committed stance on preferencing a sales tax over an income tax, which were hot topics going into the 1972 General Assembly session. The session convened on January 6th, 1972. He became one of only 22 Republicans serving in the House. Also elected that year was a delegate from northern Virginia named Wyatt Durrette, whom Miller befriended. He was placed in room 923 in the General Assembly building, about as high up as you can go, close to his fellow district colleague, Clinton Miller, whom he had no familial relations with. Clinton Miller was placed in room 916. Republicans were placed up high in the building in hopes of being forgotten about by visitors and lobbyists. The staunch Byrd Democratic Speaker of the House, John Warren Cooke, appointed Nathan to the Agriculture; Militia, Police and Public Safety; and Education Committees.

It was a contentious year. Virginia was facing a pending budget deficit of 80 million dollars. Governor Lin Holton, who was not incredibly popular among conservatives, proposed a one cent gas tax increase to finance badly needed road improvements. This was followed by a suggested plan to increase

---

[6] Murphey, Pat. "Grant Quits 16th District Race." *Daily News Record.* September 21, 1971.
[7] Laymen, Ellen. "Miller Begins Learning Assembly Today." *Daily News Record.* January 6, 1972.

the income tax and grant localities the option to permit a one cent increase in sales taxes. Both of the Millers preferred raising the corporate income taxes from five to six percent on taxable income over $12,000 instead, which would only affect seven percent of the state's population. That same year, Nathan started to take notice of Dick Obenshain and all that he was doing as he made his way through the party structure.

After an incredible first session experience, Nathan returned home to practice law and begin campaigning. During the year, he was appointed by the governor to the Milk Commission, an appropriate appointment for a farm kid from the valley. He was named Outstanding Young Man of the Community that year and was seen at nearly every local event. His name recognition continued to grow amongst his community, which resulted in his re-election in 1973. He was named to the Privileges and Elections Committee by Speaker Cooke during the 1974 session. Nobody in close circles really understood why Cooke gave Miller this appointment; it was a powerful committee appointment to be given to someone so young. However, with the election of 1973, the total number of Republicans in the House had dropped from 22 to 19. The opportunity for a balanced committee grew slimmer that year. The accolades continued for Miller, as he was also appointed by the Speaker to fill a position on the Commission on the Status of Women. Another random appointment, since he was not married and didn't have any children at this time, but Miller was happy to accept and work hard at every new challenge thrown his way. In 1974 the Republican Party chose him to be their legal counsel.

State Senator George S. Aldhizer II, a Democrat from Broadway, represented another relic of the Byrd Machine: a status quo candidate who ignored his constituency for years, banking on his experience and his incumbency. He never showed up to events such as the "Little Stanley Parade" despite annual pleas from its mayor. In politics, it is never good to get too comfortable in your position, as Aldhizer would learn in 1971, when he barely squeaked out a victory in a plurality vote with two other opponents. Republicans were feeling the tide slowly beginning to turn in state level politics. They became increasingly confident that they could take Aldhizer's seat, which would dramatically change the power structure in the state Senate and symbolically foreshadow what was to come in the Virginia Senate later that decade.

Prior to the close election in 1971, questions had been raised over Aldhizer's involvement with an independent telephone company from Harrisonburg which sought a rate increase from the State Corporation Commission. Many considered it a conflict of interest, as Aldhizer potentially stood to have made a profit off of the increase. To the surprise of Delegate Nathan Miller, the issue was not brought up during the 1971 election. Machine politics undoubtedly continued to limit the range of discussion in the local press and during debates.

Like the Republicans, Aldhizer sensed the same sweeping change which likely stalled his announcement to run again in 1975. He didn't even make his last-minute decision to run for re-election until the evening of the 26th District Democratic Convention in Luray. It came as no surprise to Aldhizer when the young Republican delegate from Bridgewater entered the race. "It didn't cause my blood pressure to rise or fall," said the old senator, but in the coming months, Aldhizer would have his work cut out for him.

The turning tide represented more of an alignment to national party politics than it did any dramatic shift in political philosophy. On specific state issues, Miller and Aldhizer barely disagreed on anything. Both men were opposed to raising taxes, bargaining, and were for a referendum on bonds only as a last resort for fixing some of the state's infrastructural issues. Nathan tried to separate himself from his opponent by highlighting his youthfulness and energetic approach to governing. Essentially, the race was about a generational gap. The age difference between the two of them was thirty-six years. Nathan continued to hammer Aldhizer for ignoring his constituents and for the 1969 utility rate increase. Nathan then attacked the Commission on Crime, a part-time commission that Aldhizer sat on, for spending over half a million dollars on its operations to date. Aldhizer enjoyed much support from insiders and the local business community. Even Republican 7th District Congressman J. Kenneth Robinson and John Dalton supported Aldhizer. Governor Mills Godwin, a new Republican but still a friend of Aldhizer, stayed out of the race altogether. The common opinion among most within the district was that Nathan had no chance of winning. Aldhizer had been a senator for over twenty years, and many insiders were still very loyal to the old guard. As Nathan continued to campaign, however, he noticed that many everyday folks he came into contact with had never heard of Aldhizer before. This made his claims of Aldhizer being disconnected from his constituents a more valid accusation.

Nathan's strength was in his personality, and in the perception that he was not a lifelong politician. As the Daily News Record put it, "By his own admission, Miller is a grassroots candidate who makes his best impression before small groups or face to face with a voter in a shopping center or country store. He's not a spellbinding speaker, but he thinks he projects sincerity…Because he entered politics more by accident than design, Miller isn't dedicated to being a politician for the rest of his life."[8] Nathan's youth worked to his advantage in that he was able to knock on more doors and attend nearly every event in the district, which allowed him those critical face to face interactions. Most found his southern drawl charming; it made him appear approachable and like one of them.

Miller's hard work paid off on election night when he received 9,586 votes to Aldhizer's 6,248 votes. His victory still came as a shock to many. The 26th Senate District was made up of Rockingham, Shenandoah, Madison, and Rappahannock Counties, with Aldhizer only winning Rappahannock. Local Republican activist Bonnie Paul won Nathan's former delegate seat along with Clinton Miller. Just to the south, in the 24th Senate District, J. Marshall Coleman of Staunton ran a similar campaign to Nathan and defeated Democrat Frank Nolen, who only served for one year. Lastly, Senator William A. Truban of Woodstock, a senior member of the Senate minority representing the 27th Senate District, held onto his seat. Joe Canada of Virginia Beach was the only other veteran senator to return to the 1976 session. These victories made the central valley region a very strong influencer among Senate Republicans. The minority members in the Senate now rose to seven out of forty.

Nathan entered the capitol building again in January of 1976, this time as a state Senator. He watched the names on the vote tally board. No longer did it read "Aldhizer" at the top, but near the middle of the 40 name listing was the name Miller. Shortly after, drama ensued. On the first day of session, there was no indication as to who would fill Aldhizer's prestigious center aisle seat. Seating charts were not available, and there was uncertainty about the Senate staffing following the decision of the Senate clerk. The moderate faction of the Senate Democrats, frustrated by their losses, did not reappoint longtime Senate

---

[8] Laymen, Ellen. "Aldhizer-Miller: The Hot Contest." *Daily News Record.* November 5, 1973.

Clerk Louise Lucas. No reason was given for his departure, but it was rumored that the Democrats were punishing Lucas for his cozy relationship with the new Republican-convert governor, Mills Godwin. Nathan quickly made waves by charging that the treatment of the majority and minority "flies in the face of fairness." There was even a move made which would have given majority leaders 1½ times the salary as that of their minority counterparts, a move the Senate Democrats claimed was not partisan but merely represented the work load of the majority in comparison to that of the minority. Senator Miller, looking out for his friend and fellow valley Republican, Minority Leader William Truban, attempted to correct the compensation deficiency, but his bill was rejected 20-17. Senator Miller later proposed another bill which would have prevented bill duplication, thus saving the Commonwealth time and money. It would have eliminated co-sponsors and have an earlier cut-off date for introduction. Though the bill seemed like common sense on the surface, it was also defeated.[9]

That year, of the 74 bills sponsored by the 7 central valley Republicans, only a handful passed both houses. Of the 10 bills that Senator Miller proposed that year, 4 were passed by both chambers, giving Miller one of highest success rates for the valley delegation. Senator Miller would head back home that year and tell his local GOP women's club, in reference to the frustrating circumstances that left Louise Lucas without a job, "If good people don't speak up, bad things start to happen." The blatant partisanship in the Senate was sharply different from what he experienced in the House for four years. That year the legislature was only able to provide 25 million of the 97 million dollars sought by the Republican Governor for capital outlay projects, which included needed services such as mental institutions and correction facilities.

The frustration many Republican state senators felt was real—and it was demoralizing. Yet it also bonded them together. Joe Canada had a different perspective regarding his first term in office. "Things were very cordial and they treated us all fairly. Things slowly became more partisan over the years."[10] Two-party competition certainly brought on the need for partisanship as the

---

[9] Laymen, Ellen. "Miller Charges Discrimination." *Daily News Record.* January 8, 1973.
[10] Canada interview.

Democratic leadership finally felt their positions of power were being threatened. Senator Canada had been a Democrat his whole life until the Henry Howell campaign forced him and many others to switch parties. He first ran for the state Senate in 1971 as a Republican, but many still knew him as a Democrat, which could also have resulted in fairer treatment for him during session. By that time there were only 8 Republican members of the Senate. Some partisanship that occurred later on could have been hyped up by the ambitions of some of the younger members of the Senate.

In 1977, Nathan garnered more statewide recognition from Republicans when he was selected to become the convention chairman of the Republican Party, but many outside of the valley were surprised by his age. One of the main tasks as chairman was to act as a mediator during the party's convention, which was setting up to be a hot contest that year. Nathan was well-liked and had the perfect temperament for the job. The experience would also help him in future endeavors, he said "It gave me an understanding of how the party worked, that was one of the things Dick Obenshain had a huge advantage [in], not only did he know the mechanics, but he knew the people; I didn't know them as well as he did."[11]

Nathan took away more from that experience than he initially thought he would. He saw how unpredictable the dynamics of a convention can be. He later stepped down as general counsel for the Republican Party and returned to focusing on his constituents in the valley. Rumors began to swirl as to who would be a candidate for the U.S. Senate as William Scott announced his retirement. Many were quick to whisper the names of Governor Linwood Holton and Richard Obenshain. Warner had also been traveling around the state for the past few years. Warner and Obenshain alone would split the party in half.

Nathan could not recall the exact moment he decided to run, but when he saw the names that were being tossed around it sparked his interest in furthering his political ambitions. He knew that he'd be a long shot in comparison to the "horse power" and fundraising potential that the other two men had, but he looked at it as an opportunity, especially if there was a large

---

[11] N. Miller interview.

voting block that would not give in to either side. The thought entered his mind that he could be the compromise candidate in a three-way race. Crazier things have happened, as he experienced the past year. He could also play up his youth, which helped get him elected to the state Senate, and the fact that he was the only candidate with legislative experience. While his mentor, Judge John Paul, a fan of Holton, was unable to counsel him at this time, Delegate Bonnie Paul encouraged Nathan. "I'll run a good, clean race." True to himself and his record in the past, he did just that.

On November 1st, 1977, in front of the steps of the Richmond Capitol building, he delivered a surprising announcement speech:

> "I am here today to announce that I am a candidate for the Senate of the United States. I come to this task from the heartland of the Shenandoah Valley, where men have always been free and are determined to remain so. My service in the Senate of Virginia and before that in the House of Delegates has confirmed for me the worth of the practical conservatism shared by most Virginians. I think I have a record of service to my party and of service in the legislature that demonstrate my ability to be elected and to do the job after I am elected. I run because our federal government is not what it ought to be. The people have judged it and found it faulty. It is too big and too powerful. The people say, and I agree, that we have too much government, too many regulations, supervision, inspections, restrictions, and collections. There is a smoldering feeling of discontent and frustration among our people. Too many promises have been made and too few kept. Too many hopes have been built and then destroyed. I run because I want to help make government what it should be, compassionate to those truly in need, encouraging to those who seek to excel, rewarding to those who work the hardest, and above all a guardian of the freedom of the individual. In the course of the campaign, I will be taking position on the issues that face us. I am not here to tell you that I have all the answers. I am here to say that I have the ability to apply the common sense of Virginia's people to the problems of our national government. I shall submit my record and qualifications to the members of my party for their judgement on my nomination to this high office. At the same time I shall demonstrate to the people of Virginia my approach to the office itself so that they can make their decision next November."

It turned out to be a more memorable and life-changing endeavor than he could have ever expected.

Chapter 16:

A Tale of Four Virginia Gentlemen

Neither wealth nor ancestry make a Virginia gentleman. The honor is bestowed to one based on his conduct. "The four of us fought hard, but we were always gentlemen; we were always straightforward. We were Virginia gentlemen. All four of us," said John Warner. "The quality of politicians in Virginia, you could set [a part], that state produced men of integrity, experience, and dedication."[1] Staffer Henry Doggett observed, "It may have got heated at times, but they were true Virginians. They knew how to behave."[2] No doubt the four candidates seeking the Republican nomination for U.S. Senate in 1978 exemplified this high ideal of the almost mythical Virginia gentleman—at least on the surface.

When Bill Scott announced in 1976 that that he would not seek re-election to the United States Senate, the fight for endorsements and votes for the 1978 Republican convention had begun. While none of the candidates

---

[1] John Warner interview, April 30, 2012.
[2] Doggett interview.

formally announced until the latter part of 1977, there was little doubt as to who two of those candidates would be. Obenshain and Warner.

For almost a decade John Warner funded Republican campaigns in Virginia, from Governor Linwood Holton to Senator Bill Scott and Governor John Dalton. Warner's financial assistance extended down to members of the General Assembly, too. While many appreciated the help, some were repulsed, alleging that Warner never looked up from his desk to hand over a check to the recipient. Warner's lavish gift-giving helped him somewhat, but it came back to haunt him when he discovered that he was perceived as a member of the D.C. cocktail elites who thought it was time to "buy themselves a Senate seat," according to Obenshain staffer Bob Hausenfluck.[3]

John Dalton had many staffers in 1977 who were working just to get enough experience so that they could work for Obenshain the following year. One of those staffers happened to be on Dalton's inaugural committee and noticed that the tickets were to be mailed to Warner at a Georgetown address in D.C. The staffer stored the information away for the right time. The Obenshain team later used the information on a flyer sent out to all of the convention delegates, nicknaming John Warner "Georgetown Johnny" and blasted him for not living in Virginia.

In July of 1977, after the hotly contested convention, Warner invited Wyatt Durrette and his wife Sharon to dinner at their townhouse in D.C. It was a delightful evening, and Durrette was captivated by how personable and friendly actress Elizabeth Taylor was. After dinner, Warner took Durrette into his study and told him that he was going to announce his run for the U.S. Senate by the end of the year. Having supported Durrette for his unsuccessful nomination at the convention, Warner expected the same in return when he said, "I'd like to have your support." Durrette was very popular and still seen as a rising star. His endorsement would have been very impactful as J. Marshall Coleman was unlikely to endorse Obenshain either. Governor John Dalton would mostly likely remain neutral. Unfortunately for Warner, Durrette could not return the favor. "I can't," he said, "I'm already committed to Dick and I'm

---

[3] Hausenfluck interview.

not going to break that commitment and I'm going to work very hard for him." Warner respected his decision.[4]

While Warner primarily earned political IOU's by monetarily supporting candidates, Obenshain was building them through personal effort. Obenshain dedicated his life to building the Republican Party from the ground up while also making it a conservative party. Most grassroots activists at the time could share similar stories of Dick Obenshain speaking at one of their Lincoln Day dinners, fundraisers, or committee meetings when there would only be a handful of people in attendance. During the primary race, an Obenshain staffer was sent on a mission to track down a professor from Lynchburg who was chair of the Lynchburg Republican Party to find out who he was supporting. Despite Dick being from Blacksburg, the mountain-valley region had always been a troublesome spot for him in terms of gaining support. The staffer, Bob Hausenfluck, who had worked for Dalton, knocked on the man's front door. After answering, the man said, "I don't think Dick will win. But I owe it to him. I ran several years ago for the House of Delegates. I got the tar beat out of me. We were having our biggest rally and I couldn't get anyone up here. This car pulls up, and Dick gets out of the car. I never will forget it; I'm with him. You can't buy that stuff."[5] Many delegates considered to be "Holton people" respected Dick for the years he spent building the party. This appreciation would help Dick tremendously at the convention.

Obenshain was still considered the favorite of the faithful party members, he was the leader of the coalition that had brought them to statewide victory for close to a decade. His service to the party over the years had endeared him to the party regulars. He was less known to the general public, though, having only run and lost for one statewide office back in 1969. In times past, he had frequently teased attempts at running for the Senate. So, it was to no one's surprise when he made his announcement on Friday, November 11th, 1977 at the Hyatt Hotel. Many of "the group," had known of his intent for weeks. The entire Obenshain family, from Blacksburg and all around, met at his home in Salisbury for the long-awaited special day.

---

[4] Durrette interview.

[5] Hausenfluck interview.

Dick's sister-in-law Marsha had never heard him give a speech before, and recalled, "Joe and I drove him and Helen. I was very interested to see how he was going to do this, because he didn't strike me as the type. We drove up and dropped him off, but before we got to the last stop light, that's when he and Helen were in the backseat working on his speech. Then all of the sudden the four of us got real quiet and Dick says, 'What if nobody comes!'"[6] His daughters Kate and Anne also remembered Dick being worried that nobody would show up. "We got out at the hotel and the place was packed; it was unbelievable," said Marsha. His announcement was attended by close to 300 people. "The instant he stepped on that platform the Dick Obenshain I knew at home was like a totally different person. His speech was just inspiring; it was amazing."[7]

Obenshain emphasized that he was running an anti-Washington campaign. His rhetoric was fiery. "I am deeply concerned about the expansion of federal power and the increasing burden of federal taxes," he said plainly. "The people of Virginia would find me to be a strong advocate for bringing the power of an impersonal bureaucracy under control, for reducing the tax burden which is taking away a fair reward for our working people." He admitted his "deepest personal aspiration" was to serve the people of Virginia in the United States Senate.[8]

The only surprise candidate, Nathan Miller, had cut in front of Obenshain and made his announcement a day before. Nobody had expected the young senator to win, but his strategy was to be everybody's "2nd choice." He thought he could be a compromise candidate if the convention went to five or six ballots. Not only was this a long shot, but it didn't quite make sense to many people either. Obenshain caught wind of a possible Miller entry into the race just a few days before the announcement and joked that he would hate to have to split the Bridgewater vote.

---

[6] Marsha Obenshain interview, July 20, 2011.
[7] Ibid.
[8] Lowery, David. "Obenshain Bid for Senate is Made Official." *Richmond News Leader.* November 12, 1977.

Many questioned his reason for running and assumed it was to lay the foundation for a future statewide campaign. The Republican populace found Nathan Miller, an Obenshain admirer, to be a likeable person with a bright future ahead of him. Besides those in valley, many Republicans did not want to see him enter this race and were dumbfounded by his reasons to do so. Holton and Warner reacted warmly to his decision as his following and platform would likely pull more voters away from Obenshain. It was rumored that this was the plan all along by those closest to state Senator Miller who were mountain valley Republicans. The few original mountain valley Republicans of old were likely fans of Holton and bitter about the influx of old conservative Democrats from around the state in recent years. Miller's announcement came as a blow to Obenshain, and a new obstacle that he did not expect. While Miller's overall chances were slim, his potential to completely derail Obenshain from his long-sought victory was great.

Governor Holton had been the third candidate to announce on December 19th, 1977. After his time serving as Assistant Secretary of State for Henry Kissinger, Holton became a partner with the Hogan and Hartson law firm, the oldest major law firm in Washington D.C. with international ties. John Warner was also a partner at this firm. Rather than quietly retire, Holton wanted back in the game. He was unhappy in his role as a senior statesman, without the spotlight and without a role to play in shaping the direction of the Republican Party. Those close to him noticed his restlessness during this time and encouraged him to get back into politics. Others whispered that he jumped back in because he wanted to stop Dick Obenshain.

Holton himself said, "I was bored. [I thought] I could easily gain the Republican nomination for Senate. I was the only person who had ever won a statewide race. 'Win Again with Lin' seemed to me to be a slogan everyone would remember and support." In his announcement he focused on just that: the fact that he had already proven his electability.[9] Holton did not think that Warner could defeat Obenshain in a primary contest. Similar to his expectation for Obenshain to essentially move out of the way, he thought that by

---

[9] Holton, p. 185.

announcing early, John Warner would also be convinced not to run. Holton again, overestimated his clout.

The last to formally announce would be John Warner. To Holton's surprise, and unlike when Warner wanted to become Secretary of the Navy, Warner never mentioned his intentions to Holton. "John's entry into that race confused it, and I was not real happy about his coming into the race, but it didn't make a great deal of difference."[10] Despite still having a following since he was elected governor, Holton had made numerous enemies within his own party. His role had been significantly diminished. His time in D.C. had also left him with even less influence in his home state.

Rather than be perturbed by this new political environment, Holton was actually confident in his chances of winning the nomination, especially after the 1977 convention showed cracks in the conservative coalition which had ousted Warren French just a few years before. Holton believed he could exploit this friction. Later, a poll taken by Virginia Commonwealth University revealed him to be the only potential nominee with a lead over Democrat political juggernaut, Andy Miller. This poll encouraged Holton to continue flaunting his electability and the fact that he was the only candidate to have won a statewide election. He thought that perhaps he could still win a general election and again reassert himself as leader of the party. Holton also didn't think that Elizabeth Taylor would be a significant asset to John Warner, but as it turned out, in his memoirs he wrote, "The glamour of John's new wife was no small asset. One of my longtime committed supporters, Ryland Heflin, told Jinks at a political rally that he would break his commitment to me and vote for Warner because Elizabeth Taylor would help him establish a race track on his property." Holton was also surprised at the funds being raised for this campaign, but felt he too was able to raise an adequate amount for himself.[11]

At the time John Warner had "parachuted into the race" his political philosophy was almost as unknown as Nathan Miller's name identification, although he was considered a moderate while Miller was considered a conservative. Miller had at least developed a voting record while serving in the

---

[10] Holton interview, September 29, 2017.

[11] Holton, p. 186.

General Assembly. Holton had been a Governor, and Obenshain had long been working at building the party from within. With each of these three candidates, voters somewhat knew the differences between them and knew what to expect. This was not the case with John Warner. Warner had no following within the party, unlike Holton and Obenshain. Therefore, his best bet for winning delegates would be to emphasize his credentials, tout his wife, and bring in a lot of new faces to the party. Warner had jumped into the race on January 5th, 1978. While he certainly had a great resume as Secretary of the Navy and head of the Bicentennial, many had come to know him as the new husband of actress Elizabeth Taylor.

"Warner came in as a celebrity candidate. He wasn't particularly ideological, but he had a lot of jazz. It came down to 'are we going to go with charismatic leader with a lot of fame and flamboyance, or are we going to go with the ideological leader of the party,'" Jim Gilmore explained.[12]

Warner had another strength at his disposal: his speaking abilities. His style was very different than that of Obenshain's, but nonetheless it was still very effective. He would take off his navy-blue blazer, refuse a microphone or a podium, and walk around a room speaking directly to his audience as if he was engaging them in a conversation. There was an attractive, laid back quality to him that had many buying in hook, line, and sinker.

Each candidate was in the early stages of building their campaign team. Congressman Joel Broyhill would run John Warner's campaign. Warner brought in consultants from outside Virginia and spent a lot of his own money. "He had the most expensive staff money could buy," said Gary Byler. He had also been working to actively peel away experienced campaign staffers that had worked for John Dalton, but most were dedicated to Obenshain.[13]

By the end of November, Obenshain still did not have a formal staff, but he did have a "committee" that helped him with campaign decisions. The slow decision-making in this area prompted Weldon Tuck to offer his help. Tuck decided to leave his comfortable position with the Department of

---

[12] Gilmore interview.
[13] Byler interview.

Commerce to come work on Obenshain's campaign. "It's time to get this off the pot and get this thing going," he told Dick. Four weeks later, he hired a driver for Dick by the name of Brad Cavedo, who had helped Dick briefly in 1969. The next order of business was to find someone to act as the campaign manager. Like the Warner campaign, they initially tried bringing in professionals from outside the state, but this didn't work out for them. While the Obenshain campaign was being led by Bill Dalton, no relation to John Dalton, it was horribly disorganized.[14] Dalton had been recommended by several friends of Obenshain, as he had run several successful campaigns out of Tennessee. The problem was that he wasn't privy to how Virginia politics worked, which led to an early psychological defeat for the entire campaign.[15]

This was uncharacteristic of Obenshain's previous campaigns, in which he led with state-of-the-art technology and had highly efficient and motivated workers. After the Obenshain team faced a major defeat at the Richmond City GOP meeting, Bill Dalton was replaced by longtime friend and successful campaign strategist Judy Peachee. When Peachee took over, she quickly whipped the team into shape. The person they hired from Tennessee was "in over his head" and didn't remain on the team very long. Even Brad Cavedo took note, and privately told Helen Obenshain and Weldon Tuck about his concerns. "It led to some heated exchanges," said Weldon, who ended up leaving the campaign around the same time. Weldon, a longtime friend of Dick's, submitted a resignation letter in which he said, "As you know, we have had strong disagreements over the conduct and direction of this campaign. I know that you are in accord with my feeling that our close personal friendship over the years exacerbated our political disagreements."[16] The two did not speak to one another for several months after.

After all of the candidates made their formal announcements, they set out to make their planned tours and debates around the state for the next six months. Early on, the four candidates agreed to many joint appearances at luncheons, district committee meetings, campus events sponsored by Young

---

[14] Tuck interview, October 2, 2017.
[15] Cavedo interview.
[16] "Resignation Given By Obenshain Aide." *Richmond Times Dispatch*. April 11, 1978.

and College Republicans, and other friendly groups. Around the springtime, they shifted gears and attended the mass meetings, which were emotionally charged. Some county and city committees were adopting resolutions which bound all of the delegates in a "winner take all" style of voting similar to that of the electoral college. The state party allowed each individual unit to make their own decisions regarding "instruction" voting.

There were still just ten congressional districts in Virginia at the time, and the Republican Party organized itself based on congressional districts. Obenshain supporters dominated in the 1st district, which was made up of the eastern shore and counties such as Gloucester and Tappahannock, as well as the 5th district, which was southern Virginia. Obenshain was also significantly strong in the 3rd district, which consisted of the surrounding Richmond area, though if the delegates were uncommitted he would only maintain a slim plurality over Warner and Holton.

As a serviceman in the Navy, Warner was mostly dominant in the 2nd district area consisting of Norfolk and Virginia Beach, an area that Obenshain always found trouble in. Warner was also aided by the support of Joe Canada, whose wife Sandy traveled extensively with Elizabeth Taylor. Warner's popularity near the shipyards and Navy vessels spilled over into the 4th Congressional District in places like Emporia and Surry County, where he was almost tied with Obenshain. Congressional District Chairman Tedd Burr recalled, "Warner had a great deal of support in the fourth district, which bothered me to no end. Somehow, the people down there had gotten it in their heads that the old Richmond establishment was trying to take over the party again."[17]

Northern Virginia, which consisted of the 10th and 8th districts, leaned close to a three-way tie between Obenshain, Warner, and Holton, while Obenshain and Holton were neck and neck in the 6th and 9th districts near Roanoke and southwest Virginia. Nathan Miller had total support in the seventh district in the northern part of the Shenandoah Valley, where

---

17 Burr interview.

Obenshain was most certainly considered a strong second, if Miller were to drop out.

The 3rd Congressional District was nearly a three-way split between Obenshain, Warner and Holton, with the bulk of Obenshain support coming from Chesterfield. State Senator Rick Ray supported Warner because, "Holton was too liberal, Obenshain was too conservative, Warner had the right background and [was the] right guy for the job." There were a series of procedural battles that took place at each local committee in Chesterfield, Richmond, and Henrico. Chesterfield had elected 105 delegates to the convention with instructions, which meant that they were not free to vote how they wanted until after the third ballot—if there was a third ballot. The instructions were to support Obenshain, which gave him the advantage in the third district. This measure however, only won by a slim vote of 48-46. [18]

All candidates were scratching and crawling their way to victory in the 3rd district. While Warner won new voters with his celebrity status, Obenshain continued to win over voters with his charm. During a reception at Parker Field a young Obenshain supporter named Carthan Currin met him for the first time. "My most vivid recollection was his wonderful way of making me feel like I was the most important person in that room, and I was probably the least important person in that room. He didn't look at other people while talking to me; he was good at giving you his undivided attention. I was impressed with that."[19]

It was clear in the early goings of the race that Dick Obenshain had set the tone, the debate, and the standard. He came out strong in favor of the Kemp-Roth tax proposal, new labor laws which would implement a national right-to-work act, and called for federal tax credits for college tuition payments.

The other candidates appeared to make the race about who was closer to Dick Obenshain's brand of conservatism, but more electable than him. The Obenshain team frequently referred to the other candidates as the "Obenshain clones." Yet the press continued to portray Dick as being an extremist. He

---

[18] "Chesterfield GOP Backs Obenshain Bid." *Richmond Times Dispatch.* March 14, 1978.
[19] Carthan Currin interview, September 26, 2017.

eventually responded to the reporters, who he sarcastically called "the great analysts and humorists of our time." He noted, "in our joint appearance they have echoed me in every particular. The phrase 'I agree with Dick Obenshain' is probably the dominant one of this campaign." Regarding his role as campaign co-chair for Godwin, Dalton, Scott, and Ford, he said, "If I was an isolated representative of some kooky fringe...If I was not in the mainstream…Why would all of the four ask me?[to chair their campaigns]"[20] The Roanoke Times and Richmond Times Dispatch in particular were never considered very friendly to Obenshain.

The debates and forums were defined by their friendliness, respect, good humor, and lightheartedness, but they still took jabs at each other. The easiest target was always John Warner. At a Giles County Republican dinner, Warner, who had inherited a farm in Middleburg which had previously been owned by the Mellon family, talked about "shoveling hay in his barn." When Obenshain came up next, he remarked, "I grew up on a farm and we always used a pitchfork for hay...we used a shovel for manure."[21] Nathan Miller also recalled another story,

> "Warner always got up to talk about being a farmer. One day at a meeting—by then we had been to about a hundred of these—he gets up in front of me and starts talking about cattle farming, so I get up and say John may be a good cattle farmer, but he's the only cattle farmer that has a swimming pool in his barn. He's a good sport, in his rebuttal he took some shots at me. I felt like overall, even if the partisan people had been more intense, the candidates themselves had a good respect for each other."[22]

The four were technically competing against each other, but it was almost as if they were running a joint campaign. They all attended the same events. They also shared flights on small private planes together from time to time. It was perhaps the most positive campaign leading up to a nomination

---

[20] Rolfe, Shelley. "Obenshain Stresses Organizational Work." *Richmond Times Dispatch*. April 17, 1977.
[21] Joe interview, July 20, 2011.
[22] N. Miller interview.

that Virginia had ever seen, and one that would be considered odd by modern political standards. The candidates focused only on their positive attributes and refrained from attacking one another as they attended endless committee meetings, potluck dinners, youth events, and mass meetings.

Warner recalled, "Nathan and Dick knew the dialogue of the Shenandoah Valley. When we got up to northern Virginia, we painted them as a bunch of hicks. Then we would go to the southwest and see Holton at his roots. He'd whack us all across the fanny there big time." Warner would reflect, "I had nothing but good will of the voters; my main strength was the centrists, the undecideds, the unaffiliated people."[23]

Holton remarked that Warner seemed like a fish out of water to political veterans like Holton and Obenshain.

> "All of us were kind of laughing at John because he was such a clown. He had obviously taken some lessons on how to campaign. Dick and I would just giggle at him. It got him awfully mad, but it was a friendly race. Dick and I had been competing a long time on these things, and we were just determined that when the nomination went to somebody it would be worth having. We were not going to have an intra-party fight on an individual, personal basis… though John tempted us with that clowning and putting out stuff that just wasn't so. We came out of it without any real problems. I talked with him pretty plainly to say, 'John, this is straight business. You don't go around trying to fool people, and there's no point in doing any acting. You're a good guy—just be yourself.' I was trying to help him, and I think it did help him."[24]

Despite having been bitter antagonists since 1969, Obenshain and Holton had developed a deeper level of mutual respect. Meanwhile the two lifelong friends and legal partners, Holton and Warner, were showing signs of annoyance with one another.[25] Warner said of his friend, "There was some

---

[23] Warner interview, April 30, 2012.
[24] Atkinson, p. 399.
[25] Cavedo interview.

friction between us on one or two occasions. It was unfortunate, but it never persisted."[26]

At the heart of this growing animosity was the feeling that one should drop out and support the other. Warner believed that as a new candidate and one with celebrity appeal that he was more capable of winning in the general election, while Holton echoed his campaign rhetoric, which was that he was the more electable of the two. Holton did not believe Warner was a formidable opponent against Miller, nor did he believe Elizabeth Taylor would have much of an impact. He couldn't have been more wrong.

Part of Warner's strategy was to employ the help of his wife's fans to flood the party with new members. An analysis of the race showed that Warner supporters were less likely to be native Virginians but were more likely to be newcomers to the state. The majority of Obenshain and Holton supporters were found to have lived in the state for longer than ten years. This showed that Warner's newness to politics was only of negative importance to native Virginians, it was not important to the transplants found mostly in the city centers, northern Virginia, and the Norfolk region. Another poll showed that a large percentage of Warner's supporters had little previous political experience, which showed that he was successful in bringing a large number of newcomers to the party.[27] While it was a different world for her and she struggled at times to keep herself together, Elizabeth Taylôr looked back fondly at her time spent in Virginia during the race. "I admit, there was something exhilarating about the experience. I could be spontaneous in public because I was working for someone other than myself, and the people of Virginia were just wonderful."[28]

Many of the conservatives feared that the two would eventually gang up on Obenshain. Throughout the campaign there was never any overt coordination between Warner and Holton, although sometimes it appeared that way. For instance, both groups staged a walkout during the Henrico County

---

[26] Atkinson, p. 399.
[27] Abramowitz, Alan; McGlennon, John; Rapoport, Ronald. *Party Activists in Virginia: A Study of Delegates to the 1978 Senatorial Nominating Conventions.* Charlottesville, VA. University of Virginia. 1981 p. 28.
[28] Taylor, Elizabeth. *Elizabeth Takes Off.* New York. Berkshire Publishing Group. 1987 p.41.

mass meeting in protest of the Obenshain factions that were in charge of the local party there. Stunts like that were getting media attention and portrayed Obenshain as an overbearing party boss. Whether it was incompetence or pride that kept them from uniting, had these factions been able to do so they probably could have prevailed over Obenshain early on in the race.

In the midst of a stressful campaign, Obenshain's staff were making small but fond memories while on the trail. Dick Obenshain was known for enjoying the little things in life. Bob Hausenfluck recalled coming back from a fundraiser in Warrenton one evening after they had been traveling all day long. It was late and the stores were closed. Dick said, "I could use a drink." Bob jokingly replied,"I think I'll just stop and get six beers." Instead, they settled on two Dr. Peppers. They were about to drive off when Dick turned on the radio and bluegrass musician Mack Wiseman was on. Bob turned off the car engine for a moment and the pair sat listening to Mack Wiseman before leaving. "Life doesn't get any better than this," Dick said. When they pulled away, he turned the station again to the VCU basketball game and "just started rattling stats off [the top of] his head," and again said, "It doesn't get much better than this; VCU on the radio and a cold Dr. Pepper." It was special because taking time to stop and the enjoy the moment was an opportunity that they usually didn't have time for.[29]

Many of the memories Dick made with his staff occurred while traveling on the road. For the Obenshain staff, there were almost as many fond memories of Dick as there were hilarious ones of John Warner. Attending many of the same events; Dick, Nathan Miller, and Linwood Holton were usually on time. John Warner usually arrived late, bestowing him the nickname "Johnny-Come-Lately" among Obenshain staffers. "Warner had a real habit of being late. There was eastern time, then there was John Warner time. Part of it was theatrical. Warner knew there is something in making a grand entrance," said field staffer, Henry Doggett. One evening Dick's driver, Brad Cavedo, was driving Dick to a reception in Williamsburg. After dropping off Dick at the front of the building, Brad pulled around to park and accidentally ended up in the receiving line on his way in to the event. When Warner, arriving late, made

---

[29] Hausenfluck interview.

his entrance and came down the line shaking hands with people, Brad Cavedo said, "Oh Mr. Warner, you remember me, I'm Dick's driver." Warner stopped and stared for a moment, then acted as if he remembered and said, "Dick! Good to see ya. Dick Driver, I'm glad you could be here!"[30]

They spent a lot of time driving in the southwest area, as did Linwood Holton. Since a lot of people were attracted to Holton because of his Big Stone Gap roots, Dick appointed his brother Joe to head the campaign in the ninth district, and Joe was able to bring in good results from Montgomery and Pulaski County and Radford. While Joe Obenshain was bringing in votes in the ninth, recently hired Obenshain enthusiast, Gary Byler was utilizing his family connections to bring votes in from Virginia Beach. His father Curly was one of the first major developers in Virginia Beach, and the family had an extensive circle of friends. Many of them might not have been involved in Republican politics for Dick Obenshain but got involved that year to help Gary Byler. The slightly more progressive area of Virginia Beach was mostly slated for Warner, with Holton running a close second. Byler took a semester off from Georgetown and went back to Virginia Beach in order to be a "spike" in the Warner operation. He aimed to water down the Warner vote by running his own campaign for chairman of the Virginia Beach Republican Party, which he won. He used that position to increase the turnout for Dick Obenshain.[31] Also helping him and Dick in Virginia Beach was a popular real estate investor named Dick Short.[32] Short had also assisted Obenshain with the Godwin negotiations years earlier.

Six weeks before the convention, all four candidates were in Harrisonburg at the Young Americans for Freedom (YAF) steak dinner. Obenshain and Miller were both board members for YAF. The Obenshain team accepted the invitation immediately. Holton declined. Warner and Miller also accepted. Bob Hausenfluck explained, "The Obenshain staff wanted to smoke this thing and outnumber the Nathan people with Obenshain supporters attending," while another Obenshain staffer replied, "That ain't going to

---

[30] Doggett interview.
[31] Byler interview.
[32] Mark Short interview, November 9, 2017.

happen, Senator Miller is really liked up here." This assessment was correct. Instead, the staffers accepted that this was Nathan Miller territory and spent the evening befriending all of "the Miller people," who they said were "genuine, decent people."[33]

At the very last minute, Warner reneged on his invitation, which the Obenshain staff was quick to capitalize on. They later sent out a mailer to all of those in attendance with a local headline article titled, "Warner Disappoints Valley Youth." The event was attended by some 200 people, all of whom had been delegates to the previous year's convention. Dick showed up without intending to pull voters away from Miller, which there was a slim chance of doing anyway. Instead, he stole from the Miller playbook and tried to position himself as the best number two option. He spoke in front of the crowd and did the usual, "Great to be here, back where I went to school," routine.

The only two candidates who showed up flipped a coin to see who was going to speak first. Miller won the toss but deferred to Obenshain, so Obenshain approached the podium and spent the majority of his speech talking about what a wonderful state representative Nathan Miller was. It "blew the roof off the Holiday Inn," said Hausenfluck. Nathan got up and said, "Well thank you, Dick." He had prepared himself a speech as to why he should be the nominee, but Dick had already said everything about him, so there was nothing left to talk about. The Obenshain staff made a point to stay in close contact with the delegates from the Shenandoah Valley after that.[34]

While the candidates remained cordial on stage throughout the campaign, some of their staffers and supporters had a strong dislike for their opponents, especially the Obenshain and Holton people, who had been competing with one another for such a long period of time and remembered all of the hurts, victories, and defeats suffered at each other's hands. A lot of the animosity was taking place among the delegates on the field at the county mass meetings. The Obenshain campaign sent one of their operatives to a unit meeting in the City of Hampton, where they often lacked support. The meeting

---

[33] Hausenfluck interview.
[34] Ibid.

started at 7 p.m. and lasted until 4 a.m. The Obenshain supporters won after much back and forth and an extended procedural battle.

Meanwhile, Chairman George McMath was preparing for the upcoming convention by fractionally dividing the delegate votes, which meant that no delegate would have a full vote. He did this to encourage a larger convention in order to build enthusiasm for the party. He came up with a specific formula for dividing the votes for each of the counties and cities. This increased the vote total to 3,081. It was approved by the Republican State Central Committee.

When the first round of attendance numbers came in, McMath ended up with an amount far larger than he had intended. McMath made a call to the Republican National Headquarters to get some advice on how to handle a convention of such size and told them, "We came up with a plan, but we are going to have 8 to 9 thousand delegates. What can you do to help us for organizing this thing?" The response was not what he wanted to hear. The person on the other line at the RNC said, "We've never had a convention that large; we can't help you." George McMath was on his own to figure out how to organize such a massive event. But McMath was selected as state chair because he was a master organizer. His skills would be put to the test.

> "We came up with a plan: we'd have all of the delegates' seats together, and if they said they had 40 delegates we might have only 10 on each row, as voting procedure, we'd have the chair[man] at the end of the row on the aisle, and each of the delegates on each row of the aisle would go and cast their ballot and then go back to their seat. The day before we went into session, we had a meeting with all of the county and city chairmen and gave them instructions on how the voting was going to occur and went through the whole process exactly as to how we were going to get the job done."[35]

By mid-May, loyalty, favors, and hard work over the course of many years finally looked to have paid off in the lead-up to this one moment in time for Obenshain. When he was confident that he had 1200 committed votes, he

---

[35] McMath interview.

turned his attention towards attacking the likely Democratic nominee: his former foe, Andrew Miller. He attacked Andy Miller for not being a "superstar," for being a Carter favorite, and promised him "a real licking" in November. The attacks showed that Obenshain was going to wage a much tougher and more aggressive campaign than he did in 1969. He consistently referred to Andrew Miller as a liberal who tried to hide his true positions.[36]

Since the party had chosen a convention as a nominating method, the four Republicans were battling for 3,081 votes dividing among over twice as many people. As is the typical rule, each vote could be split by five, allowing for more attendees. The party rules also stated that a county convention (which chose delegates to the state convention) could bind all of their delegates to vote for one candidate as a bloc vote. The bloc vote method worked magically for Obenshain and his candidates in 1972, but it was feared that Holton and Warner would turn it into an issue at the convention and move to have the rule rescinded, making them appear as the anti-establishment forces trying to loosen up strict rules, despite those rules having been in place for over a decade. The Warner faction and the waves of people he brought to the convention were also causing an uproar, as a lot of them were new Republicans, unfamiliar with these longstanding rules.

A week before the convention, Obenshain held a news conference in Richmond saying that he was releasing the delegates that had been instructed to vote for him. The decision made sense, as the Warner forces were preparing to wage a passionate attack at the convention. Obenshain was slightly vulnerable to the "elitist" attack after the 1977 campaign had gone awry. But this was a moral win for him, and one that would only cost him around 40 votes. He only had the promise of 1200 votes at this point, with the magic number being 1541 to win. At the conference Obenshain said, "Nothing could do more to destroy GOP unity than to allow a bitter battle."[37] His brother Joe

---

[36] "Miller Promised 'A Real Licking'". *Richmond Times Dispatch.* May 11, 1978.
[37] Latimer, James. "Obenshain Frees Delegates Bound By Instructions." *Richmond Times Dispatch.* May 26, 1978.

reflected, "Dick was wise to release his committed voters. His opponent tried to use that to classify him as a party boss riding rough shot."[38]

His good fortunes continued on May 31st when Governor Mills Godwin officially endorsed Obenshain who he thought "has the best chance of winning the coalition of moderate and conservative Virginians." Governor Godwin remained officially neutral until a day before the great indoor primary, but there was never any doubt that Godwin would endorse Obenshain. The timing of the endorsement had been carefully contrived as a way of building momentum heading into the convention.[39]

---

[38] Joe interview, July 20, 2011.
[39] Latimer, James. "Godwin Supports Obenshain." *Richmond Times Dispatch.* June 1, 1978.

Chapter 17:

A Political Battle Royal

The night of Friday June 2nd, 1978 was filled with excitement and anticipation. Friends, family and neighbors; people from all walks of life, young and old, rich and poor, either drove or were bussed in from all around the state. It was friends against friends. Emotions ran high. It was a frenzy.

Two of Nathan Miller's supporters who were newlyweds postponed their honeymoon just to make it to the convention and cast their vote.[1] Many former Republicans that left the party in 1972, had returned to support Linwood Holton. But it was the Obenshain supporters who were the most passionate. One die-hard Obenshain supporter biked all the way from Norfolk. Another delegate, a college student studying photography printed a large negative image of Obenshain's face, placed the cut out on his skin while tanning and burned a bright image of Obenshain on his back. Another delegate from Roanoke had been diagnosed with cancer and had also just lost her husband.

---

[1] Beck, Jody. "Capital Buldging at the Seams with 8,000 Delegates" *Washington Star.* June 3, 1978.

Yet she made her sister bring her to the convention, and she stayed until the very end, just so that she could vote for Dick Obenshain. Sadly, she passed away a few months later.[2]

Televised news networks from across the country set up their equipment outside the John Marshall Hotel and the Richmond Convention Center, which were only a few blocks from each other. Even some international networks such as the British Broadcasting Corporation (BBC) had sent their reporters to cover the event. The incredible number of attendees only heightened the electricity in the air. The estimates vary, but most counted the total figure at well over 10,000 people: about 8,522 delegates, 1,176 alternates, and hundreds of staff and convention workers, guests, and news crews. Not only was the world watching, but the Republican factions that existed throughout the United States were certainly watching. The emerging neo-conservatives and the Eastern Establishment Republicans undoubtedly had their favorite candidates, as did the Barry Goldwater and Reagan conservatives. Virginia, with its close proximity to Washington D.C., it's off-year election cycles, and its political heritage, had always been a good measuring stick for predicting the future mood of the nation. The reports came in and the Republican Party Chairman George McMath said it was the largest political convention in American history. Possibly in the history of the world. Only primaries could get this kind of turnout, which is why McMath labeled it "The Great Indoor Primary."[3]

Preparing for the massive event had been an enormous task according to the Richmond Coliseum events manager, Grady Mathias. He informed his employees to be ready to work a 24-hour event. Concession stands prepared 14,000 sandwiches for the opening day. Mathias noted that the coliseum contracted with a telephone company that had been working for three straight days finding space and trying to get additional phones ready so that each campaign could conduct their operations in secrecy. One candidate wanted to rent the coliseum management offices while another wanted to rent the coliseum restaurant for extra space. "Every room in this coliseum is

---

[2] Huffman interview.

[3] McMath interview.

occupied…In fact, if we had 10 more rooms we could use them," said Mathias. The vote-counting rooms themselves were locker rooms which used the large showers to store tally sheets and signs. Holton's people used their large shower as a conference room, complete with a ten-foot table inside.

Approximately three thousand hotel rooms were filled. Most were booked from Ashland to Petersburg. Finding available parking close to the coliseum was next to impossible and most delegates had to be bused in. A few days before, there was a crisis regarding the delegate's badges. Too many last-minute delegates and alternates were added to the attendee list, which had to be entered into a private firm's computer database. The rushed entries resulted in many misspellings which had to be corrected. This tedious task was essential to properly identifying the delegates. Even worse, the original number of printed badges for delegates was short by nearly 2,000. The total delegate lists were entered late on Thursday night and the remaining badges were finally shipped on Friday morning. This avoided what could have been an organizational catastrophe.[4]

On Friday afternoon, arriving in front of a 100-car motorcade, John Warner stepped out of his limousine donning red and blue suspenders accompanied by Elizabeth Taylor wearing a sailor hat, blue jeans, and a Warner campaign t-shirt. The crowd erupted. Together they greeted their fans for a noon rally outside of their hotel. The crowd swarmed around them. Eyes were locked on Taylor while ears were fixed on Warner's welcoming speech.[5] The pair stole the show again that evening at the hotel ballroom where they made another appearance. Many wanted to get a glimpse of the star couple. There were certainly many delegates in attendance who wouldn't mind having a little bit of Hollywood as a permanent fixture in Virginia politics.

Friday evening was composed of congressional district meetings, last minute strategizing, and heavy drinking before the big day. Straw polls were taken. Many were close, but one in particular favored Obenshain as the strongest candidate by 65%. The four candidates spoke at each congressional meeting. Holton's final pitch accentuated that ex-governors are the most

---

[4] Beck,"Capital Buldging at the Seams with 8,000 Delegates." June 3, 1978.
[5] Ibid.

effective senators; he also made an apology, all too late, for not appointing more Republicans during his time as governor. Warner kept his speech light-hearted and fairly lackluster. Obenshain talked about how liberalism was failing the country and articulated his political philosophy. Miller emphasized his youth and energy.

The four Senate hopefuls also hosted parties in their suites at the John Marshall building, which was customary for candidates to do the night before a convention. Dick had a suite on the top floor of the John Marshall to host his supporters, friends, and family. Bill Hurd, who organized the event, said, "We were trying to get every opportunity to interact with a large number of delegates and demonstrate the campaign's strength to those delegates to either reinforce or change their opinion."[6]

In between shaking hands and convincing attendees, the Obenshain family made many memories that Friday night before the convention. During the party, Dick's sister-in-law Marsha presented Dick with a poster of himself that she wanted him to sign. "He looked at me like I was crazy," she said. "I want you to do it for Kathryn [Dick's niece], you know, for posterity." Dick obliged and wrote on his own poster a note to his niece which said, "To Kathryn, a true friend of the free market economy." A photographer captured this moment of Dick talking to his young niece. The photo gave Mark Obenshain the idea for Dick's campaign slogan "Obenshain Listens To Virginia." Joe and Marsha stayed at Dick's house later that night, and Dick's daughter, Kate, proudly showed them a letter her dad had given her the night before while she was sleeping. After he had come home late from the campaign, he took the time to write a note which read, "Dear Kate, I love your new haircut," and continued to express about how much he loved her. They fondly remembered, "With everything he had going on, people pulling him in different directions, he took the time to write his ten-year-old daughter a note."[7] It was a touching display of calmness before the approaching convention chaos, and the culmination of his life's work.

---

[6] Hurd interview.

[7] Marsha interview.

Nathan Miller's team also had a reception that night, followed by a covert operation delivering look-alike "Time" magazine covers to hotel rooms that had a picture of Nathan on the cover and a caption that read "The Man of the Hour." "I had to get something to grab their attention," said Miller.[8]

On Saturday morning, while most of the attendees slept quietly in their rooms, the Obenshain campaign was hard at work. "I remember getting up super early," said Kate.[9] While the other campaigns were telling the delegates that the nomination would be finalized early after three ballots, the Obenshain campaign staffers slipped a newsletter under the room doors at the John Marshall Hotel that prepared delegates to expect a long and epic day with multiple ballots. Obenshain's newsletter assured victory in the end, but the purpose of the letter was intended prevent his supporters from leaving prematurely. One of Warner's staffers picked up the newsletter that morning and considered it a desperate plea by a desperate campaign.

The Obenshain staff assembled another group that morning. A team of five volunteers, led by Bill Klinge (no relation to Kenny Klinge), running a newsletter operation inside the John Marshall Hotel. Bill Klinge was a journalist from northern Virginia and knew how to operate a press on a mini-graph machine. The team was responsible for printing off a newsletter as new endorsements were coming in and to send them down to the convention floor during the voting. John Paul Woodley recalled having to run between the John Marshall building and the Convention building trying to track down Kenny Klinge for approval before each print.

> "I remember the look of annoyance on Kenny's face every time I found him. We wanted to get an issue out between each ballot. There was no time to lose. But he had to clear it, make sure it wasn't going to cause problems, and make sure it wasn't going to offend anybody. Highlighting the changing sides, we had to make sure it wouldn't make someone else against us. We printed about ten of these. It was like

---

[8] N. Miller interview.
[9] Kate interview.

factory work; I don't think we slept, I don't think we ate. We were working very hard."[10]

People began arriving at the Coliseum at 8:00 a.m. Various interest groups and campaign workers stood outside the front doors waiting to hand out their candidate's literature or their group's points of interest. A white banner could be seen stretching across one of the doors which read "Young Americans For Freedom," a group that had given Dick Obenshain an award the previous year. Beside them, a banner with a red background and white letters read "Obenshain" across the top with a picture of Dick smiling, holding his eyewear by the temple, caught in the active motion of removing them.

As delegates and guests shuffled inside, they were greeted by a line of tables ready to register them to the event. "It was tightly run, and commended for its impeccable organization," said Chairman George McMath.[11] After being handed their official "delegate" name tag the attendees were then bombarded by an army of volunteers flashing their candidates' signs and distributing pamphlets. Dicks signs were red, with a large "O" in the middle with his last name at the bottom, a concept that was designed by his driver, Brad Cavedo, but slightly altered by the campaign "board."[12] Obenshain supporters were handed clickers which made a "cricket" noise when utilized in mass. Bill Hurd explained, "We found them at a bunch of Halloween stores; they were little metal shells that would bend and click when you pushed on it. We thought we had to have something for people to express their support for our campaign."[13]

As the convention assembled, the most ardent fans could be seen wearing odd-looking hats with their candidate's name placed on the front. Warner hired a Virginia Beach group called Mr. Flim Flam's Singing Telegrams to randomly sing "Hello Dolly" to wandering attendees. Others brought stuffed Republican elephants along with their own makeshift pins, shirts, and signs. Those with blue and green hats that said, "Win Again With Lin" kept their distance from those wearing pins which said, "Kiss Me, I'm for Obenshain."

---

[10] Woodley interview.
[11] McMath interview.
[12] Cavedo interview.
[13] Hurd interview.

Those taking themselves more seriously arrived in formal attire despite the heat. Inside, the convention was just as hot from the thousands of people scurrying about. "The convention for me was like being at a rock concert," said attendee Carthan Currin.[14] It was indeed a spectacle.

Regardless of whether Obenshain won or not, he had to have been proud looking out across a sea of Republican voters, a sight that was unimaginable just several years ago. His dream had been to have this opportunity, but his life's work of realignment had manifested itself before his eyes on this day. For a man whose political and theocratic philosophy had placed an emphasis on the power of individual choices, Dick must have been pleased at having made the right choices to lead him to this moment.

At 10:00 a.m. the delegates took to their seats. Dick made his way to the top middle rafters where his own Chesterfield delegation was being seated. People were yelling his name, wanting to shake his hand and talk to him as he made his way up the steps. Many were shouting with signs and banners above, but the distractions below kept him from seeing the fans in the nosebleed sections. Brad Cavedo said to him, "Dick, wave to all of your supporters up there." Dick looked up, smiled, and waved to all of those in the stands above him. The moment was captured by a photographer with the Richmond News Leader and was used in the headline the next day.[15]

The rest of the Obenshain campaign split into two groups: those down below working the convention floor, and those in the stands communicating with the delegates. Wyatt Durrette was Dick's floor leader. Judy Peachee was above, directing the team's activities. A young political consultant, many have now heard of named Paul Manafort, was also brought in by the campaign to assist with the floor operation. His future consulting partner Roger Stone, was also in attendance as a floor leader for the 10th Congressional District.

George McMath was having conversations with all of the candidates, keeping them informed with procedural action and what was taking place. McMath also came up with the idea to have a documentary film team cover the

---

14 Currin interview.

15 Cavedo interview.

convention. John Dalton and Bill Royal were in the governor's boxed seat above. "It was a pumped atmosphere, it was something to see," said Royal.[16] Weldon Tuck, who began the campaign working for Dick, was accompanying Senator Bill Scott near the top of the stadium. They weren't active participants but merely observers. Tuck recalled Scott's wife knitting the entire time. Dick's former driver, Stan Maupin, was working for Marshall Coleman, observing the events from a skybox seat above as well. John Alderson recalled what it was like being in the strategy room above with Peachee, "We had to make a lot of personal visits and come back with a report. We went all day without eating."[17] Bill Hurd was also in the strategy room, which he called, "The Crow's Nest." "We had a section where we could see things, we had walkie talkies. It was a vote counting operation where people were assigned to go and talk to certain people and find out who they were leaning for and what we had to do to get them."[18] To their surprise, some Holton supporters had Dick as their second choice going in that day. The Holton people felt that Dick had "paid his dues." The Crows Nest would also send their staffers down to motivate people. The staffers tasked with these jobs wore Obenshain hats so that they could be spotted in the crowd.

Around mid-morning the coliseum attendees began to settle down. A large mysterious black screen was lowered behind the podium from the top of the stadium and loomed in the background. Governor John Dalton gave the opening first speech calling for unity after what promised to be a very long and hard day. The Republican National Committee Chairman delivered the keynote speech, emphasizing the need to return all hope to the U.S. Congress as opposed to one man, i.e. the president. As a result of Obenshain releasing his committed delegates a few days before, the convention rules for the day were passed with no objections. Everyone viewed the competition that day as a fair fight. Convention Chairman and State Senator Herb Bateman, a parliamentarian genius, ran the convention smoothly. Bateman predicted, along with McMath, that the convention would continue until Sunday.

---

[16] Royal interview.
[17] Alderson interview.
[18] Hurd interview.

Next were the nominating speeches. Congressman Bill Whitehurst from the 2nd Congressional District provided the nominating speech for Linwood Holton and used his popularity as an attempt to cut into Warner's lead in that district. Each candidate was allowed to have a demonstration afterward, which was a visual way of displaying support for the candidate. Holton had a small group march to the podium chanting "We Want Lin." Former 10th District Congressman Joel Broyhill from northern Virginia gave the nominating speech for John Warner. Warner himself came on stage to second his own nomination. Warner's demonstration was a little more exciting. Warner's march included himself and Elizabeth Taylor, wearing a sailor's cap, marching around the building to "Anchor's Away," the official Naval Academy fight song.

Dick was next. Former Governor Mills Godwin gave the nominating speech, crediting Obenshain as being the architect of the realignment, statewide election victories, and the modern Republican Party. Obenshain was seconded by a local doctor named James Wendell Bean, an African-American who commented that Democrats "far too long have taken black American's for granted," and ended with, "Lets send Dick to the Senate!"[19] Bill Hurd was in charge of the demonstration and sent thousands down to storm the front of the podium; a sea of red signs with large "O"s could be seen everywhere. Chants of "We Want Dick" continued for several minutes and erupted in waves throughout the rest of the day even after the demonstration had ended.[20]

Nathan Miller took an unorthodox approach. A few weeks before the convention his team rented a large screen from the Virginia Museum of Fine Arts. This was the screen that had confused many of the delegates for the past several hours. Rather than having a speaker, Miller's team prepared a fifteen-minute video introducing the state senator to the crowd, again fashioning him as the Man of the Hour, along with clips from his announcement speech. The coliseum darkened. The audio-visual presentation began and after several minutes finished with "the future is now-Miller is next." Nathan Miller walked up to the podium and the lights came back on. It was theatrical and dramatic.

---

19 "Obenshain Leads on Fourth Ballot." *Richmond Times Dispatch*. June 4, 1978.
20 Hurd interview.

After the presentation a group of his supporters marched down below in the same fashion that the other candidates had arranged. His signs were amazingly similar to Obenshain's, with white letters across a red backdrop at the top and a black and white portrait of the candidate below.

The first ballot was circulated at 12:00 p.m. Two and a half hours later the results trickled in. Convention staffers counted the votes individually by counties first, then would report by congressional districts. "One district had someone who voted for Elizabeth Taylor's first husband, Eddie Fisher, then on the next ballot it was Richard Burton; it got to be real funny as they reported it on the microphone each time," said Stan Maupin, who was way up in the nosebleed section of the coliseum with Governor John Dalton. Elizabeth Taylor could be seen putting her hands in her face as the crowd burst out in laughter. "She seemed to be having fun with it; who knows how she felt deep down" said Stan.[21] Other than that, it was of no surprise that Obenshain finished first and received almost 1,200 votes. However, he came up a few votes shorter than he had predicted, which made him slightly uneasy. Warner and his army of new Republicans came in second with 853 votes, followed by Holton at 780 and Miller at 252. Obenshain reflected back to his first political convention in 1952, when he learned the unpredictable turns a convention can take. He wondered how many delegates would heed his warning from that morning: "do not leave until this is over for sure." After the first ballot, the candidates made a few rounds around the building, greeting delegates and attempting to convince those who may be on the fence. Campaign staffers also spent their time greeting delegates while also counting and recounting projected vote totals in their "control rooms." "I knew it was over for me [after the first ballot]," said Holton, "but I went through the motions of visiting several delegations in the stands, seeking support based on what I proclaimed was my best asset: the ability to win the general election in November. But the only positive reaction I got was from one little group who promised I would gain one hundred votes on the next ballot if I would announce support for their anti-abortion position." Holton said he took inner satisfaction in declining the

---

[21] Maupin interview.

offer.[22] John Warner used this interim to motivate his base by standing up and waving his Navy hat to the crowd in between each vote tally.

As the second ballot was nearing an end, the main question centered around who would finish in second place and who would continue on to the third round. If either Warner or Holton dropped out now and gave their votes to the other, one of them could potentially win. If Miller dropped out and released his delegates, that would likely put Obenshain within reach of the 1541 votes needed to win. The Obenshain and Warner campaigns were frequently meeting with the Miller campaign throughout the day, "They've both promised me the coliseum and everything in it. But I want votes. I'm sticking [in it]," said Nathan Miller.[23]

No candidate would drop out and none would gain much momentum. At 4:00 the second vote was tallied. Obenshain gained almost 70 new votes while Warner also gained about 55. Holton lost almost 30 votes and Miller experienced the largest drop of 93 votes, most of which likely went to Obenshain. It was rumored that Obenshain, Warner, and Holton told some of their most trusted delegates to vote for Miller on the first ballot and then switch their votes on the second ballot as a way of building the perception of having momentum.

Dickenson County was giving Obenshain a lot of problems over in the 9th Congressional District. They were almost unanimously for Holton. If Dick could manage to peel away some of their votes, others in the 9th might begin to follow, but this did not happen either.

Obenshain was strongest in the 3rd Congressional District where he resided, with the exception of Richmond which was a stronghold for Holton and Warner. He also did well in southern Virginia. He split with Holton in the 9th district, where they were both raised. In the 6th near the northern Shenandoah Valley, Obenshain split with Nathan Miller, but he had a surprising

---

22 Holton, p. 185.
23 Rosenfeld, Megan. "Politics, Show Biz, And Cast of 10,000." *The Washington Post*, June 4, 1978.

show of strength up in the northern Virginia districts, where he carried about 30%. As expected, Warner was strong in the Navy-heavy areas of Virginia Beach.

Obenshain's delegates, like him, were determined. They were the most die-hard supporters in the building that day. The conservatives had found their leader—their own Ronald Reagan. He had done all he could do over the course of many years to get here; now it was up to his friends and supporters to carry him through.

The third vote was taken shortly after 4:00 p.m. Supporters from all campaigns were beginning to get hot, tired, and cranky. It was turning into a battle of will, as most groups were pretty entrenched. Wyatt Durrette said, "It was exhausting. I was constantly doing something. We were trying to decide where to focus people. Who's wavering? Who's going to talk to us?"[24]

As the votes came in, Obenshain increased his vote totals again, as did Warner. The total vote count now stood at: Obenshain 1,338; Warner 996; Holton 520; Miller 122.

Many thought Nathan Miller would quit, but it was Governor Holton who bowed out of the competition first. He gave a speech in which he echoed Henry Howell, saying, "Let the convention work its will." As he gave his speech, many Holton supporters could be seen crying and visibly angry. If Holton and Warner had merged their forces more effectively it may have resulted in a win for either man, forcing Obenshain out of the race.

On the surface, Holton seemed to have gracefully accepted his role as an "elder statesman," but behind the scenes he and his people were upset. Obenshain and Warner factions swarmed the freed-up delegates, vying for their support. One disappointed Holton supporter told an Obenshain supporter named Boyd Marcus, "You may have won this battle, but you will lose the war."[25] Another Warner supporter was overheard saying "you don't want to vote for Obenshain and all [of] those born again Christians they've got in with them, do you?". A visibly upset Holton supporter shouted to a Warner

---

24 Durrette interview.
25 Currin interview.

supporter, "Get out of here, leave me alone, I mean it!"[26] Even though Holton didn't tell his supporters what to do, many feared that they were encouraged to support his friend, John Warner. If this was attempted, it was not entirely transparent in the results that followed.

Ray Garland, who made an unsuccessful attempt at the U.S. Senate against Harry Byrd, Jr., was a Holton supporter from Roanoke, but was one of those who respected Dick and came over to his side after Holton dropped out. The Dickenson County delegation also threw their support behind Obenshain. They remembered the "black satchel" case back in 1969 when Dick provided the legal defense for several local party officials free of charge.

The 1st Congressional District was holding strong for Obenshain thanks to a waterman named Carol Prosdale. He was overseeing seven counties on the eastern shore within that district. In the 2nd district, Gary Byler had successfully turned many of the Holton supporters into Obenshain supporters.

Many thought that the fourth ballot was sure to give Obenshain the victory, but it didn't happen. He only picked up 170 of Holton's 620 freed-up votes. His total was now at 1,521. Just 20 votes away from being one step closer to the prize he had sought since his youth. It was on this fourth ballot that things began to happen—or didn't happen, depending on who you ask. The convention was now going into the early evening. Some were beginning to go home. Obenshain staff tried relentlessly to maintain their lead. Dick's son Mark remembered feeling nervous, "walking up and down the corridor in the underground section of the Colosseum."[27] The biggest concern was that a lot of the older delegates, who had further to travel back home, were from the 9th Congressional District in southwest Virginia, which were predominantly Obenshain voters now that Holton had dropped out. Warner gained a whopping 342 votes on the fourth ballot. The vote count now stood at Obenshain 1,521; Warner 1,338; Miller 201.

Despite Miller having picked up nearly eighty votes, Judy Peachee was confident that his supporters were not as committed as Obenshain's, and she

---

[26] Beck,"Capital Buldging at the Seams with 8,000 Delegates." June 3, 1978.
[27] Mark interview.

held onto the view that Dick would win on the next ballot, seeing that he was now so close to reaching that pinnacle amount. This didn't stop many on the Obenshain side from fuming at Miller. Obenshain supporters were shouting at Miller supporters. Some told Nathan Miller himself not to come to their county looking for support in the future. "Nathan, take my word please, we will stay here until hell freezes over. Nobody is going to desert Dick; we love him. You're crazy, it ain't going to happen," Durrette said to his friend and colleague in the General Assembly.[28] Miller now felt emboldened now in the belief that his dark horse strategy might truly work.

While Miller remained in the battle royal, it was essentially down to Obenshain and Warner, with Warner gaining momentum. After a lull period, the atmosphere began to rustle again. Had C-SPAN been established a year earlier, this would have been a popcorn-worthy event. It was getting more intense.

Obenshain's long-awaited victory was but a handful of votes away. A swarm of what sounded like locusts could be heard during the count as the Obenshain people reaffirmed their support with their clickers. The crowd began to cheer in perfect harmony and rhythm, "Obenshain! Obenshain! Obenshain!" Then, "We Want Warner" emerged from the midst of the crowd and overtook the convention stadium.

Warner's campaign manager convinced him that in order to sway the momentum he needed to go on the convention floor and wave his jacket around his head. Conventions are like circuses, anything and everything might work to change the tide. So he did it. It was not characteristic of Warner's reserved nature as he came onto the floor looking like a war general firing up the crowd. His campaign manager told him to wave his jacket around one time, but Warner did several times as the crowd reacted positively to his wild display of emotion.

The concession stands ran out of food and drink; they weren't prepared for the event to go on this long either. Joe's wife Marsha was one of the most uncomfortable delegates in the building. She was pregnant with their son Chris

---

[28] Durrette interview.

at the time. The day was excruciating for her as well, "Dick was busy working the crowd. Helen was busy communicating with floor leaders. Marsha was [sick] in the bathroom…they'd have to find her and tell her to come back out and vote," Joe fondly remembered.[29]

Meanwhile, Obenshain remained in the strategy room with his team. He could hear the roars from the crowd and the "We Want Warner" chants. In this moment, one of his friends decided to take him aside and said, "Dick, we need to pray." They closed the door in a small room and began to pray for several minutes. This was a welcomed moment of peace amidst a constant storm of loud commotion. Before they could finish, a staff member pounded on the door before rushing in and shouting, "Come on out, Dick. We need you right away!" The staffers were growing worried about how slow the vote counts were coming in. Obenshain stepped outside to look upon the thousands of delegates who were still there after nearly twelve hours and said, "Goodness gracious, I'm surprised we're getting any totals at all." Obenshain joined the public and returned to his seat up in the rafters. A friend from Fairfax, Delegate Guy Farley Jr., escorted Dick through the crowd and before departing with him, Farley whispered, "God is on your side."[30]

On the fifth ballot, now going well into the evening, the votes came in. Dick had lost several votes and Warner had gained 55. The totals were now Obenshain 1,516; Warner 1,393; Miller 166. It looked like the momentum was shifting. Fear for Obenshain supporters set in for the first time the entire evening, although Dick said that he "was worried all day and night."[31] Obenshain supporters who were older were beginning to leave. Many were beginning to wonder how long this would go on, and it was the first time all day that Obenshain had lost votes while Warner had gained a tremendous amount, not from Obenshain supporters but from Nathan Miller's. The longer the deadlock continued the stronger Warner became. Little did anyone know

---

[29] Joe interview, July 20, 2011.
[30] Atkinson, p. 409.
[31] Rolfe, Shelley. "Obenshain Won't Shift His Ground." *Richmond Times Dispatch.* June 15, 1978.

that Nathan had given the Warner campaign his word earlier that he would not drop out of the race.

"It's in the Miller vote," Dick Lobb overheard Governor Godwin saying.[32] By this time, Mills Godwin had lost his patience with Nathan Miller. The elder statesman was an intimidating force and had a presence of authority that surrounded him. When he spoke, people listened. He marched over to the Miller campaign room, and while some described him as "persuading" Nathan to drop out, it was more like commanding him to. Others had visited Nathan Miller throughout the day and delivered the same message but without the same impact as Godwin. That message clear: Nathan had a bright future in politics, but if he wanted to keep that future he'd better drop out. Nathan seriously pondered on that for a while, and he learned that Godwin didn't ask you what to do, he told you what to do.

Nathan Miller decided that since he was now losing votes and didn't want to be a spoiler in the race, that perhaps it was best to end his campaign. He conceded shortly after. Judy Peachee contended that if Nathan hadn't withdrawn, his support would have fallen apart regardless. With his support already cracking, remaining in the race would have been an even bigger blow to his future in the party.[33] Like Holton, when Nathan withdrew, he chose not to endorse either Warner or Obenshain.

Bob Hausenfluck rushed over to the 7th District delegation with a bunch of Obenshain lapels in hand. He began passing them out to everyone in the stands and greeted those he had met several months before during the Young Americans for Freedom dinner that he attended. "Remember me?" he kept saying, reminding them that Obenshain had attended their event when Warner did not.[34]

Underneath the floor of the convention, the Warner team gathered together and discussed the possibility of trying to delay the next vote using parliamentary procedural rules. The strategy was that since many of

---

[32] Lobb interview.
[33] Wason interview.
[34] Hausenfluck interview.

Obenshain's supporters were religious, especially from the Shenandoah Valley, they would soon be going home to honor the Sabbath. These Obenshain supporters would not remain in the building if the Warner campaign could delay the next vote until midnight. The move would have ensured a Warner victory. After a heated discussion, John Warner rejected the idea and let the sixth ballot proceed.[35]

The final vote was taken around 10:00 p.m. At this point delegates had been at the convention center for close to fourteen hours. The votes began to trickle in, and the numbers looked much the same as they had all evening, with the Warner and Obenshain battle getting tighter. The crowd was anxious. People could be seen standing with their fingers crossed as the votes were counted. Dick sat patiently talking to reporters from the stands.

Obenshain's campaign was confident that at least half of Nathan Miller's leftovers would switch to their camp. It continued to be a nail biter until Fairfax County's vote totals came in and Obenshain was launched well over the 1,541 votes needed, marking an end to one of the longest, largest, and most intense political conventions the world had ever seen. The final vote tally put Obenshain at 1,579 to Warner's 1,472, with a few protest votes remaining for Holton and Miller.

Fortunately, the moment Obenshain reached the top was captured on video. People patted him on the back and raced to be the first to congratulate him, but the first thing he did when he stood up was to hug his wife, Helen. It had been a shared adventure, with endless ups and downs over the years. It was not a journey that any spouse could handle with as much grace, understanding, and enthusiasm as Helen had. She had been his rock on the home front through the whole journey, and now he had done it. He did it the right way, from the ground up, through sweat and tears, honesty, long hours, long trips and long nights. It paid off in that moment. It was a victory for the both of them. As Joe Obenshain put it, "[it]was not the result of chance, but was something he had

[35] Atkinson, p.410.

devoted the whole course of his life to and had worked for and stuck to throughout his career."[36]

John Warner took to the podium and moved to make the decision unanimous. In a gracious speech, he commended Holton as a great elder statesman, Nathan Miller for being a great state senator with a future and Obenshain for being a great future U.S. Senator.

Finally, at 12:01 a.m. Sunday morning, Dick and Helen made their way up to the stage clutching each other by the hand. Anne recalled seeing the enormous amount of people going down to the floor after they called his name. "It felt good; it really brought into focus how big what he was doing outside of us really was."[37] With his family, friends and supporters all gathering, Obenshain gave his acceptance speech, in which he said, "the deepest, longest, most exciting, most tenacious competition we've ever had in Virginia...the greatness of this party, the reason we've been stacked here to the rafters with this enthusiasm, is because of our commitment to the great historic fundamental principles of Virginia, and thousands of Virginians are here today because of that commitment of our party, and thousands and thousands more are waiting around the state of Virginia for this campaign to take to them the message of the principles and the strengths that the Republican Party of Virginia offers to this state and also offers for constructive leadership to the United States of America."[38] His daughter Kate recalled, "I loved hearing him speak. I never wanted him to stop speaking; I just loved listening to him, and I understood the spirit. The only other person who had that effect on me as a speaker was Ronald Reagan. He reminded me of my father…mesmerizing, the captivating skill that he had that is so rare and unique. It seemed like an extension of him. It never surprised me to see him up there; he was definitely a firebrand in the spirit of Patrick Henry."[39] As he finished his speech, he grabbed Helen's hand again and raised it to the air in victory.

---

[36] Joe interview, July 20, 2011.
[37] Anne interview.
[38] Convention Video on file with the Republican Party of Virginia.
[39] Kate interview.

Nobody slept before 3 a.m. that night. Joe Obenshain recalled, "It was almost the most stressful day I ever had in my life at that point because it was so back and forth." The three brothers, Dick, Scott, and Joe, all shared a beer together and joined the rest of the family for steak and eggs.[40]

---

[40] Joe interview, July 20, 2011.

Chapter 18:

A Spirit of Fire

"He had charisma, conviction—real fire in his soul about what he was doing…and he could get that across to people," said Lawrence Lewis Jr. "The fire that burned inside him—the passion that stirred inside him and guided his unrelenting efforts—was philosophical more than partisan," said Frank Atkinson.[1] "Dick was one of those folks who was in it for the right reasons. He wasn't in it for fame. He had this incredible personality to go along with it," said Wyatt Durrette.[2] These and many other qualities are what helped him win the nomination the morning of Sunday, June 4th.

On a day typically reserved as a day of rest for the Obenshain family and many Virginians, Dick wasted no time beginning his campaign and hit the the ground running. Folks gathered early on the morning of June 4th for a victory breakfast at the John Marshall building, many without a wink of sleep from all of the celebration. Not all were thrilled with his nomination. The unity

---

1 Atkinson, p. 267-268.
2 Durrette interview.

breakfast was organized as a way of bringing together all of the groups and factions that had battled the day before. Even Linwood Holton attended. He remembered,

> "It was tough to lose, but it had been a positive campaign—no mudslinging—and all of us remained friends. Jinks and I didn't hesitate to join the 'unity' breakfast the Obenshain folks scheduled for the John Marshall Hotel on Sunday morning following his nomination Saturday Night. We didn't expect that Warner and Taylor would appear but, somewhat to our surprise, they were getting out of a car in front of us when we pulled up to the hotel. As we moved from the street to the hotel, Elizabeth leaned over to Jinks and whispered, with her unity smile in full glow, 'Shit Jinks—just shit!' and so the candidates went in, all smiles and charm, to the unity breakfast."[3]

Whatever their true thoughts were, the candidates appeared good-natured about the loss. John Warner made good on his promise the night before and handed Dick a check for $1,000 to kick-off his campaign. "Dick won fair and square," he said. "It was midnight at the ballot. I went to a quickly arranged fundraiser the next morning. I know I made two appearances with him, and I know I did speeches for him."[4]

As a way of bringing his opponents to the table and making them feel as though they had a stake in his campaign, Dick established the group "Friends of Dick Obenshain" and appointed Linwood Holton, Nathan Miller, John Warner, and Mills Godwin as honorary co-chairs of the group. The group was also chaired by former Democrat Delegate Roy Smith, Congressman Caldwell Butler of Roanoke, and former Democrat Delegate French Slaughter.

Next, the campaign established their symbol. Dick chose an "O" with the state of Virginia drawn inside to reflect that he was thinking of all Virginians. His slogan became "Obenshain Listens to Virginia" after an internal campaign poll confirmed that the most important thing to voters was that they wanted to be heard by their elected representatives.

---

[3] Holton, p. 187.
[4] Warner interview, April 30, 2012.

Dick's son Mark developed the slogan the night before the convention and was beginning to take more of an interest in politics and policy himself; he remembered learning all about supply-side economics and the Kemp-Roth tax plan. He once asked his father who he would have supported if he hadn't won the nomination, but Dick refused to answer, saying he was running because he believed that he was the best candidate.[5]

The momentum Dick had after the convention was astonishing. It was the result of years of effort converging at one time. As a result, the campaign moved at break-neck speed. They began hiring more staffers and were finally able to pay other staffers who had been working for free, such as Gary Byler. They added a scheduler, Rene Maxey, as well as a few field staffers, like Henry Doggett. Others were "loaned" to the campaign by Governor John Dalton, such as Dick Lobb and Steve Mahan. The campaign also continued to receive counsel from a "board" that had been a part of the Obenshain group for many years. In addition to that, Obenshain inspired an army of volunteers and those willing to provide free travel by plane or a free place to stay for the night during long and late trips. This was crucial to the campaign as raising money had been their biggest obstacle at the time.

As the campaign began to focus their attention on the general election, they paid an outside consulting firm to conduct research on what the campaign needed to do in order to win. Staff called it the "Finkelstein" report, named after the consulting firm. The study concluded that; Obenshain still had a name recognition problem with the general public, that Miller was not a polarizing figure, that there were limited finances for the Republican Party, that there was still a mostly conservative financial establishment that had to be convinced into donating to an individual candidate and finally that Obenshain couldn't overcome his name identification problem without the support of this financial establishment. Regarding his opponent, Andy Miller, whom he had lost an election to nearly a decade ago, the study found that Miller was no longer seen as an invincible candidate after his loss to Henry Howell in 1977. Yet, he was able to bounce back in 1978 as he defeated a handful of other contenders for

---

[5] Mark interview.

the Democrat Senate nomination. Using the Finkelstein report the campaign reached these conclusions:

1. Miller was well known but perceived as standing for little, which made him vulnerable to a candidate that took a hard stance on issues.

2. A direct attack on Miller would backfire and make Obenshain look like a right-wing zealot.

3. For the same reasons, he shouldn't directly attack President Carter's policies.

4. Obenshain needed to show great understanding of the issues and create a positive image with the press.[6]

Miller's vagueness as a candidate was noted on one of his campaign pamphlets, which said that America should, "recognize our enemies," "respect human rights," and "reduce conflict whenever possible."[7]

The report put the contest into focus. In order to win, Obenshain needed to first gain the financial support that he needed and then use that support to raise his name identification with voters, take a strong and intelligent position on the issues, refrain from any attacks on Miller or Carter, and warm up to the press, which frequently referred to him as an "ultra-conservative." That title angered him. He never understood why the press never labeled Henry Howell an "ultra-liberal."

The first point of action proved to be difficult for raising money outside of the state, but a little easier with the Richmond financial establishment, who already knew who Obenshain was. Right after the convention Obenshain rejected money from various pharmaceutical companies that vied for his attention, which would have provided a good boost to his campaign.[8]

He made the Roth-Kemp tax bill the center of his campaign and vocalized his desire to reduce the income tax by 33% over a three-year period

---

[6] Virkler, p. 124.
[7] "Miller is Called Fuzzy on Issues." *Richmond News Leader.* April 24, 1978.
[8] Byler interview.

and thought economics were the key issue of the year. His strong position on taxes won him the essential support of the Richmond establishment early in the campaign. This allowed just enough money to perform a ten-day, thirty second radio advertising blitz scheduled in July. The radio spots featured leading figures in each region including Dalton, Holton, Godwin, and others. Dick used the same strategies that he had previously used to get others elected.[9]

Next, the campaign suggested that the candidate begin to appeal more to voters who were in the center of the political aisle while also changing his appearance to look more modern. This was no easy task. Judy hired a marketing consultant from Richmond who suggested a few things while Dick Lobb helped Obenshain refine his speeches a little bit to sound more appealing to a general audience. "Judy tried to get him away from wearing the glasses or [to] change the look of his glasses. They had to talk him into it," said Renee Maxey. Begrudgingly, he went with a new pair of wire rim glasses.[10] He might not have liked it at first, but his daughter Kate may have changed his mind. "He walked through the front door one evening and I ran with all of my might and jumped into his arms and told him how much I liked his new glasses. We were all aware that the time that he was home was very special," Kate remembers fondly.[11]

Bob Hausenfluck and Gary Byler recalled policy meetings regarding agricultural subsidies. Agriculture was a big part of the Virginia economy, and some farmers relied on those subsidies. "He [Dick] hated agricultural subsidies," Gary recalled, but they tried to get him on board with just a few. "Ya'll are trying to make a liberal out of me!" he shouted. Eventually, he agreed to support two small incremental subsidies. While maintaining his strong conservative streak on most issues, he came out with some policy positions that were unique and often creative.[12] The primary objective was to provide an opinion on as many issues as possible in order to contrast himself with Andy Miller's perceived lack of position. Obenshain advocated for having the federal government cover 80% of the bill for a D.C. Metrorail system, called for greater coal-related technology, saying standard of living should not be dependent on

---

[9] Atkinson, p. 417.
[10] Renee Maxey, interview September 23, 2017.
[11] Kate interview.
[12] Byler interview.

foreign sources, believed in college tuition tax credits in order to encourage middle-class families to pursue higher education, endorsed arms reductions, criticized Carter's approach to S.A.L.T (not Carter himself as advised, though later he did attack Carter for having the Saratoga built in Philadelphia instead of Newport News, which he said would weaken privately owned shipyards and cost thirty million dollars more), called for a constitutional amendment requiring a balanced budget, like the requirement in Virginia, and even reached out to groups that he knew would not endorse him.

He had a meeting with AFL-CIO leaders and planned to speak to their group in late August. Regarding the meeting, the AFL-CIO President said, "His presence, humor, and candor were appreciated by the assembled labor leaders." Dick made "a mutual commitment with labor to assure greater economic growth, despite disagreement on specific political issues.[13] The campaign also made arrangements for him to speak with leaders of the 7th District Black Caucus in Winchester, and at the Virginia Education Association PAC, a group that never supported Republicans. When asked about his unusual decisions, he said he'd "be delighted with teachers' endorsement, but I'm not playing that game…I don't have any inflated expectations ...I prefer a one on one approach with voters but will accept invitations from any groups."[14] He would essentially go anywhere and speak to anyone and everyone. He said he preferred a one-on-one approach to reaching voters, adding that, "all hard-working Virginians," are interested in improving the economy and have ideas. [15]

His schedule was intense but Brad Cavedo noted that he always seemed relaxed. In fact, the whole staff noticed his calm nature. "He was always nice and pleasant, I never saw a temper or a negative side of him at all. He was kind and gentleman-like, and only positive," said Renee Maxey.[16] Gary Byler said, "I addressed him as sir; he didn't like that. He said, 'if you keep calling me sir I'm going to start calling you Peppermint Patty!'" (in reference to the Peanuts and Peppermint Patty cartoon strips).[17] Nothing ever seemed to really upset him.

---

[13] "Obenshain Vote of Labor Pledge." *Richmond Times Dispatch.* August 22, 1978.
[14] "Obenshain Not Chasing Endorsements." *Richmond News Leader.* July 28, 1978.
[15] Ibid.
[16] Maxey interview.
[17] Byler interview.

He was jubilant just to have the opportunity to chase his dream. Henry Doggett recalled,

> "Shortly after I was hired, there was an event called the Pork, Peanut, and Pine Festival. It was always the third weekend in July, hot as hell. At the time, they discouraged political campaigning, but they didn't mind candidates coming there to campaign, just no signs, no stickers, but your candidate could wear his own lapel. Dick did not like to campaign on Sundays, so I tried to get him there on a Saturday. There was conflict, but somehow he got wind of the invite and said, 'I'd like to go to that, it's not that far from Richmond to Surry County.' That Sunday morning, the skies opened up and the rain poured. I tried to call the headquarters [to tell them] that the event was cancelled, but I couldn't get in touch with anyone since it was their day off. So, I went over there and profusely apologized. I could tell Brad was angry; it was his day off and they had driven all the way down. Dick could not have been nicer. He put his arm around me and said 'don't worry about it, this kind of stuff happens. This isn't anybody's fault. Nobody controls the weather.'" They ended up salvaging the day by visiting the Surry House Restaurant. "That told me a lot about the guy; he could've easily looked at me like a bug, but he didn't."

Doggett was also impressed by how many people Obenshain already knew by simply walking into a random restaurant.[18] Ted Burr recalled similar characteristics, "He had the amazing ability, if he met someone one time, he'd know them five years later if he didn't see them again. It was fascinating." Similar to Doggett's story, Ted remembered, "I went to a campaign event at the county fair in South Hampton County, next to Emporia. He was going through the crowd saying things like, 'I met you four years ago at such and such event.' People liked that, that was a fascinating plus."[19] "He was the perfect candidate," said Kenny Klinge. [20]

---

[18] Doggett interview.

[19] Burr interview.

[20] Klinge interview, September 8, 2017.

Renee would often schedule him to stay at other people's homes, usually with friends and supporters of his, while he was on the circuit in order to save the campaign money. He was always frugal. John Alderson recalled him staying at their home. "Dick would have to be some place at a certain time; he'd know the timeline and would wake up very early. He'd say, 'you have to give me plenty of time in the morning because once I get going it will be a long 15-hour day before I can shut down again.'"[21] Getting up early was always something he struggled with as a young man, but that changed when he became actively involved in politics. His brother Scott said, "We were all surprised. That's how we knew how serious he was."[22] "He'd get up at 4:30 a.m., drive some place, shake hands, make appearances, give speeches," said Brad Cavedo.[23]

When answer policy questions, Miller was often either evasive or gave too much detail. Obenshain accentuated this, "We were certainly making efforts in the direction of painting Andrew Miller as a liberal," Dick Lobb reflected. The staff was actively looking for civic groups to sponsor debates in order to get around the equal time rule, a rule that required TV and radio stations to provide the same amount of air time for campaigns who requested it. The staffs from both campaigns got together and agreed on three debates. The Obenshain campaign wanted to hold them all early, while the Miller campaign wanted to spread them out over the course of the campaign. The Obenshain team finally conceded to spacing the debates out over time, but the two campaigns were at an impasse when it came to which civic groups to accept invitations from.[24]

The Miller campaign seemed overconfident, as did the Democratic party as a whole. Democratic Chairman Joe Fitzpatrick later said, "At our convention, many of the delegates were jubilant. They said it's Johnson vs Goldwater again. I told them not to be so cocky, 'You don't know him like I do.' I told them that Obenshain was smart and tough and that he was the strongest possible candidate that the Republicans could have nominated. I felt

---

[21] Alderson interview.
[22] Scott interview.
[23] Cavedo interview.
[24] Lobb interview.

Obenshain would have defeated Andrew Miller by a wider margin than Warner."[25]

The business community in Richmond had lined up to support Obenshain, although not all of them had prepared the funds yet, and the campaign found themselves in debt early. The campaign team decided to hold a late-July event in northern Virginia in order to raise money. The fundraiser drew many from within the influential circle of Richard Viguerie, a top Republican financier from Falls Church who started the monthly magazine called "Conservative Digest" as well as the National Conservative PAC, the Conservative Caucus, and Gun Owners of America. It was a successful event and the first of many more scheduled that would help the campaign regain financial footing. Viguerie and his magazine endorsed Obenshain that same week, saying Obenshain "has been a leader in the conservative movement in Virginia…and in the nation…a potent force."[26]

After the big fundraiser in Manassas, Dick, Judy, Kenny, their spouses, and several friends went out for a late dinner close to the motel they were all staying in off of Interstate 66. Kenny, who was working at the RNC, informed Dick that they had conducted a poll and it showed that Dick was already within two percentage points of Andy Miller in the race. As they were leaving the restaurant, seemingly out of nowhere Dick turned to Kenny and said that he had been "born again," to which Kenny jokingly replied, "I thought you were doing pretty good already." Dick responded with his signature crooked smile. The same testimony was confirmed by Delegate Guy Farley several months prior, who had a spiritual conversation with Dick in which Dick indicated that he considered himself "born-again," and had put his personal faith in Jesus Christ.[27] Kenny never followed up with him on the issue, but he reflected that to him, Dick was always a Christian, though he didn't wear his faith on his sleeve. The two then made plans to get together again for Kenny's birthday on

---

[25] Virkler, p. 132.
[26] "Conservative Digest Supports Obenshain." *Richmond News Leader*. July 27, 1978.
[27] Virkler, p. 4.

August 4th. Dick and Helen were eager to finally take a few days off from the campaign, something they had been intending to do since the convention.[28]

Several days later, Dick was invited to a Farm Bureau event in Winchester, which he accepted. The initial plan was to fly, but he received an invitation to Charlottesville on the same day, which he also accepted. "We didn't have to coax him into anything, he was always eager and interested in showing up where people wanted him," said his scheduler Renee. She recalled having trouble finding a pilot for that day. She went down the list of pilots that they were actively using; Gary Bengston, who flew Dick frequently, had a conflict. Rene then called upon Dick's friend Rick Neel, who agreed to it.[29] Brad met Dick at his home in Salisbury on the morning of August 2nd in order to switch vehicles and begin what was to be almost a twenty-hour day. Brad left his car at Dick's house and the two rode to the West End Kiwanis Club meeting together in the campaign vehicle, then to the Charlottesville event. The campaign car itself was leased, one of the controversial financial decisions that former campaign manager Bill Dalton had made. Brad said they had put 50,000 miles on that car in just a few months.

Dick gave a moving speech in Charlottesville that day. The two then traveled to Winchester to address the Frederick County Farm Bureau. [30]On the way Dick said to his driver, "If every day could be like this, there'd be no stopping us!"[31]

He was in high spirits the entire day. As Dick prepared to speak, he hearkened back to his roots. Brad had heard hundreds of Dick's speeches, but this one was different and one that he had not heard before.

> "Two German farmers who were brothers came down from Pennsylvania in the late 1800's. One stopped in Augusta County; the other—who was my ancestor—went down to Botetourt County around Fincastle and Troutville. My dad grew up there, and to make a

---

[28] Kenny Klinge interview, January 2, 2019.
[29] Maxey interview.
[30] Cavedo interview.
[31] Atkinson, p. 415.

> long story short, he ended up on the faculty at VPI teaching others, as well as myself, that farmers don't work with dirt, but with soil...So I grew up on a farm outside of Blacksburg and my heritage, despite the fact that I became a lawyer, is deep in the soil of Virginia...I am a man whose highest aspiration is to carry the voice of American agriculture to where it needs to be heard. Every time the American farmer has been tempted to think that government can solve his problems, that farmer ends up under the thumb of the government. . . The American citizen is paying 42% of everything we earn to federal, state, and local government...We have to let the nation hear the voice of Virginia, the voice of freedom, just as the nation heard it two hundred years ago!...When the needs of Virginia and agriculture are hanging in the balance, the people of Virginia will know that they have a friend who talks the farmer's language."[32]

It was considered one of the most emotional and moving speeches he had ever given. Democratic Delegate Lewis Fickett, who was in the audience, said, "His speech last night was exceptionally moving; it evoked and touched everyone's heart." Later he described it as "one of the most moving speeches I've ever heard. The essence of the speech was the necessity of individual freedom and the vitality of private initiative, which are the cornerstones of American democracy."[33]

Brad and Dick sat waiting at the airport in Winchester that night. The pilot was late. The plan was for Dick to fly to Chesterfield and be picked up by a man named John Marshall while Brad was to drive back to Richmond to retrieve his personal vehicle from the Obenshain house. Close to an hour later, they saw an aircraft approach. It didn't land immediately but instead circled around the airport one more time before landing. The pair shared a look of confusion. Eventually, the plane landed and two men exited the aircraft: Richard Neel, the pilot, and Ronald Edden, the flight instructor. Edden hurried past Dick and Brad, heading straight for the phonebooth to make a call, likely to check the weather. After exchanging pleasantries, the three men took flight.

---

[32] Bageant, Joe. "Candidate Spoke Here Last Night". *Winchester Star.* August 3, 1978.
[33] "Last Speech Is Spirited, Humorous." *Richmond News Leader.* August 4, 1978.

Brad headed for Richmond, enjoying a bright full moon and a clear sky through his front windshield along the way.

Brad arrived in Salisbury around midnight to quietly switch vehicles and avoid waking the sleeping Obenshain family. As he walked towards his car, Helen stepped outside. She had a look of concern on her face. Then she called out to him, "Where is Dick?"[34]

---

[34] Cavedo interview.

Chapter 19:

Nunc Dimittis

Campaign staffer Henry Doggett set out to drive for over three hours from his home in Surry County to the city of Danville on the evening of August 2nd, 1978. His vehicle was loaded up with brochures, bumper stickers, lapels, and red campaign yard signs marked with a large "O" in the center of them. He was scheduled to meet with local Republican leaders in Danville the next day and provide them these campaign materials to distribute as well as update them on the progress of the campaign. It was more than worth it to him. As he told his boss, Bob Hausenfluck, "I would clean toilets if it would help get Dick Obenshain elected." His enthusiasm is likely what landed him the job.

He had only briefly met Mr. Obenshain once or twice prior to taking a position with his campaign for U.S. Senate, but during those few interactions, Henry, like many others, had been impressed with Mr. Obenshain's charm, kindness, and his ability to remember names after just one introduction. He considered Obenshain to be about as close as one could get to the perfect candidate: good looking, good natured, a family man who was articulate, young, principled, genuine, and smart. Of course, it helped that he agreed with Dick's politics. Henry started out as a local unit chair for Surry County and bothered his Congressional District Chair Ted Burr, every other day for an interview for a possible job on the campaign. After weeks of tormenting Burr, he finally got his wish and was hired on July 5th, 1978.

He found an Econo Lodge off of Route 29 North for $10 a night and checked into his hotel room late that evening. Once settled, he made his routine call to the campaign headquarters. Before the days of cell phones, if a person wanted to make an outside call they would have to pick up the phone and the front desk would have to make the call. A lady by the name of Marie Quinn answered the phone. Henry told her where he was and gave her the number of the hotel, which was standard operating procedure. Exhausted and uncomfortable, he went to sleep late that night.

The next morning around 6 a.m., Henry was stepping into the shower when he heard three urgent-sounding knocks outside his door. "What in the world is going on?" he thought. "Is there a fire?" With a towel draped around himself, he cracked open the door. There stood a Danville policeman. Henry wondered what he did wrong. "Excuse me, I hate to bother you so early, but are you Henry Doggett?" the officer asked. "Yes sir," replied Henry. "Are you the Henry Doggett with the Obenshain Campaign?" the officer clarified, to which Henry again replied, "Yes sir," this time thinking someone in his family had died.

"I got a message for you. You need to call your office in Richmond immediately; there is an emergency." The officer walked away while Henry stepped out into the hall with his towel still draped around his waist. "Do you know what the emergency is?" The officer stopped, lowered his head and said, "Well, I hate to be the one to tell you this, but Mr. Obenshain was killed last night in a plane crash just outside of Richmond at the Chesterfield Airport."[1]

Henry immediately turned on the television. The local Roanoke news station was already reporting it. He called the headquarters and staffer Steve Mahan answered the phone. He confirmed the worst. "Look, there are a lot of people gathering here, the only thing I can tell you is to bring your materials

---

[1] Doggett interview.

and come on back. Call all the people you are supposed to meet with and cancel all of your appointments."

Mahan, now a judge, had worked for Governor Linwood Holton during the Republican nominating process. Afterwards he was brought on board as the Obenshain campaign made an effort to bring elements from other campaigns into their circle. Originally from Richmond, Mahan grew up in Virginia Beach, part of the 2nd Congressional District where Holton had a lot of support due to his friendship with that district's Congressman, Bill Whitehurst. He and Bill Hurd were tasked with calling the rest of the campaign team.

The campaign's scheduler, Rene Maxey, was working late at the headquarters that night. The staff had become accustomed to working until 10 p.m. as the campaign began to head into the final stretch. When Dick won the nomination, she and her father expressed their excitement by making their own bumper stickers before the campaign could create and distribute the official ones. "Don't distribute those, we're going to get some real professional looking ones," Judy Peachee told her, but Rene was too thrilled.

She went out to dinner nearby that night with several other staffers. It was a convenient ritual as Rene was renting a room at her aunt's house near the campaign headquarters. It was a warm night and the skies were clear. When she came home, her aunt had already gone to bed, but left a note on the staircase which read, "Call the campaign office. The plane has crashed."[2]

The Press Secretary Dick Lobb was listening to a tape recording of Dick giving one of his speeches that they had worked on together. "Boy, that sounded good. We are really doing well here," he thought. Lobb had also worked for John Dalton's campaign and was put on "loan" to the Obenshain campaign. He helped write two speeches for Dick as they prepared to transition from the primary to the general election, attempting to appeal to a wider audience.

---

[2] Maxey interview.

He went to bed that night content and proud of the progress the campaign was making. After drifting off to sleep, the sound of a telephone ring startled him awake. An agitated Lobb answered the phone, and it was a reporter from the Richmond Times Dispatch who asked,

"Do you know where Dick Obenshain is?"

"I think he's in Winchester somewhere giving a speech, but he's coming back tonight," Lobb replied.

"Yeah, but do you know where he is right now?" the reporter persisted.

"No," Lobb paused. "Why? What's going on?"

"Well…" said the reporter, "there's been a plane crash in Chesterfield, and we want to know if its him."

Lobb hung up the phone and yelled for his roommate, John Paul Woodley. John rolled out of bed and the pair jumped in the car and zoomed to the headquarters. Others were gathering there around the same time. That is where Lobb and Woodley learned the facts: that the wing number on the plane had matched that of Obenshain's. Lobb called his colleague Bill Hurd, who called Jim Gilmore. Gilmore and his friend Jack Reed showed up at the headquarters soon after. Lobb also called Smitty Ferebee while Woodley tried to track down Dortch Warriner.[3]

Just south of Virginia Beach, Dortch Warriner was enjoying an annual vacation with his family in Duck, North Carolina. Dortch had been a longtime friend and confidante of Dick Obenshain; the two went back many years and were nearly identical in their political philosophy at the time. There was no-one Dick trusted more politically than Dortch. Since Warriner had been appointed as a federal judge, he was no longer actively engaged in the political process. Occasionally, he would get the latest scoop from his law clerks, Ted Burr and John Paul Woodley.

Woodley was tasked with giving him the tragic news. Woodley had the street address where the judge was staying but not the phone number, so he

---

[3] Lobb interview.

called the local police and told them, "I have an urgent message for a federal judge, if you can get him to please call the Republican Party of Virginia. I have a message I can't give to anyone else." Eventually, Warriner called the headquarters and after Woodley informed him of what had happened, Dortch was silent for a moment, then said, "Why do the good ones have to die young?" before abruptly hanging up.[4] While word was spreading, nobody in Richmond could bring themselves to call Dick's close friend, Kenny Klinge.

At 2:00 a.m. Kenny's wife answered a phone call from Charlie Black, who was working with Ronald Reagan. "It's Charlie," she said to Kenny. He grabbed the phone and heard, "Kenny, I got some bad news. Dick's been in an accident. The plane crashed, and he is dead."

"I just went to pieces," said Kenny. It took him an hour to pull himself together before he opened up his red notebook of phone numbers which included members of the Obenshain group from around the state, including Don Huffman, John Alderson and Weldon Tuck. He began every conversation with the only words he could bring himself to say: "He's gone. Dick is dead." Each time, a silence would follow. It was difficult for him to deliver such devastating news, but it was Judy Peachee who was given the hardest task of all: that of informing Helen Obenshain.[5]

One of the last to receive word that early morning was Dick's longtime rival, Andrew Miller, who was awakened at 3 a.m. by reporter Shelley Roffe of the Richmond Times Dispatch. It was one of the worst phone calls he said he had ever received. He stayed up and waited until it was a reasonable hour to visit the Obenshain residence, which wasn't far from his own home. Many people were gathered around, still in shock, not sure what to do or say. Andrew Miller offered his condolences to Helen, which to him didn't feel adequate. He followed with, "If there is anything I could ever do for the family, I will do it."[6]

The family had a lot of visitors for those few days after. George Hinnant, Dick's law partner, was at the beach when he got the news, and rushed

---

[4] Woodley interview.
[5] Klinge interview, September 20, 2017.
[6] A. Miller interview.

home to see the family the next day. He recalled someone making the comment, "Why in the world would God take a life that was ready to make such a contribution?" He replied, "Maybe it was because he was too far ahead of the crowd." Helen found some small comfort in that.[7] When Rene Maxey visited the home, Helen showed her a porcelain clock that stood six inches tall on her dresser. It stopped working at the time that Dick had died.[8]

The GOP headquarters on the 16th floor of the Fidelity building was silent, only interrupted by the infrequent ringing of the main office telephone. Donuts and coffee were scattered everywhere in the main conference room where staffers Lorna Hatlock and Ben Naslund spent the early morning hours taking calls and informing party officials around the Commonwealth. Covering the office walls were posters of several prominent Virginia Republicans. On the wall in the conference room was a giant poster of Dick Obenshain holding his glasses in one hand, smiling, his eyes seemingly fixed on the workers below.[9]

The worst was true. On the night of August 2nd, around 11:00 p.m., a Piper PA34 crashed a quarter of a mile from the Chesterfield County Airport as the pilot attempted a landing. All three persons onboard were killed. Richard Neel was forty-two years old, Richard Obenshain was less than three months away from his forty-third birthday, and Ronald Edden was twenty-eight. The National Transportation Safety Board concluded that the crash was due to pilot inexperience and error, exacerbated by bad weather.

On Friday August 4th, Dick's funeral service was held at Richmond's Second Presbyterian Church at 5th and Main. The church that holds 900 people, was packed full. "It was a moving eulogy," said Dick Lobb. He was buried at Mill Creek Baptist Church in Botetourt County, where most of his family had been buried for generations.[10]

Judy Peachee took the lead in dealing with the political business that nobody wanted to think about during that time of shock and mourning. Still, it

---

7 Hinnant interview.
8 Maxey interview.
9 Edmonson, George. "Headquarters Mood Quiet, Stunned." *Richmond News Leader*. August 3, 1978.
10 Lobb interview.

had to be dealt with quickly. The next day Judy, Wyatt Durrette, and a few other members of the group met at Don Huffman's home. The consensus of the group was that they wanted Mills Godwin to take Dick's place, or possibly even Congressman J. Kenneth Robinson. Both were perceived as being very conservative. Holton had already notified party chairman George McMath that he was not interested in the seat now that he had officially declared himself an "elder statesman." Nobody was seriously considering Holton anyway, but many of the party faithful would have rather had him than Warner, about whom they knew almost nothing. Durrette was even considered, but he made it clear that he too was not interested. Judy was to contact Godwin and Robinson. Robinson was the first to say no on Saturday. She wasn't able to get in touch with Godwin until Sunday and Godwin responded with, "I'll let you know on Monday."[11]

Durrette had been the liaison between John Warner and the Obenshain campaign for the past several weeks. He knew that Warner was probably already preparing to announce his intention to be the nominee, so he arranged a meeting between Warner, Judy Peachee, and Finance Chairman Bob Russell. "Judy, I've gotten to know John well, and he's ramping up," Durrette told her. "He may do something tomorrow morning before we hear from Mills, and if he does…you know Mills is not going to compete for the nomination. It's going to be a coronation or he ain't going to do it. So, if Warner is out there seeking the nomination and Mills said no, even if he was going to say no anyway, Warner will be perceived as having cut Mills off. If that happens, Warner will never be the nominee, and we know it has to be Warner if we are going to win." However, there were many in the party and on state central committee who would not be open to Warner at all. Durrette called Warner, and as he suspected, Warner's campaign manager was already in the process of launching telegraphs to the delegates that had attended the great convention in June. The telegraphs stated that Warner would be seeking the nomination. Warner was planning on sending them out on Monday morning. "We stopped him," said Durrette. "John, the only way you get it is to not do anything and if Mills says no." Godwin did, of course, say no the next day.

---

[11] Durrette interview.

On Thursday of that week the core group met with all of the Obenshain supporters and convinced them that Warner was the only way they could win. The Obenshain campaign didn't have any money concerns leading up to the convention, but after the convention they were spending more funds than they were raising. The campaign had accrued $80,000 in debt that they expected to pay off after a Labor Day boost when voters started paying attention. It was obvious that whoever took the mantle had to have the ability to raise funds quickly. Warner was able to do just that.

On August 8th, a large group of Obenshain supporters grilled Warner on various issues, prying him in every way they could. One activist stood up and said to Warner, "We don't trust you, and we really don't like you." Other potential candidates were discussed, but none seemed viable. The committee saw Warner as an "interloper" and "not a real Virginian." Much of the content of the meeting reflected a general theme: is this what Dick Obenshain would have wanted? By most accounts, Warner handled himself well that day. He was able to win most of the support he needed, though the support was not enthusiastic. Many viewed him as an adversary. He officially declared his candidacy the next day.

Warner agreed to keep the Obenshain staff for his own campaign, but many of them had already planned on walking away if Gary Byler was not a part of the team. Warner had disliked Byler for turning him down twice, a year prior when Warner had offered him one-thousand dollars a month to come work on his campaign. Gary chose to work for Obenshain, starting out for free. Gary wasn't willing to continue with the Warner campaign until Helen Obenshain persuaded him. Gary agreed, but with a stipulation of his own: if Warner broke any of his promises, he would walk. Warner spent the first two weeks trying to find a reason to fire Gary, but he was unable to. It was difficult for much of the staff to work for someone they had only recently spent months attacking. Several days after the accident, the campaign's accountant reached out to Gary and told him that he needed to cash his last check from the official Obenshain campaign. Gary was never able to bring himself to do so, and to this day still has the check.[12]

---

[12] Byler interview.

By law, the Republican State Central Committee was responsible for selecting a new nominee. On August 12th they chose John Warner. On November 7th, 1978 he defeated Andrew Miller for the U.S. Senate, completing a zero-sum game of rock, paper, scissors amongst the three of them: Miller once defeated Obenshain, Obenshain defeated Warner, Warner defeated Miller. After following Obenshain's campaign strategy, Warner won by less than 5,000 votes but would go on to hold the seat for thirty years until he retired in 2009. He kept a framed portrait of Dick Obenshain in his office for the entirety of his service. During his first term, Warner voted very conservatively, similar to how a Senator Obenshain would have voted. As time went on, many conservatives expressed disappointment and frustration with his voting record.

Linwood Holton never ran for public office again. He spent the majority of what was left of his political clout supporting and endorsing liberal Democrats. In 2006 his son-in-law Tim Kaine, a Democrat, became Governor of Virginia.

Only one staffer disaffected from the Senate campaign after Obenshain's plane went down. Some begrudgingly carried on, while others believed they were honoring his legacy by staying and winning the election in November. They all dealt with the loss in their own way, and many to this day still have a difficult time talking about the events of 1978. The people who surrounded Dick Obenshain were like a family who had just lost their patriarch.

On the ride back from the private burial service in Botetourt, Dick's old friend Weldon Tuck pondered the same question he had since the tragedy, "Had it all been worth it? Dick had lost two campaigns and lost his life in the third campaign. Was it all worth it?" A spirit of comfort and certainty swept over him. He concluded that yes, "Surely, it has all been worth it."[13]

---

[13] Tuck interview, October 2, 2017.

Chapter 20:

Vindicated

In an instant, Richard D. Obenshain's life came to an end and so soon after his greatest triumph. It was a tragic loss, but those who knew him personally found solace in the fact that he died chasing his dream—a dream that was within his reach. Being a voice for freedom is what he loved doing.

Obenshain's death brought people together; friends and foes, from all political stripes on both sides of the aisle and in a special way. It was a tragedy they had all experienced…together, and the Commonwealth mourned... together. After countless conversations and interviews with those who had been involved during this time in Virginia's history, they all agreed that to know Dick Obenshain was a special and unique privilege. On August 5th, 1978, in solidarity, thousands of Virginians wore his campaign buttons that said "Obenshain is my friend." Groups of people who would not have ever interacted with each other found themselves mourning together. One of those who came to mourn at the Richmond's Second Presbyterian Church that Friday, noted how he found himself in line next to a "liberal Jewish physician, a conservative Presbyterian lawyer, and Mayor Henry Marsh," Marsh was seen as a "Black Power" symbol to many white Richmonders. But Mayor Marsh spoke for them all: "Dick was my friend, one of the most decent human beings I have known...one of the few lawyers whose company I enjoyed,"[1] which received much laughter from the crowd.

In 1980, the Republican Party of Virginia announced that they would name their new headquarters, the "Richard D. Obenshain Center." The dedication event was held on May 9, 1981. National figures were in attendance for the event including; Lyn Nofziger, assistant to President Reagan, Senator John Warner, Senator Jesse Helms of North Carolina and Governor John Dalton. A block of Grace Street in downtown Richmond was roped off for the public. The ribbon cutting was performed by Helen Obenshain. The event was attended by hundreds of Republicans from all corners of Virginia. [2]

Obenshain's death created a void in Virginia politics that can't be overstated; one that the Republican Party is still recovering from to this day. Without a clear leader, realignment at the local level halted, and the coalition Obenshain had assembled splintered in the 1980s. The split affected members of "the group" as well, some of whom are now Democrats. After Dalton's term ended in 1982, Virginia would not see another Republican governor until 1994, nor were Republicans able to elect a lieutenant governor or attorney general throughout the decade. Republicans did continue to win presidential elections and won another U.S. Senate seat with Paul Trible in 1983. As Richmond reporter Ross McKenzie put it in 1981, "Virginia Republicans are like the Washington Redskins in not having any draft choices."[3]

Naturally, questions swarmed around various "what could have been" scenarios. Would Obenshain have become a U.S. Senator? How long would he have served? How would Virginia politics be different today? Would he have eventually run for president?

He and his team certainly shaped the campaign strategy which helped get Warner elected and the Republican Party was barreling forward, full of momentum. Andy Miller believed that after running three times for statewide

---

[1] Pudner, Peter. "Richard D. Obenshain of Virginia, Nunc Dimittis." Tribute.
[2] Carico, Melville. "Obenshain Honored At Dedication." *Roanoke Times.* May 10, 1981.
[3] Virkler, p. 162.

office he had more natural momentum, and since he was running as a centrist Democrat, "The odds are I would have prevailed again."[4] There is certainly legitimacy to his sentiment, but this centrist Democrat recipe for victory worked better for candidates at the state level than it did for candidates running for federal office. It also had more success in the 1980s than in the 1970s before the Virginia Democratic Party was more united. The Virginia Republicans became fractured again in the 1980s. President Carter's approval ratings were also tanking and on the verge of their lowest point, which occurred in March of 1979.

Although physically nearsighted, Dick intellectual vision was 20/20. He could see a political alignment unfolding in Virginia and in the South as a whole, and he knew that the Byrd Machine would crumble. He was able to capitalize on this adjustment. He envisioned that the ideas of Barry Goldwater would win the day eventually. Despite losing the primary in 1976, Dick knew Reagan had the right ideals and abilities to become President of the United States. He was vindicated when this movement he was a part of culminated in the Reagan Revolution that swept the country in 1980. George Allen said, "When Ronald Reagan won the Presidency in 1980, Dick Obenshain was with us in spirit, because our band/group of 1976 rebels stayed together and grew with new recruits. Persuading and welcoming more people to our positive conservative cause was the Dick Obenshain winning way."[5] While Obenshain himself may not set his eyes on the ultimate dream, others liked to ponder the thought of an Obenshain presidency. His likeability, Reagan-esque qualities and commitment to conservative principles were not out of fashion in 1988 or in 1992. Senator Orin Hatch approached Helen Obenshain at the 1980 Republican National Convention and said, "He would have been on the ticket."[6] Whether that would have occurred that quick, undoubtedly his name recognition would have grown and he would likely have at least been re-elected to the U.S. Senate several more times, as John Warner was.

---

[4] A. Miller interview.

[5] George Allen interview, December 5, 2018.

[6] Helen interview.

He was always doing what was best for the party while remaining principled and committed to his own beliefs. He understood that politics is a process and you have to fight to have your values impressed on a party or an institution.

The Obenshain family continued their involvement in politics. It was, after all, a family affair and a family mission. After the tragedy, Helen worked hard at convincing people to throw their support behind John Warner. Helen also became a National Committeewoman from Virginia and served as a co-chair for Ronald Reagan's presidential campaign in Virginia with Paul Trible.

In 2003 Helen and Dick's son Mark was elected to the Virginia State Senate representing the northern portion of the Shenandoah Valley, where he still serves today. In 2013 he followed in his father's footsteps and ran for attorney general, losing by little more than one hundred votes. Andrew Miller fulfilled his promised to help the family whenever they needed it and endorsed the son of his former opponent.

In the mid-1990s his daughter Kate served on the State Council of Higher Education for Virginia to help implement the reform measures of Governor George Allen and Governor Jim Gilmore. In 2004 she served as the first chairwoman of the Republican Party of Virginia. Today she is on the board of the Young Americans for Freedom organization, author of several books, and has been a featured guest on various national news programs.

While speculation is always fun, it remains just that: speculation. No one will ever know what would have been. One thing is clear: despite the relatively short time he spent building a Republican Party in Virginia, Dick Obenshain's influence is still felt today, and it left a permanent mark on Virginia. If he had more years, it is hard to say how far his influence would have gone.

His dream of becoming a U.S. Senator was merely a vehicle for his life goal. On his tombstone it is written, "The most important goal in my life is to have some significant impact in preserving and expanding the realm of personal freedom in the life of this country." Through his efforts, character and inspiration to others, he managed to achieve exactly that. He may not have achieved his dream, but ultimately, he achieved his goal.

Listed are quotes from some of the people who were influenced by Dick Obenshain.

"When you asked Dick a question you always got an honest answer. He responded candidly. This is unusual in politics. Because he was set in his viewpoint, he felt no need to shilly shally."

—Hugh Robertson, Richmond News Leader Reporter, January 5th, 1981.

"Dick Obenshain was an anomaly in politics. He was philosophical and thoughtful in a profession that is often pragmatic and cynical. He was a visionary in an age of short-sightedness. He was a faithful and loyal friend in a trade where shifting alliances are often the coin of the realm. But he inspired his followers to pursue a better way. And I am one of those followers."

—Judge Bradley Cavedo, October 3rd, 2002

"When I think of the life of the truly honorable Dick Obenshain, three words in a phrase describe this gentleman of character: principled, fearless, and energetic leadership in the pursuit and advancement of freedom. In sum, Dick Obenshain was a freedom fighter in Virginia. After Dick Obenshain's tragic passing, for generations after, many of us benefited from the positive foundations he built during his truly consequential life."

—Governor and U.S. Senator George Allen, December 5th, 2018.

"History will say he was a pivotal figure because he altered the Republican Party to make it a conservative party, and that stayed even though John Warner became the senator. John Warner did not try to influence the party back to the left. He did not do that. The true believers that were surrounding Dick Obenshain carried on after that and continued to make the Republican Party in Virginia a conservative party."

—Jim Gilmore, Governor of Virginia, October 3rd, 2017

"He inspired a generation of young Virginians to not only become Republicans, but to become active Republicans. He deeply touched those whose lives were forever altered. They became active Republicans with a sense that the old dominion could change, and it was his quiet charisma that did that. The common nexus for a lot of them was that they had been active for Dick Obenshain."

—Karl Rove, author, Senior Advisor and Deputy Chief of Staff to President George W. Bush, December 9th, 2016

"He had core convictions and always spoke to them and let those convictions guide what he was doing. He was a conviction politician. Many people don't know what a politician's convictions are these days."

—Dick Lobb, November 8th, 2017

"It was not a wishy-washy philosophy; he was a rock solid conservative. He could've been president—he *should've* been president. The whole moral of the Republican Party might have been different, not just in Virginia, but nationally, had Dick lived. He had everything you could ask of a politician: good looking, well spoken, solid in his convictions, good family man—everything you could ask for."

—Donald Huffman, June 18th, 2017

"What he did, at that time and since, he introduced a new generation of political leaders to the Republican Party and brought in a new wave of people and a definite conservative political philosophy. His contribution to Reagan in 1976 should not be minimized. It was people like Dick who were the young enthusiasts who paved the way for the group in 1980 and had a lot to do with him getting the nomination."

—Ed Meese, 75th Attorney General of the United States, November 12th, 2018

"He was one of the seminal figures in my life. I have never met anyone close to him. For Dick it was not about him. It was about the cause. If he ever got upset, it was not because you let him down, but because you let the cause down."

—Gary Byler, December 26th, 2009

"I am basically a yellow dog Democrat, but for many years I was a card-carrying member of the Virginia Republican Party on account of Dick. I think many others, like me, were attracted to his character and ability, even if we were not in his philosophical camp. Dick had great strength of character and conviction. He was also very likeable and managed to be clear and forceful but never strident when he set forth his views. I think that made him unique."

—Larry Dagenhart, December 4th, 2009

"I served with Barry Goldwater and used to have talks about the roots of conservatism and where they came from. Clearly, Dick Obenshain was one of those, not only for Virginia, but [he was] known since he was a party chairman by Republicans across the country as one of the fathers of the motives of the conservatives. He understood the balance and how you took your philosophy and pushed it forward, but at the same time, you didn't try and murder the other guy. He was an ideologue for the roots of conservatism but not a fierce partisan and ruthless intransigent ideologue like what we are seeing today. He was an intellectual, dealing with the roots of a conservative movement that was moving in this country."

—Former U.S. Senator John Warner, April 30, 2012.

"Dick was one of the real pioneers of the Republican Party in the dominion state, having the courage to run for attorney general in 1969. He was truly one of the greatest men I ever knew, and I took his death very hard."

—Roger Stone, December 29th, 2018

"Dick was one of the most influential people in my life. His intelligence, commitments to his beliefs, and the respect he showed everyone he met were things that made a big impression on a 21-year-old starting off in his career."

—Stan Maupin, September 14th, 2017

"Dick's personal legacy was integrity. Moral uprightness. Dick was a Christian, and his personal standpoint would be the hallmark of lasting integrity, honesty, morality; [he] was a stand-out and it was so easy to accept him, to be able to enunciate in a very clear way the principles that enabled us to become the people that we are. His impact was his fierce embracement of the principles of the founds [sic]. That's what he left us. He wasn't looking to become rich or famous. He just wanted to make a difference."

—John Alderson, Republican Activist, September 19th, 2017

"His smile could light up the whole room. He was one of the most joyful people that you would ever hope to know, no matter what the adversity might be facing him or the seriousness of the issues. He had an absolutely charming mountain-valley accent. I don't remember him without a smile on his face; he always had one."

—Judge John Paul Woodley, July 10th, 2017

"His legacy in my mind will be having a vision of what the Republican Party in Virginia could be and dedicating himself to making it happen. Knowing the ingredients that it took, the philosophy, the effort. He knew that you could have all the principles in the world but if you didn't have people as precinct chairs, knocking on doors, making the phone calls and all those things that go into winning elections, you aren't going to win elections. Of all the people I know in politics, he combined the qualities of a principled leader and a practical politician."

—Wyatt Durrette, December 16, 2016

"I knew and admired your father and am very proud to have these inscribed words of his here on my desk. I shall be guided by them."

— President Ronald Reagan letter to the Dick Obenshain's children, May 14, 1981

A modified and shortened version of a Buddhist text reads, "Thousands of candles can be lighted from a single candle, and the life of the single candle will not be shortened." No other phrase could better describe how Dick Obenshain influenced so many during his lifetime. His notable passion, character, conviction and fiery rhetoric will stand out in the minds of many Virginians and the nation for years to come.

Chapter 21:

Lessons From Dick Obenshain

Throughout his life, Dick Obenshain was consistent with his habits and his principles. One can learn much by reading between the lines through all of the secondhand accounts of people who knew him well. These are some lessons that I gathered throughout my research, though I am sure there are many more to be found in his tale.

Speak from the heart. Dick didn't memorize or write down his speeches. He spoke completely off the cuff, and it allowed his words to match his emotions. It came across to the audience as genuine, which is why he was such a powerful orator.

Know the importance of listening. Dick did a lot of talking when he was in front of an audience, but mostly listened when he was one-on-one. His brother Scott didn't necessarily always agree on the issues, but he noted how his brother would take the time to listen to his opinion. Right or not, sometimes people just want to be heard, and many were flattered by how he could make an individual feel like the most important person in the room. Taking the time to listen can go a long way in building rapport.

Make time for your family. Dick's kids found a list of his goals in an attic. At the top of that list included spending more time with family. Knowing this was a priority for their dad impacted how his children made decisions in their own lives. Mark declined to run for attorney general in 2009 because he wanted to wait until his children were older, as they were still at home and needed him around. When Dick was home, he also made a point to spend quality time with just himself and Helen.

Live life with a purpose. As it was said at his funeral, Dick lived more life in forty years than most do in eighty. He had a goal, to become a U.S. Senator, since the time he was a young man. Having this goal in mind guided him to take risks and do things he would have never had a reason to do without this purpose in life. When you find a purpose, you are truly living your best life.

Stay true to your principles but keep an open mind. Dick let his principles guide him personally, but he often supported candidates that didn't quite share his vision, like Linwood Holton, or candidates that had previous "sins," like Mills Godwin. Supporting people you don't always agree with does not have to mean that you are sacrificing your principles.

Read. His closest friends and family frequently commented on how well-read Dick Obenshain was. It was evident in his speeches, and he was well-versed on the issues, which commanded respect from an audience and from his opponents. Know your topic or vocation inside and out.

Tell the truth. According to his daughter Kate, he didn't even want his children watching television that endorsed telling white lies. Dick took honesty seriously. Honesty and trust are a two-way street; if you want people to trust you, you have to earn their trust.

Enjoy debate, but don't take things personally. DPV Chairman Joe Fitzgerald said, "Sometimes tough-talking and usually serious in his speeches, Obenshain was rarely personal in his charges and had an unusual reputation for both hard politicking and fairness, as well as candor in his dealings." Dick maintained countless friendships and working relationships with people he didn't agree with, and he maintained a richer life for it. Emulate his ability to debate, then pause to enjoy a baseball game with the one you're debating with.

Have a brain trust. Throughout the years, Dick always had a group of several people around him giving him counsel. The best leaders know that they don't always have the right answers and can learn and grow from the perspective of others.

Cultivate the young. Dick's legacy was cemented due to all of the young people he helped inspire and made time for. Jim Gilmore recalled how he could not believe Dick would invest time in making sure those around him were taken care of. Dick never overlooked the importance of including the youth in his campaigns and frequently made time for Young Republicans Clubs and treated them as equals. Dick understood that the future always rests in those who follow us after.

Bibliography

Books & Publications

Abramowitz, Alan; McGlennon, John; Rapoport, Ronald. *Party Activists in Virginia: A Study of Delegates to the 1978 Senatorial Nominating Conventions.* Charlottesville, VA. University of Virginia. 1981.

Atkinson, Frank B. *The Dynamic Dominion: Realignment and the Rise of Two-party Competition in Virginia, 1945-1980.* Lanham, MD: Rowman & Littlefield Publishers, 2006.

Gates, Ernie. "May Days, 1970: The week that would change UVA forever." UVA Magazine. March 7, 2018.

Heinemann, Ronald L. *Harry Byrd of Virginia.* Charlottesville, VA: University Press of Virginia, 1996.

Holton, Abner Linwood. *Opportunity Time.* Charlottesville, VA.: University of Virginia Press, 2008.

Kashner, Sam; Shoenberger, Nancy. *Furious Love: Elizabeth Taylor, Richard Burton, and the Marriage of the Century.* p. 37. HarperCollins Publisher 2010.

Key, V. O. *Southern Politics in State and Nation*: (2. Print.). New York: Alfred A. Knopff, 1950.

Morton, Richard L. "The Virginia State Debt and Internal Improvements 1820-1838." Journal of Political Economy 25, no. 4, April 1917:

Nash, George H. *The Conservative Intellectual Movement in America since 1945.* Wilmington, DE: ISI Books, 2008.

Quigley, Carroll. *Tragedy And Hope: A History Of The World In Our Time.* Macmillan, 1974.

Rove, Karl. *Courage and Consequences: My Life as a Conservative in the Fight.* Threshold Editions. New York, NY. 2010.

Taylor, Elizabeth. Elizabeth Takes Off. New York. Berkshire Publishing Group. 1987.

Virkler, John S. "Richard Obenshain: Architect of the Republican Triumph in Virginia" Unpublished Thesis, Auburn University, 1987.

Wilkinson, J. Harvie. *Harry Byrd and the Changing Face of Virginia Politics: 1945-1966.* Charlottesville: University Press of Virginia, 1984.

Wright, Crystal. *Con Job: How Democrats Gave Us Crime, Santuary Cities, Abortion Profiteering and Racial Division.* Regnery Publishing, New Jersey, 2016.

Newspapers

Daily News Record

New York Times

Richmond Times Dispatch

Richmond News Leader

Roanoke Times

Washington Post

Washington Star

Winchester Star

Online Resources

Guthrie, Benjamin J. "Statistics of the Presidential and Congressional Election of November 3, 1964." Accessed September 18, 2018. http://clerk.house.gov/member_info/electionInfo/1964election.pdf.

Heidelberg Castle. Accessed April 02, 2019. https://www.heidelberg-marketing.de/en/experience/sights/heidelberg-castle.html.

Nichols, John. "The Nation: Why Do GOP Bosses Fear Ron Paul?" NPR. December 22, 2011. Accessed April 02, 2019. https://www.npr.org/2011/12/22/144122913/the-nation-why-do-gop-bosses-fear-ron-paul.

Mewbar, Mary K. "Real Estate News." The Washington Life Magazine. May 2005. http://www.washingtonlife.com/issues/2005-05/realestate/

Spoehr, Thomas. "Remembering Reagan's Army Secretary, John O. Marsh, Jr." The Daily Signal. February 4, 2019. Accessed February 10, 2019. https://www.dailysignal.com/2019/02/04/remembering-reagans-army-secretary-john-o-marsh-jr/

Virginia State Board of Elections. 1969 Report. https://www.elections.virginia.gov/resultsreports/election-results/index.html

"Walker, Gilbert Carlton" Accessed March 4, 2017.

http://bioguide.congress.gov/scripts/biodisplay.pl?index=W000054

Misc.

"Dortch Warriner" biographical sketch on file at Republican Party of Virginia Archives.

Convention Video on file with the Republican Party of Virginia Archives.

Maupin, Stan "Driving Dick Obenshain" personal papers.

Pudner, Peter. "Richard D. Obenshain of Virginia, Nunc Dimittis." Tribute.

Ronald Reagan Letter to Obenshain family, May 14, 1981.

Interviews

Alderson, John, September 19, 2017

Allen, George, December 5, 2018

Bowman, Pasco, April 14, 2017

Burr, Ted, June 19, 2017

Byler, Gary, December 26, 2009

Campbell, Polly, September 16, 2013

Canada, Joe, December 16, 2016

Cavedo, Brad, May 13, 2010 & January 7, 2019

Clemens, Tommy, October 18, 2017

Currin, Carthan September 26, 2017

Dagenhart, Larry, December 4, 2009

Doggett, Henry, September 13, 2017

Durrette, Wyatt December 16, 2016

Gilmore, Jim, October 3, 2017

Gregory, Carlisle, July 12, 2017

Hausenfluck, Bob, October 3, 2017

Hildebrand, Barbara, March 3, 2010

Hinnant, George, October 11, 2017

Holton, Linwood, September 29, 2017

Huffman, Donald, June 18,2017

Hurd, Bill October 3, 2017

Klinge, Kenny, February 9, 2010, March 3, 2010, September 8, 2017 & January 2, 2019

Layman, Rodman, August 17, 2011

Lobb, Richard (Dick), November 8, 2017

Maupin, Stan, September 14, 2017

Maxey, Renee September 23, 2017

McMath, George, November 14, 2017

Meese, Edwin III, November 12, 2018

Miller, Andrew, December 10, 2016.

Miller, Nathan, June 29, 2011

Obenshain, Beth (Betty), July 20, 2011 & September 13, 2017

Obenshain, Helen, August 7, 2009

Obenshain, Joseph, July 20, 2011 & September 1, 2017

Obenshain, Kate, September 19, 2018

Obenshain, Mark, March 23, 2018

Obenshain, Marsha, July 20, 2011

Obenshain, Scott September 18, 2017

Paul, John, December 7, 2016

Rove, Karl, December 9, 2016

Royal, Bill, September 15, 2017

Short, Mark, November 9, 2017

Tuck, Weldon, September 26 & October 2, 2017

Warner, John, April 30, 2012 & April 13, 2017

Woodley, John Paul, July 10, 2017

Wason, Judy, March 3, 2010

Zumbro, Anne, October 15, 2018

About the Author

Joel Hensley was born and raised in the Shenandoah Valley in western Virginia. He received his Bachelor's Degree in Political Science from James Madison University and worked as a legislative aide in the House of Delegates for six years. He is currently pursuing a Master's degree at Virginia Commonwealth University while owning and operating a small business just outside of Richmond.

Made in the USA
Middletown, DE
23 July 2021

44667075R00146